Pragmatism, Statesmanship, and the Supreme Court

Pragmatism, Statesmanship, and the Supreme Court

GARY J. JACOBSOHN

Cornell University Press

ITHACA AND LONDON

First published 1977 by Cornell University Press.
Published in the United Kingdom by Cornell University Press Ltd., 2-4 Brook Street, London W1Y 1AA.

International Standard Book Number 0-8014-1071-1
Library of Congress Catalog Card Number 77-1921
Printed in the United States of America by York Composition Co., Inc.
Librarians: Library of Congress cataloging information appears on the last page of the book.

To the memory of my parents
Hilda and Hans Jacobsohn

Acknowledgments

The views presented in this book will not be shared by some readers. They owe their dissatisfaction to me and not to the scholars who generously encouraged my efforts. At various stages of the manuscript I received sage advice from Walter F. Berns of the University of Toronto, Werner J. Dannhauser of Cornell University, Robert J. Harris of the University of Virginia, Harry M. Clor of Kenyon College, and James MacGregor Burns and Vincent M. Barnett, my colleagues at Williams College. I am grateful for their counsel, although any errors in the book are my own. I owe the deepest gratitude to Janice Cook Jacobsohn, whose lawyerly skills, keen editorial eye, and considerable patience proved invaluable in the preparation of the manuscript.

Slightly different versions of some of the material in Chapters 6, 7, and 8 have appeared in the *Emory Law Journal* (Vol. 23, No. 1, 1974) and the *New York University Law Review* (Vol. 49, No. 1, 1974). Permission to incorporate this material is gratefully acknowledged.

GARY J. JACOBSOHN

Williamstown, Massachusetts

Contents

Pragmatism, Statesmanship, and the Supreme Court

Introduction

This book is about the Supreme Court and constitutional adjudication. It is an inquiry into the pragmatic school of jurisprudential thought, which has made a substantial contribution to the development of our constitutional law. It also tries to illuminate the meaning of statesmanship in the judicial context.

The term "statesmanship," of course, has strongly normative connotations, and in this age of cynicism and scientific realism the use of such a value-charged word may raise a number of skeptical eyebrows. A statesman, after all, is commonly recognized as a politician with whom one agrees, or as Speaker Joe Cannon once put it, a politician who has been dead for a long time. Liberal indulgence in the debunking mode is as fashionable today as was the uncritical acceptance of received opinion in earlier times; the blind veneration that made statesmen out of ordinary politicians has been replaced by a cold objectivity that makes ordinary politicians out of statesmen. Statesmanlike attributes, to the extent that they are worth talking about, exist in the eyes of the beholder, which means that to describe these traits is, in effect, to enumerate the essentials of one's own particular ideology and political preferences.

Occasionally, however, our attention is drawn to an event that causes even cynics to flinch. When, for example, Senator Roman Hruska came forward to speak in behalf of President Richard Nixon's nomination of G. Harrold Carswell to be an associate justice of the Supreme Court, he ruffled the sensibilities of the most hardboiled observers of varied political persuasions. Said the senator from Nebraska: "Even if [Carswell] is mediocre there are a lot of mediocre judges and people and lawyers. They are entitled to a little representation aren't they, and a little chance? We can't have all Brandeises, Cardozos, and Frankfurters, and stuff like that there."[1] Senator Hruska was, in part, correct. There are a lot of mediocrities in the categories he mentioned, and we cannot have all Brandeises, Cardozos, and Frankfurters. The point, which apparently escaped Mr. Carswell's defender, but which seemed implicit in much of the reaction to his statement, is that, regardless of the immediate political implications of an individual's appointment, we have a right to expect excellence in nominees for the Supreme Court. That right inheres in the nature of the responsibilities associated with the position and in the remoteness of the judges from direct popular control. As far as our expectations of public officials are concerned, if the people of Nebraska determine that their elected representative's remarks constitute evidence of his own mediocrity, they may require that he seek alternative employment. Common sense suggests that the ease with which we are able to reverse a previous error, and the magnitude of the damage that may issue from such error, will affect the elevation of our expectations.

It becomes necessary, whatever our reservations about value preferences, to develop and refine the criteria by which excellence may be identified. Moreover, it is useful to render excellence synonymous with statesmanship. The more than rhetorical import of this rendering is suggested by an observation of the great nineteenth-century student of American politics and society, Alexis de Tocqueville. "Not only must the Federal judges be good citizens, and men of that information and integrity which are indispensable to all magistrates, but they must be statesmen, wise to discover the signs of the times, not afraid to brave the obstacles that can be subdued, nor slow to turn away from the current when it threatens to sweep them off, and the supremacy of the Union and the obedience due to the laws along with them." Tocqueville's reflections about the judges of the federal courts were intended to have a special meaning when applied to those

1. Quoted in Henry J. Abraham, *Justices and Presidents: A Political History of Appointments to the Supreme Court* (New York, 1975), pp. 6–7.

sitting at the pinnacle of the federal judicial structure. "If the Supreme Court," he said more than twenty years before the *Dred Scott* decision, "is ever composed of imprudent or bad men, the Union may be plunged into anarchy or civil war."[2]

Tocqueville, of course, was writing for a European audience eager to learn about the new American experiment in democracy, and thus his remarks about the federal judges were very likely received with considerable interest and curiosity. Nowhere in Europe was it possible to attach so much significance to the responsibilities of the courts and to the consequences of judicial action. Statesmanlike qualities were attributes one looked for in political leaders, and for the French observer's primary readership, political roles were to be clearly distinguished from judicial roles. Tocqueville, however, with his usual perspicacity, appreciated the fact that the Supreme Court, in regulating the relations of government and citizenry, exercised "prerogatives . . . almost entirely political."[3] By this he did not mean that the Court was political in a partisan sense, or even in a specifically legislative sense, but rather that the broad sweep of its authority—its power extended to all cases arising under the Constitution—and the finality of its decisions, guaranteed that its resolution of individual disputes would have profound effects upon the distribution of power and influence in American society.

As a result, the Supreme Court demanded more of its members than the traits typically associated with judicial office. It demanded a statesmanship tailored to the distinctive nature of the circumstances defining its rather unique political position. The "political prerogatives" of the Court were different from those of the other political institutions, as Tocqueville indicated when he said of the Supreme Court, and only the Supreme Court, that "their power is enormous, but it is the power of public opinion."[4] Lacking the powers of purse, arms, and votes, it could not long suffer a loss of prestige. Without popular respect for law and for the Court's

2. Alexis de Tocqueville, *Democracy in America,* trans. Phillips Bradley (New York, 1945), I, 157.
3. Ibid., p. 156.
4. Ibid., p. 157.

decisive role in expounding and interpreting the law, it would be impotent. Further, the vulnerability of the Court's position meant that its output, the decisions and opinions through which the judges governed without electoral accountability, would necessarily be subject to the most exacting public scrutiny.

While the Court's power endured as long as public opinion accepted it, it was to be exercised by judges whose carefully circumscribed independence was designed to place them beyond the easy reach of popular will. "The complete independence of the courts of justice," as Alexander Hamilton had put it, "is peculiarly essential in a limited Constitution." This, though "[the judiciary] may truly be said to have neither FORCE nor WILL but merely judgment; and must ultimately depend upon the aid of the executive arm even for the efficacy of its judgments."[5] Somewhat paradoxically, then, the power of the Court was to rest ultimately upon public opinion, and yet the justification for the Court's exercise of power rested, in large measure, upon an immunity from the pressures of public opinion that would have been considered intolerable were it to have been affixed to any other political institution. How the justices performed within the political-judicial context created by this tension would provide essential information for an appraisal of their statesmanship.

Public opinion represents something considerably larger than the findings of a Gallup poll. While it may include such findings, it refers to all those pressures and demands produced by societal change. In terms of twentieth-century public law adjudication the central problem for judicial statesmanship can thus be stated most simply as follows: Is it possible to interpret an eighteenth-century document in such a way as to render it adaptable to a complex modern society, a society whose economic and social problems are radically different from those that existed at the time the document was written? At least three answers to this question are possible. One could say that the meaning and application of the Constitution never change, and that if one disapproves of the social consequences of this view, one's only recourse is through

5. Alexander Hamilton, James Madison, John Jay, *The Federalist Papers,* Number 78.

constitutional amendment. On the other hand, the meaning of the Constitution can be seen as varying according to changing circumstances so that the substantive content of the Constitution's most important clauses cannot be established in advance and in the abstract. The argument of this book is that a third alternative, one that falls between these two extremes, is the position of judicial statesmanship. The statesmanlike judge will adapt the Constitution to changing social realities without altering the meaning of the document. The substantive content of constitutional principle thus remains fixed, but prudence demands that judicial doctrine (which consists of the application of principle to facts) reflect the social realities of the moment.

Historically, this issue came to a head at about the turn of the century when the prevailing orthodoxy in constitutional adjudication (represented best in the person of Justice Stephen Field) sought to sanctify and preserve a status quo favorable to the great industrial interests through an appeal to fixed principles of natural right. The dissatisfaction that resulted in response to the social consequences of this jurisprudence gave rise to the pragmatic movement in American jurisprudence, a movement dedicated to the goal of achieving congruence between the law and the pressing needs of a society undergoing rapid flux and transition.

Many years passed before the impact of this new jurisprudence was reflected in the decisions of the Supreme Court, and even longer before it was enthroned as the new constitutional orthodoxy. The justices of the Warren Court, wrote Alexander Bickel, were the judicial offspring of the "Progressive realists," those men who had, in their writings, so effectively waged war against the constitutional traditions of the past. Bickel's point was that these judges are best understood as following in a tradition that began with the scholarly writings and judicial opinions of Oliver Wendell Holmes, Jr., was developed in the work of Benjamin Cardozo and Roscoe Pound, and was refined in the jurisprudential school that came to be known as American legal realism. The principal thrust of that tradition was that law must not stand in the way of progress, and that the Constitution was not a document embodying immutable principles but one whose meaning was made to depend upon the circumstances of time and place. While the justices of the Field era were consistently in step with the movements of a burgeoning commercial aristocracy, the justices of the Warren Court marched to the tune of egalitarianism.[6]

The connection between the egalitarianism of the Warren Court and the jurisprudential tradition of "progressive realism" is easily seen. Progress in this century has come to be defined in terms of equality. Thus to the extent that the Court adopted a jurisprudence that facilitated progress, it also placed its imprimatur upon the goal of an egalitarian society. The importance, however, of pragmatism in the development of American constitutional history in the twentieth century is only in part reflected in the egalitarian decisions associated with the Warren Court. Perhaps more significant is the extent to which egalitarian considerations were manifested in the interpretive process through which these decisions were announced. The Field Court and the Warren Court were equally result-oriented; however, the fact that they were oriented toward different results does not lead to an understanding of their distinctive characters.

That is to say, although it is customary to see the pragmatist as someone whose principal concern is with results, pragmatism as a philosophy represents a systematic approach to solving problems. This approach has had a decisive influence on modern jurisprudence and judicial decision making, and is the focus of concern in the pages to follow. The objective is to explore the theoretical underpinnings of this orientation, to describe the integration of pragmatic philosophy into a system of norms for judicial decision making, to evaluate pragmatic jurisprudence as it functions in the field of constitutional law, and to suggest, in the course of critical review, a more appropriate standard for the resolution of public law questions.

That standard seeks to accommodate the demands of stability and change in constitutional adjudication. It is basically an elaboration of the Tocquevillean definition of statesmanship—the judicial statesman being one who, at a minimum, is "wise to

6. Alexander M. Bickel, *The Supreme Court and the Idea of Progress* (New York, 1970), pp. 19, 103.

discern the signs of the times" and yet "slow to turn away from the current when it threatens to sweep [him] off." It also takes seriously a further observation of Tocqueville, that one of the functions of the Supreme Court is the defense of "the public interest against private interests." Statesmanlike adjudication adapts the public law to the times without giving in to the "fickleness of the democracy."[7] To succeed in this delicate process, however, requires that the idea of the public interest be accorded more serious consideration than it has received of late from students of politics and jurisprudence. Pragmatic jurisprudence, for example, conceived of the public interest as a sum of individual private interests, all of which made demands upon the public sector. In calling for the judicial accommodation of as many of these demands as was practically possible, pragmatic jurisprudence did not provide judges involved in constitutional interpretation with a strong enough reason or incentive to be "slow to turn away from the current." On the other hand, the elevation by the judges of the Field persuasion of a private right of capital accumulation into an absolute civil right failed to account for social change and thus also, albeit for quite different reasons, abandoned the public interest. The assumption implicit in this work is that the public interest is identifiable, that it is not a mystical concept fathomable only by a court of Platonic guardians, and that it is discernable through careful analysis and application of constitutional principles to the social realities reflected in the signs of the times.

Following this introduction, Chapter 2 sketches the three basic alternatives confronting those responsible for judicial decisions in constitutional cases. The principal features of Justice Field's natural rights approach, which froze meaning and application of the Constitution within narrow, inflexible limits, are discussed with a view toward a more detailed consideration of the pragmatic rejection of this older jurisprudence. Perhaps the most important message of this chapter is that to find fault with the pragmatic alternative, as we will, does not entail a return to the Fieldian solution. The third alternative, represented in this chapter by

7. Tocqueville, *Democracy*, I, 157.

the first Justice John Marshall Harlan's dissenting opinion in *Lochner* v. *New York,* illustrates that it is not necessary to repudiate the political principles embodied in the Constitution in order to accommodate social and economic change. In the final chapter a more detailed account of a similar statesmanlike stance is presented in an analysis of Chief Justice Charles Evans Hughes's majority opinion in the famous Minnesota mortgage moratorium case. For both Harlan and Hughes, constitutional adjudication required prudence, the possession of noble convictions, and an understanding that in political life convictions must be acted upon with moderation and caution.

Chapter 3 shows that the relationship between equality and pragmatic jurisprudence is best understood through analysis of the egalitarian assumptions that are an integral part of the philosophy of pragmatism. Indeed, the judicial implications of this relationship become clearer upon reflection on the writings of the founders of the pragmatic movements in American philosophy. But the keenest insight into the logic and implications of pragmatism was made prior to its emergence as a philosophical school. Alexis de Tocqueville's description of the philosophical method of the Americans bears a striking resemblance to the pragmatism later developed by John Dewey, William James, and others. The relationship depicted by Tocqueville between American philosophy and equality of condition elucidates the pragmatism that was in time to assume such great importance in the judicial context. This chapter explores, through a juxtaposition of Tocqueville's reflections and the writings of Dewey and James, those features of the philosophy of pragmatism, which, when relocated to a judicial context, become essential elements of the jurisprudence of pragmatism.

Chapter 4 examines the convergence of pragmatism and jurisprudence in the writings of Benjamin Cardozo and Roscoe Pound. The egalitarian theme is evident in the thought of both of these judicial philosophers, and the question then arises whether the principles of pragmatic jurisprudence serve the ends of constitutional interpretation well. That these principles prove inadequate does not speak to any inherent flaw in pragmatic jurisprudence but only to the failure of their advocates to distinguish between private and public law. Thus, in the case of a natural rights document such as the Constitution, the application of pragmatic principles—principles hostile to the natural rights tradition—leads to serious problems in constitutional adjudication. Pound and Cardozo allow us to observe the role that the principle of equality plays in this process of adjudication, which in turn leads to a fuller appreciation of the work of the modern Court.

One of the most important issues confronted by the Warren Court (according to Chief Justice Earl Warren, *the* most important) was the reapportionment controversy. To illustrate the application of pragmatic principles to constitutional interpretation, and to indicate some of the problems associated with this application, Chapter 5 evaluates the substance and implications of the Court's equal-population principle. As in the analysis in Chapter 2, three positions are outlined, and once again the least-quoted opinion (in this case by Justice Potter Stewart) most closely approximates the posture of judicial statesmanship. It is important to note here that in both situations (Harlan in *Lochner*, Stewart in *Reynolds* v. *Sims*) the opinions lead immediately to the same egalitarian result found in the pragmatic opinions (Holmes in *Lochner*, Warren in *Reynolds*). However, since the reasoning within the two sets of opinions is grounded on different premises, the long-range results are not at all the same. This is particularly evident in the prevailing view of the reapportionment majority where egalitarian considerations were reflected not only in the result but also in the process leading up to the decision. This resulted in the dogmatization of the Court's "one-man, one vote" doctrine, impeding, in the long run, flexible and prudent judicial response to the districting dilemma.

The third position discussed in Chapter 5 is the alternative of judicial avoidance that has come to be identified with Justice Felix Frankfurter and, in terms of reapportionment, with his dissenting opinion in *Baker* v. *Carr*. Frankfurter's position was neither pragmatic nor statesmanlike. The analysis in the next two chapters directs us to a similar conclusion with regard to his judicial performance in general. But our interest in these two chapters is only in part one of understanding Justice Frankfurter. The reevaluation of the justice's judicial philosophy presented here seeks to provide a clearer picture of judicial pragmatism as well as a path upon which we may go beyond pragmatism toward an understanding of excellence in constitutional judgment. Chapter 6 discusses Frankfurter's attempt to grapple with the concept of judicial statesmanship in his many extrajudicial writings. Chapter 7, examining Justice Frankfurter's judicial opinions, argues, counter to the standard interpretations, that he should *not* be viewed as a judicial pragmatist in the mold of his great hero, Justice Holmes. Indeed, the differences between the two men shed valuable light upon both judicial pragmatism and judicial statesmanship.

Finally, the concluding chapter sketches the broad outlines of a constitutional jurisprudence that reflects the unique political character of the Supreme Court. It will be helpful, in this regard, to consider Thomas Jefferson's reflections on jurisprudence. Whereas Frankfurter is sometimes mistakenly identified with pragmatic jurisprudence, Jefferson has been viewed, on occasion, as a precursor of pragmatism. This view, grounded in Jefferson's empiricism and well-known championship of progressive change, is flawed by its failure to appreciate the significance of Jefferson's commitment to fixed principles of natural right. Although in Jefferson's case we do not have an opportunity to analyze the implementation of statesmanlike considerations in the course of actual adjudication, we are provided with eloquent reminders of the way judges must proceed in their efforts to accommodate the demands of the past and those of the future. In Chief Justice Hughes's masterful opinion in *Home Building and Loan Association* v. *Blaisdell* we see the practical extension and modern application of Jefferson's teaching on change and stability. Indeed, this example, occurring in the midst of the great economic crisis of this century, suggests a model of judicial statesmanship that will also serve the Court well in times of lesser national emergency.

CHAPTER 2

Between Field and Holmes

JUDICIAL ENFORCEMENT OF NATURAL RIGHTS

In 1873, John Dewey was a precocious youngster growing up in Vermont, and Stephen J. Field was a justice of the United States Supreme Court. The two had little in common, except perhaps that Field had been born and raised in the same part of the country as Dewey. The area had changed little since Field's boyhood some forty-five years earlier. Indeed, today its soft, rolling green countryside still retains much of the rustic simplicity it possessed at the time of its original settlement. Yet, in the intervening years, an industrial revolution had commenced, and by the early 1870's it was in the process of radically transforming the American landscape. While examples of this upheaval were not especially obvious in Dewey's Vermont, in other parts of the country one could find much evidence of important economic and social change.

In New Orleans, a "carpetbag" state legislature, exercising its police power, established a slaughterhouse monopoly ostensibly for the purpose of protecting the health and welfare of the citizens of that city. The constitutionality of the legislation was upheld by the Supreme Court in 1873, but not without the vigorous dissents of Justice Field and Justice Joseph Bradley—dissents which ultimately proved to be turning points in American constitutional law.[1] In stating their case the justices made reference to

1. *Slaughter-House Cases,* 16 Wallace 36 (1873). The importance of the *Slaughter-House Cases* is known to all students of American constitutional development. Robert G. McCloskey, for example, has described Field's dissent as "the point in our intellectual history at which the democratic strain in the American tradition begins its subservience to political conservatism." McCloskey, *American Conservatism in the Age of Enterprise, 1865–1910* (New York, 1951), p. 1.

fixed principles, to a priori standards, to natural rights. Young Dewey was presumably not aware of the opinions of the dissenters in the *Slaughter-House Cases*—in due time, however, his philosophy would respond to their arguments.

Eleven years later, when the philosopher of pragmatism was a graduate student at Johns Hopkins, and was as yet not settled upon any one philosophical path, the Supreme Court was once again confronting the slaughterhouse issue. Since it had last decided, the state of Louisiana had repealed the statute creating the monopoly involved in the *Slaughter-House Cases*. The Court sustained the action, and in a concurring opinion, Justice Field provided a splendid example of how the political philosophy of the regime could be applied to protect economic barons (or in this case, butchers) in their quest for ever-increasing capital profits. Said Field:

As in our intercourse with our fellow men certain principles of morality are assumed to exist, without which society would be impossible, so certain inherent rights lie at the foundation of all action, and upon a recognition of them alone can free institutions be maintained. These inherent rights have never been more happily expressed than in the Declaration of Independence, that new evangel of liberty to the people: "We hold these truths to be self-evident"—that is, so plain that their truth is recognized upon their mere statement—"that all men are endowed"—not by edicts of emperors or decrees of parliament, or acts of Congress, but "by their Creator with certain unalienable rights"— that is, rights which cannot be bartered away, or given away, or taken away except in punishment of crime—"And that among these are life, liberty, and the pursuit of happiness, and to secure these"—not grant them but secure them—"Governments are instituted among men, deriving their just powers from the consent of the governed."[2]

To appreciate the pragmatic revision in American jurisprudence, and to understand the judicial salience of the philosophy of pragmatism as developed by Charles Peirce, William James, and most particularly, John Dewey, this excerpt requires some consideration.

In the first place, one notices that Field's appeal is to the past,

2. *Butcher's Union Slaughter-House and Live-Stock Landing Company* v. *Crescent City Live-Stock Landing and Slaughter-House Company,* 111 U.S. 746, 756–757 (1884).

to the rights inscribed in the Declaration of Independence. These rights are not given to man by his government, as Field was careful to emphasize, but belong to man because of his very nature. They include the right to accumulate property; or as Justice Bradley claimed in the *Slaughter-House Cases,* rights "to life, liberty, and the pursuit of happiness are equivalent to the rights of life, liberty, and property."[3] Without contesting, for the moment, the correctness of this alteration of the Declaration to the original Lockean language,[4] it should be noted that the critical source of Field's view resides in the prepolitical, that is, to those inalienable rights which are possessed by all men prior to the establishment of civil society. Thus the inequality associated with capitalist accumulation is perfectly compatible with the Declaration understood in Lockean terms; civil society is perceived as an organic development away from the state of nature where the equality of all men is an actual fact.[5] The role of government, in this view, is essentially a negative one, ensuring the unimpeded exercise of man's natural rights. There is a sense, then, in which Field represents a sort of hybrid of John Locke and Charles Darwin, the beneficiary of this amalgam being the individual who, in the exercise of his natural rights, emerges triumphant from the competition with his fellow citizens.[6]

3. *Slaughter-House Cases,* at 116.

4. Professor McCloskey, in reflecting on Field's "gloss" on the Declaration, maintained that the "Jeffersonian theory of democracy was rooted in spiritual and humane, rather than material and economic, values." McCloskey, *American Conservatism,* p. 2. This judgment may be correct, although it clearly does not portray the views of many of Jefferson's influential contemporaries, such as Madison and Hamilton, who did not draw the issue so sharply between economic and spiritual concerns. For the view that the substitution of the pursuit of happiness for property in the Lockean trilogy of rights constituted a fundamental change in meaning see Cecilia Kenyon, "Republicanism and Radicalism in the American Revolution: An Old-Fashioned Interpretation," *William and Mary Quarterly,* 3d ser., 19 (1962).

5. This understanding of the Declaration borrows from Harry V. Jaffa's analysis in his *Crisis of the House Divided* (Garden City, N.Y., 1959), especially Chapter 14.

6. The best treatment of the Darwinian side of laissez faire capitalism is to be found in Richard Hofstadter, *Social Darwinism in American Thought* (Boston, 1944). Darwin, as will be seen, also looms large in the pragmatic rejection of natural rights.

Related to this appeal to the past is the reference to fixed principles of morality, principles that are "assumed to exist," meaning that their existence is to be ascertained through the use of reason. The exercise of this reason is not the special preserve of the philosopher, for the principles are so self-evident that "their truth is recognized upon their mere statement." In other words, any reasonable man will be able to determine that free institutions require a basis in the recognition of natural right.

The Declaration, however, speaks in generalities. The accumulation of capital may in fact be an inalienable right, but is its specific manifestation always a self-evident truth? Is it so obvious that the establishment of a slaughterhouse monopoly makes civil society impossible? If there is a basis for the state to believe that its policy will prevent disease and death, and thus preserve that right of self-preservation which is, after all, the prerequisite to all other rights, then who is serving the ends prescribed in the Declaration? The question, at this point, is only rhetorical. It does, however, introduce us to the problem of formalism.

The formalistic judge, committed to strict adherence to a prescribed model, arrives at a particular judgment through a mechanical process of deductive logic. For Field, the Declaration of Independence began the deductive process. If all men are endowed by their Creator with certain inalienable rights, and if the uninhibited accumulation of property is such a right, then the state of Louisiana cannot create a slaughterhouse monopoly. The conclusion, of course, depends upon the substance given the forms. Here the words of the Declaration are like vessels into which liquid is poured. Justice Field was determined to fill up his vessels—life, liberty, and the pursuit of happiness—with a liquid distilled from the labors of private enterprise.

We shall return to the question whether this particular receptacle was designed for the substance introduced into it by Justice Field. For present purposes, however, it is only necessary to indicate the character of the reasoning by which the justice arrived at his decision. It was a type of reasoning not unique to the legal setting, but one, certainly, that had found the judicial world of precedent, traditionalism, and rationalism a particularly agreeable and harmonious environment in which to become firmly entrenched. The construction of the constitutional defenses of vested interests relied upon a good measure of ingenuity and creative legal imagination, but it did not require the adoption of a new set of epistemological assumptions. For centuries there had been a nexus between ethical and political systems based upon an acceptance of first principles and a mode of reasoning that was rigorously Euclidian in its deductive logic.[7] The jurists of a newly industrialized nation placed this complementary tradition in the service of capitalist accumulation.

To recapitulate: Field's jurisprudence (which was soon to become the prevailing judicial approach) was characterized by an appeal to the past, for the purpose of deriving absolute principles grounded in Nature, by which conclusions could be deduced, with certainty, regarding the inequality of man in civil society. For those left unhappy with the ends secured by this approach, an opposite approach required development—an appeal to the future, for the purpose of deriving relative principles grounded in experience, by which conclusions of a tentative nature could be inductively assembled regarding the equality of man in civil society—in other words, judicial pragmatism.

TWO RESPONSES

Justice Holmes's famous dissenting opinion in *Lochner* v. *New York* reflected the pragmatic reaction against the jurisprudence that Justice Field helped to create. If the latter (or in this case, Justice Rufus W. Peckham) could use natural rights principles to sanctify laissez-faire economics, he, Justice Holmes, could abandon all reference to such principles in order to deny that the Constitution incorporated any economic theory. "A constitution is not intended to embody a particular economic theory, whether of paternalism and the organic relation of the citizen to the State or of *laissez faire*. It is made for people of fundamentally differing views."[8]

Holmes's dissent was a logical outgrowth of the position out-

7. For an illuminating discussion of this question see Edward A. Purcell, Jr., *The Crisis of Democratic Theory: Scientific Naturalism and the Problem of Value* (Lexington, Ky., 1973), pp. 47–74.
8. *Lochner* v. *New York*, 198 U.S. 45 (1905).

lined twenty-five years earlier in his classic work on the common law. Then he penned the now-familiar words that have inspired the work of many subsequent legal scholars. "The felt necessities of the time, the prevalent moral and political theories, intuitions of public policy, avowed or unconscious, even the prejudices which judges share with their fellow men, have had a good deal more to do than the syllogism in determining the rules by which men should be governed."[9] As the basis of his critique of the majority view in the *Lochner* case, this observation led him to conclude that the right of "liberty of contract," which Field and other judges had derived from the Fourteenth Amendment, was in fact a derivative of the prevailing economic and political philosophies of these judges and their beneficiaries in the business world.

The *Lochner* case was the high-water mark of judicial reinterpretation of the due process clause. In striking down a New York statute that had established a ten-hour working day for bakery employees the Court was completing the "surgery by judicial metaphysicians operating on the recently adopted Fourteenth Amendment."[10] Due process was now a substantive guarantee against "unreasonable" legislative intrusion upon the rights of property subsumed under the rubric of liberty of contract.[11] Specifically, the issue before the Court was whether the challenged enactment constituted "a fair, reasonable, and appropriate exercise of the police power of the State."[12] Its invalidation by the Court meant that a majority viewed the statute as an unreasonable exercise of this power.

9. Oliver Wendell Holmes, *The Common Law* (Boston, 1963), p. 5.
10. Leonard Levy, ed., *American Constitutional Law: Historical Essays* (New York, 1966), p. 129.
11. In 1897, in *Allgeyer* v. *Louisiana*, 165 U.S. 578, the Court first invalidated a state law on the ground that it infringed upon the "liberty" guaranteed by the due process clause of the Fourteenth Amendment. Thus were vindicated the earlier dissents of Justices Field and Bradley [for example, *Slaughter-House Cases*, 16 Wall. 36 (1873); *Munn* v. *Illinois*, 94 U.S. 113 (1877); *Davidson* v. *New Orleans*, 96 U.S. 97 (1898)]. It should be noted that perhaps the most influential writing in the development of the doctrine of liberty of contract appeared off the Court in Thomas M. Cooley's *Treatise on Constitutional Limitations,* published in 1868.
12. *Lochner* v. *New York*, at 56.

Unlike most judicial pragmatists, Justice Holmes was not concerned with the facts of the particular case (the plight of sickly bakers did not move him); however, since the Constitution, in his view, was an essentially neutral document, the legislature was free to enact any legislation that its study of the facts suggested was necessary. Indeed, legislative experimentation, designed, in pragmatic terms, to render a problematic situation unproblematic, would be incompatible with a constitutional theory that upheld a laissez-faire economic philosophy.[13] Thus, although Holmes left Justice Harlan to talk about facts (i.e., the working conditions of bakers), it was his opinion, with its extreme judicial deference, that afforded the greatest scope for the application of pragmatic doctrine.

Harlan's empirical analysis did not deny the majority's principles of interpretation, but rather interpreted the facts differently and granted a somewhat greater presumption of constitutionality to the legislation. His dissent, in point of fact, was closer to the majority view than the dissent by Justice Holmes. In a much earlier case, *Mugler* v. *Kansas*,[14] dealing with the constitutionality of a state prohibition statute, Harlan had made abundantly clear the distinction between his philosophy and that of his future colleague. Once again he upheld the legislation under the police power of the state, but in this case he made an important statement regarding the limits of judicial deference.

It belongs to [the legislature] to exert what are known as the police powers of the state, and to determine, primarily, what measures are appropriate or needful for the protection of the public morals, the public health, or the public safety.

It does not at all follow that every statute enacted ostensibly for the promotion of these ends, is to be accepted as a legitimate exertion of

13. Richard Hofstadter maintained that Dewey's skepticism about laissez faire was a logical extension of his experimental philosophy. If knowledge was a function of direct participation in an event, a philosophy that prevented any social intervention would constitute an impediment in the way of truth. Hofstadter, *Social Darwinism*, p. 138. Holmes's opinion was calculated to open the way for the kind of unbridled experimentation that Dewey's pragmatism was advocating.

14. 123 U.S. 623 (1887).

the police powers of the state. There are, of necessity, limits beyond which legislation cannot rightfully go.

. . . the courts must obey the Constitution rather than the law-making department of government, and must, upon their own responsibility, determine whether, in any particular case, these limits have been passed.[15]

That Harlan took his dictum seriously is suggested by the number of cases where he voted, under the rubric of economic due process, to strike down legislation. Unlike Holmes, then, Harlan held state experimentation to a severe standard of constitutional adequacy, and the judge, not the legislator, was to prescribe the applicable constitutional limitations. Harlan might very well have agreed with Robert McCloskey's concern that substantive, economic due process, no longer a viable constitutional standard (a fact that can be traced to Holmes in *Lochner*), can be as instrumental to freedom as the procedural due process which presently enjoys the favor of the Court.[16]

It is somewhat ironic that Holmes and Charles Beard, the foremost pragmatic revisionist in historiography, who thus had much in common with Holmes, should have disagreed on the economic interpretation of the Constitution. Holmes claimed that no economic theory is embodied in the Constitution; Beard maintained that "the Constitution was essentially an economic document based upon the concept that the fundamental private rights of property are anterior to government and morally beyond the reach of popular majorities."[17] Doubtless both overstated their

15. Ibid., at 661. Harlan rejected Mugler's due process argument without denying that due process was the relevant constitutional standard. He failed to be swayed by the hysteria of counsel—this excerpt from the brief of attorney George G. Vest is a representative sample: "If a state convention or legislature can punish a citizen for manufacturing beer, or wine, or bread, not to be sold or bartered away, but for his own use, then instead of civil liberty, we are living under the most unlimited and brutal despotism in history."

16. McCloskey, "Economic Due Process and the Supreme Court: An Exhumation and Reburial," in Levy, ed., *American Constitutional Law*. "It is one thing," McCloskey wrote, "to argue that economic liberty must be subject to rational control in the 'public interest;' it is quite another to say in effect that it is not liberty at all and that the proponent of the 'open society' can therefore regard it as irrelevant to progress." Ibid., p. 173.

17. Charles A. Beard, *An Economic Interpretation of the Constitution* (New York, 1941), p. 324.

cases—Beard in his controversial book and Holmes in his Court opinions. Even Beard's severest critics, however, do not deny the importance of economic factors, though they attribute much less importance to them.[18] While it can be said that the contradiction between Beard and Holmes is only an apparent one, that to cite economic origins need not imply a specific economic theory, Beard's history (despite its gross exaggeration) does suggest very definite constitutional limitations regarding legislative activity affecting property rights. This is the important point, for the question still remains: Was Justice Field's interpretation of natural rights and property correct? If so, Holmes's pragmatic alternative may be the only way to avoid the practical implications of that interpretation.[19] Or can one assent to the natural rights–constitutional basis for property rights and yet differ from Field's interpretation? Can one, in short, steer a middle course between Field and Holmes?

History provides some insight into this question. In the late nineteenth century the major thrust of egalitarian movements was directed against the massive accumulation of industrial capital. Earlier in the century, at the time of Tocqueville's visit (during the height of Jacksonian democracy), equality and private property had not been in conflict; in fact they were, as the Frenchman observed, very much related. The expansion of political and social democracy was paralleled by the accelerated development of an ethos of acquisition. For example, as Benjamin Wright noted in his study of the contract clause, the same men who in their constitutional conventions were advocating a broader suffrage and the abolition of all property restrictions upon office holding, were also

18. See especially Forrest MacDonald, *We the People* (Chicago, 1958), and Robert E. Brown, *Charles Beard and the Constitution: A Critical Analysis of "An Economic Interpretation of the Constitution"* (New York, 1956).

19. For a good example of a scholarly analysis that reflects the Holmesian alternative and then proceeds to develop a pragmatic understanding of the relationship of the Supreme Court to the Constitution see Arthur Selwyn Miller, *The Supreme Court and American Capitalism* (New York, 1968). For Miller, "the idea of the 'living' Constitution is a justification for adaptation of the basic document to fit new social situations. The words remain the same—they are both timeless and ambiguous—but their content changes." Ibid., p. 23. See also, in this regard, Walton H. Hamilton, "The Path of Due Process," *Ethics,* 48 (1938).

voting to include in their new state constitutions clauses prohibiting the legislature from passing any law impairing the obligation of contracts.[20] This clause, in the federal Constitution, was the instrument, prior to later due process interpretation, used by the courts to protect private property against legislative intervention. Unlike the Field-Bradley interpretation of the due process clause, the contract clause was not perceived, for most of its active history, as an antidemocratic or antiegalitarian device.[21] There was no sharp antithesis, then, between the unequal accumulation of property by members of society and the working principles of democracy. This is a major theme, too, in the work of Louis Hartz, who, following Tocqueville, traced the development of the liberal philosophy of democratic capitalism.[22]

John Locke's political philosophy, as Hartz correctly noted, lies at the root of this democratic capitalism. Indeed, "Locke dominates American political thought, as no thinker anywhere dominates the political thought of a nation. He is a massive national cliche."[23] The relevant question here is whether for Justice Field, Locke was simply a cliche, a stereotype of little significance, so that the pragmatic reaction against natural rights principles may very well have been, historically speaking, a reaction against their misapplication.

Locke's doctrine of property represents the core of his political teaching.[24] With regard to the rapid expansion of industrial capital in post–Civil War America, two aspects of this doctrine should be mentioned. First, there is an important distinction recognized in the theory between possession and acquisition. The latter constitutes the more fundamental right. That is to say, the public interest

20. Benjamin F. Wright, Jr., *The Contract Clause of the Constitution* (Cambridge, 1938), p. 254.

21. This does not mean that the clause was unimportant in the early contests between propertied and non-propertied interests. Often the small land-owning democrat was the most concerned with legislative interference with his private property. The protection of vested interests was not a concern of any *one* class in society.

22. Louis Hartz, *The Liberal Tradition in America* (New York, 1955). See especially pp. 89–114 and 203–228.

23. Ibid., p. 140.

24. For the discussion of this interpretation see Leo Strauss, *Natural Right and History* (Chicago, 1953), pp. 234–252.

is best served by unleashing the acquisitive instincts of private individuals. This is facilitated by the invention of money, which removes the limitations upon acquisition that necessarily existed in prepolitical society.[25] Of course, government is supposed to protect one's possessions, but the larger purpose to be served by such protection is the further acquisition of property. As one noted scholar has written, "the property which is to be 'preserved' by civil society is not 'static' property—the small farm which one has inherited from one's fathers and which one will hand down to one's children—but 'dynamic' property."[26] In Chief Justice John Marshall's Lockean jurisprudence this means that "the haves are protected in what they possess, but the road to having is opened to all by a fundamental protection of acquisition, not possession."[27] Unequal accumulation of property is made compatible with democratic equality when equality is specified to mean equality of opportunity (for acquisition).

Locke's theory was developed prior to the industrial revolution. Of what importance is this historical fact? One could argue, as Edward S. Corwin did, that "the property which Locke had in mind . . . did not comprise anything closely analogous to modern investment capital."[28] This argument makes a distinction between property of a personal nature, such as a person's land, house, and furniture, and property of an impersonal nature, such as characterizes the absentee ownership of corporate enterprise. Whereas the courts, in protecting the former against legislative intrusion, were upholding Lockean natural rights principles, they were not obliged, according to the same principles, similarly to intervene

25. "And as different degrees of industry were apt to give men possessions in different proportions, so this intervention of money gave them the opportunity to continue and enlarge them." John Locke, *Second Treatise on Civil Government*, chap. 5, sec. 48.

26. Strauss, *Natural Right*, p. 245.

27. Robert K. Faulkner, *The Jurisprudence of John Marshall* (Princeton, 1968), p. 24. According to Faulkner it is this protection of acquisition that renders Marshall's judicial interpretation of property rights intelligible.

28. Edward S. Corwin, *The Twilight of the Supreme Court: A History of Our Constitutional Theory* (New Haven, 1934), p. 197. This theme was elaborated upon in several of Professor Corwin's other books as well. See his *Liberty against Government* (Baton Rouge, 1948), *Constitutional Revolution Ltd.* (Claremont, 1941), and *Court over Constitution* (Princeton, 1938).

when the property in question was of the corporate kind. Hence the resort to these principles by the "liberty of contract" jurists involved a fundamental distortion of Lockean philosophy. The distortion is highlighted, so this interpretation goes, by confusing obligation of contract (which had to do with vested rights) with liberty of contract (which did not).

Unfortunately, the argument creates a distinction not suggested in Locke. While Locke may not have anticipated John D. Rockefeller, Jay Gould, and Andrew Carnegie, his doctrine of property certainly provides a philosophical basis for investment capital. If Corwin were speaking only of Locke's reflections on pre-money property his distinction would be valid, though irrelevant. The invention of a basic unit of exchange assumes investment expansion beyond that which an individual obtains by mixing his labor with the natural resources common to all. But this does not mean that the difference in the two types of property is of no consequence.

One must recall that the right of acquisition is to be protected by government. As James Madison put it in *Federalist* 10, the first object of government is the protection of the "different and unequal faculties of acquiring property." Protection partakes of positive as well as negative action. For Locke, the right to acquire was instrumental; property was essential for liberty (self-government) and not the reverse. Capitalist property is something all can share; it is not divisive. This is so because capitalist property is acquisition, and acquisition becomes the substitute for morality—becomes, in effect, the basis of civil society. No longer, for Locke, is the moral thread that binds together the fabric of society the gift of an aristocratic elite dedicated to the pursuit of virtue. Rather, a public morality, less edifying perhaps, but more solid than what earlier prevailed, could be expected to result from the private interest in accumulating wealth. Acquisition would lead to general well-being, which in turn would eventuate in security, which is the only environment that will successfully accommodate peace and tolerance. Moreover, the satisfaction of the acquisitive instinct does not lead to bloodshed because, according to Locke, everyone can acquire under capitalism. If private factors are themselves responsible for the infringement upon the right of acquisition, then it is the obligation of government to intervene in behalf of those individuals whose exercise of a natural right is being denied. This is in part the theory behind the police power of the state.[29] The protection of the natural right to property, or acquisition, is an appropriate basis for state action designed to remove such obstacles to acquisition as subsistence wages and dangerous working conditions. The unlimited acquisition of the few may have to be regulated in order to secure the basic right of acquisition of the many. Thus the case against Field can be made in Lockean terms.

Even Daniel Webster, that arch defender of private property, whose views on the subject were an important influence on John Marshall, recognized the relationship between government action and the right of acquisition. In the Massachusetts Convention of 1820, after arguing that it was "the part of political wisdom to found government on property," Webster declared that "the freest government, if it could exist, would not long be acceptable, if the tendencies of the laws were to create a rapid accumulation of property in few hands, and to render the great mass of the population dependent and penniless."[30] Webster was hardly an egalitarian, but he realized that a just political order guarantees its members at least a minimum of dignity and independence. The problem with so many of the Supreme Court decisions upholding the sanctity of the contract between employer and employee was the

29. The term "police power" first appears in Chief Justice Marshall's opinion in *Brown* v. *Maryland*, 12 Wheat. 419 (1827). However, the term acquired its present-day meaning in the opinions of Marshall's successor, Chief Justice Roger B. Taney. See especially his opinions in *License* cases, 5 How. 504 (1847); and *Charles River Bridge* v. *Warren Bridge*, 11 Pet. 420 (1837). In this latter case he wrote, "While the rights of private property are sacredly guarded, we must not forget, that the community also have rights, and that the happiness and well-being of every citizen depends on their faithful preservation." Ibid., at 548. "The power," as one scholar has written, "is that to prevent or restrain exercises of private rights which may be noxious to others." Bernard Schwartz, *A Commentary on the Constitution of the United States—Part II: The Rights of Property* (New York, 1965), p. 40. "The police power, under the traditional approach, may be paraphrased as society's natural right of self-defense." Ibid., p. 41.

30. Quoted in Corwin, *The Twilight of the Supreme Court*, p. 64. Appropriate here is Professor Faulkner's discussion of Marshall's jurisprudence: "Built into the individualistic doctrine he shares with Lockean liberalism . . . is the presupposition that personal property may be regulated in accord with the requirements of commercial society and of a government capable of protecting that society." Faulkner, *John Marshall*, p. 27.

failure to understand this basic fact—that the relationship of government to liberty implies a positive as well as a negative dimension. Ultimately, therefore, the constitutionality of economic and social legislation is a question of judgment. What prevents this from being a simple truism is the history of Fieldian and Holmesian opinions, which, more often than not, involved prejudgment rather than judgment. Harlan, on the other hand, understood that constitutional judgment involves the careful application of principle to a given set of facts. This implies the legitimation of legislation that, on balance, supports the operative principle (in this case the right of acquisition) and rejection of legislation, the thrust of which is to undermine the principle.

A second and related aspect of the Lockean doctrine that is relevant here is the idea of the public interest. Ultimately, it is the procuring of this interest which justifies the inequality of possessions. All members of civil society, not just those who have amassed the greatest fortunes, will benefit from the protection of the natural right to acquire property. This is also the argument behind the theory in *Federalist* 10, where Madison indicated that the public good would be secured through the pursuit of private commercial self-interest. The development of a commercial society is thus intimately related to the success of the American experiment in republican self-government. However, since the end in view is not the possession of property but rather a common good for men living in civil society, the natural right of acquisition requires certain modifications when it is converted into a civil right (without destroying the essence of the right). This is nowhere better expressed than by Sir William Blackstone, who defined civil liberty (which is the end of civil society) as "natural liberty so far restrained by human laws (and no further) as is necessary and expedient for the general advantage of the public." On the preceding page he had indicated that the "first and primary end of human laws is to maintain and regulate [the] *absolute* rights of individuals."[31] In civil society, then, regulation of rights is necessary

31. Sir William Blackstone, *Commentaries on the Laws of England* (New York, 1859), I, 125, 124. For an excellent account of Blackstone's views on this question see Herbert J. Storing, "William Blackstone," in *A History of Political Philosophy*, eds. Leo Strauss and Joseph Cropsey (Chicago, 1966). Storing related this conversion of natural rights into civil

for the maintenance or rights. This was true in Blackstone's day; it was also true in Field's.[32]

This is precisely what Field did not understand. It was not so much his misinterpretation of natural rights as it was his misapplication of natural rights philosophy that flawed his constitutional jurisprudence. His frequent citation of the Declaration of Independence is not to be decried; however, as a judge interpreting the Constitution, his function was to civilize the rights inscribed in that natural rights document. And this, in most cases, he did not do. As Corwin put it, "to [Justice Field] the individualistic tenets of the Declaration of Independence were an evangel of eternal verities, and what they meant was that individual initiative was not to be curbed by government so long as it did not take form in actual violence or the grosser species of fraud."[33] To this must be added relief from disasters and prevention of calamities. "Except in cases," reads Field's dissent in *Munn* v. *Illinois,* "where property may be destroyed to arrest a conflagration or the ravages of pestilence, or be taken under the pressure of an immediate and overwhelming necessity to prevent a public calamity, the power of the state over the property of the citizen does not extend beyond such limits."[34] In time, and with great reluctance, Field came to accept the constitutionality of limited state regulations. In another Illinois case six years later, he concurred in the opinion of Chief Justice Morrison Waite upholding the railroad rate legislation, still, however, voicing total disagreement with the decision in *Munn,*

---

rights to the role of the judiciary. "How far and in what respects the general advantage requires restraint of natural liberty is not a question that can be answered, except in a way that reformulates the question, by some general principle or rule. And free government depends on the maintenance within it of a central place for the judiciary, that peculiar body of men who are capable, by tradition, political position, and training, of judging well." Ibid., p. 542.

32. Professor McCloskey wrote that as the Constitution stood until 1870, "the rights of the man of property were subsidiary to the higher consideration of the public interest [as understood by the founders]." McCloskey, *American Conservatism,* p. 73. While the public interest was the highest consideration, McCloskey was mistaken if he meant to suggest by the word "subsidiary" that property rights and public interest were understood to be two distinct things. Rather, property rights, properly regulated, were central to the attainment of the public interest.

33. Corwin, *Court over Constitution,* p. 107.

34. *Munn* v. *Illinois,* 94 U.S. 113 (1877).

but arguing instead on grounds of precedent.[35] Characteristically, Justice Harlan's concurring opinion disagreed with the majority's contention that the subject of reasonableness was not a question for judicial inquiry. He was the Blackstonian of that period of Supreme Court history, a believer in the same eternal verities as his colleague, Justice Field, but with one difference. As a judge, he recognized that justice would be achieved only by placing reasonable limits upon the exercise of any absolute right.[36]

More will be said of this approach to constitutional questions in the succeeding chapters. It is certainly not a novel jurisprudence. For example, the old common law judges in England had transformed the ideas of the law of nature into progressive principles of legal growth by adapting them to changing social and economic conditions.[37] The failure similarly to adapt these principles to the legal problems emerging out of the industrial revolution of the nineteenth century gave rise to the pragmatic reaction against "mechanical jurisprudence." From an historical perspective Fieldian jurisprudence gave natural rights philosophy a bad name. It suggested stagnation, a lack of vitality in legal principles, and aloofness from the conditions of the real world.[38] And in doing so it provided grist for the pragmatic mill.

35. *Ruggles* v. *Illinois,* 108 U.S. 526 (1883).

36. Carl Brent Swisher made a revealing comment concerning Field's view of how the public interest could best be achieved. "He almost never emphasized the need for protecting the masses against the superior strength of the few. Instead he stressed the need for protecting the strong, who were bringing about superior achievements in the business and industrial world, against the restraining activities of the public. Perhaps he reasoned that ultimately the public at large was immeasurably benefited by the achievements of the few, and, on the whole, had no cause for complaint." Swisher, *Stephen J. Field: Craftsman of the Law* (Washington, 1930), p. 427.

37. This development is discussed in Charles G. Haines, *The Revival of Natural Law Concepts* (Cambridge, 1930), p. 44.

38. Professor Felix Frankfurter expressed this very well in an article entitled "Mr. Justice Holmes and the Constitution," *Harvard Law Review,* 41 (1927), 141–142: "Though speaking the language of abstractions, the opinions of Mr. Justice Field reflected adequately enough the vital elements of the social and economic order in which he grew up. But his society was in process of drastic transformation, and indeed had largely passed, certainly when Mr. Justice Peckham wrote Mr. Justice Field's dissents into the opinions of the Court."

CHAPTER 3

Pragmatism and Democracy

PRAGMATISM AND THE EQUALITY OF CONDITION

"The Americans," wrote Tocqueville, "have no philosophical school of their own; and they care but little for all the schools into which Europe is divided, the very names of which are scarcely known to them."[1] Tocqueville was writing in 1835 when, it is true, the Americans had not as yet developed a philosophical school of their own. They had, however, developed a philosophical method which the Frenchman described in careful detail. This description is significant in relation to the present inquiry, for in all essential respects it serves extremely well as an account of the philosophy of pragmatism. Tocqueville's analysis of the American approach to philosophical questions constitutes an anticipation of pragmatic philosophy, often described as the only original philosophic contribution produced in America. This anticipation is hardly coincidental. Rather, as so often in Tocqueville, the accuracy of the prophecy is attributable to the author's understanding of the essential characteristic of democracy, the equality of condition. Indeed, pragmatism is the philosophy of the equality of condition.[2]

Tocqueville described the American philosophical method in the following way: "To evade the bondage of system and habit, of family-maxims, class opinions, and, in some degree, of national prejudices; to accept tradition only as a means of information, and

1. Tocqueville, *Democracy*, II, 3.
2. Critics of pragmatism, such as W. Y. Elliott, *The Pragmatic Revolt in Politics* (New York, 1928), have written of the adaptability of pragmatic doctrine to a variety of governmental regimes, just and unjust. Perhaps the major point of Tocqueville's book is that equality of condition can prevail with equal ease in regimes characterized by freedom as well as those characterized by despotism. The connection, however, between pragmatism and equality of condition has not, to my knowledge, been made; although Tocqueville suggests it.

existing facts only as a lesson to be used in doing otherwise and doing better; to seek the reason of things for oneself, and in one-self alone; to tend to results without being bound to means, and to strike through the form to the substance—such are the principal characteristics of what I shall call the philosophical method of the Americans."[3]

These "principal characteristics" are useful in describing the philosophy of pragmatism as well, and to the extent that they bear significantly on jurisprudential matters, they will receive analysis in the discussion that follows.[4] Inevitably, the limited purpose of this brief excursion into philosophical exegesis leads to a certain degree of distortion. In referring to pragmatism, for example, an impression may be conveyed that the spokesmen of pragmatic philosophy spoke with a unified voice—that there is *a* philosophy of pragmatism. This, of course, is not the case; and even between James and Dewey, the two philosophers most often identified with the movement of pragmatism in American philosophy, there existed a considerable area of disagreement.[5] Nevertheless, for present purposes it will suffice to speak of pragmatic philosophy in the singular, concentrating on those general themes that unite, rather than divide, most pragmatists. To some extent this unity is artificially achieved by focusing most attention on the work of John Dewey, by singling out Dewey as the spokesman for American pragmatism. In so doing, however, the importance of Charles

3. Tocqueville, *Democracy*, II, 3.
4. The effort will not be to summarize all the major doctrines of pragmatism, but rather to depict those elements of the philosophy which illuminate constitutional decision making.
5. The disagreement between James and Dewey derives from differing attitudes toward the place of subjectivity in the definition of truth. James was much less "rigorously empirical" than Dewey, and he was much readier to accept the validity of propositions unsupported by scientific evidence. A comparison of James's "The Will to Believe," in *Pragmatism and Other Essays* (New York, 1962), with Dewey's *Logic: The Theory of Inquiry* (New York, 1938), provides ample illustration of their divergence on this matter. James was also much less concerned with the problem of reconstruction, or radical reform in the society. Consider Morris R. Cohen on this point: "Dewey and his followers are essentially moralists, interested in philosophy as an instrument for social betterment. James is a spiritualist, interested in what constitutes well-being rather than well-doing." Cohen, *American Thought* (Glencoe, Ill., 1954), p. 290.

Sanders Peirce and William James to the pragmatic movement in philosophy should not be overlooked.[6] Rather, Dewey is chosen because pragmatism reaches full maturity in his writings, and because the connection between the philosophic doctrine and its application by the Court is most readily apparent in Dewey's work.[7]

Tocqueville's insight into the philosophic method of the Americans suggests a framework for the presentation of pragmatic doctrines. His description can conveniently be segmented into four elements, each one elaborated in other parts of his book: reconstruction (the rejection of tradition), change, experience, and antiformalism. Pragmatism lends itself to analysis according to the same division. What follows, then, is a juxtaposition of Tocqueville's reflections on the relation between philosophic method and equality of condition and Dewey's exposition of a pragmatic ap-

6. Indeed, by the time Dewey began writing systematically about pragmatism, the major groundwork had been prepared by Peirce and James. Peirce, the philosopher of science, originated the term (derived from the Greek word for "action") in his quest for an appropriate method for defining general concepts. His ideas are best elaborated in a number of articles, most notably "The Fixation of Belief," "How to Make Our Ideas Clear," and "What Pragmatism Is," to be found in the *Collected Papers of Charles Sanders Peirce,* eds. Charles Hartshorne and Paul Weiss (Cambridge, 1960), as well as in several anthologies of pragmatism. James, who explicitly acknowledged his debt to Peirce, developed and popularized the latter's ideas, and was the key figure in defining pragmatism as a serious movement in American philosophy. According to one student of pragmatism, "the movement [of pragmatism] did not become of dominant concern to philosophers until after the publication of James's book *Pragmatism* in 1907." Edward C. Moore, *American Pragmatism: Peirce, James, and Dewey* (New York, 1961), p. 135. Another wrote that "it was James more than anyone who gave pragmatism its mother tongue, its characteristic vocabulary, its identifying phrases and stock of illustrative materials." H. S. Thayer, *Meaning and Action: A Critical History of Pragmatism* (Indianapolis, 1966), p. 145. Finally, Cohen wrote that "James seems to have been what the chemists call a catalytic agent in American philosophy." Cohen, *American Thought,* p. 290. Continuing the analogy, for our purposes, Dewey constitutes the critical element in the pragmatic equation.

7. Or, stated differently, Dewey's substantive concerns coincide with those of the advocates of judicial pragmatism, whereas the work of Peirce is most immediately relevant to linguistic analysts, and the work of James, to students of religion and psychology. However, for an interesting analysis of the influence of Peirce on judicial pragmatism see Note, "Holmes, Peirce, and Legal Pragmatism," *Yale Law Journal,* 84 (1975).

proach to philosophic questions. The rationale for such a juxta-position is that the linkage between pragmatism and equality of condition will prove instructive in the subsequent consideration of the Supreme Court and its role in American political life.

Reconstruction

Reconstruction in Philosophy is perhaps Dewey's most ex-plicit statement of the place of philosophy in modern society. The objective of the book is to bring philosophy down from the clouds in order to make it effective in the resolution of pressing social problems. For Dewey, the initial step in producing this descent was to expose the deception that surrounded the history of philo-sophic thought. Thus, "under disguise of dealing with ultimate reality, philosophy has been occupied with the precious values embedded in social traditions."[8] The great philosophers are no longer seen as independent thinkers pursuing truth, but rather as defenders, rationalizers, of the social system of which they are a part. Dewey shared with Karl Marx the view that philosophy is a reflection of a society's particular social arrangements. More specifically, he maintained that philosophy prefers the heavenly environs because in that way it deflects the attention of society's less fortunate members from the conditions which define their station in life. Accordingly, Justice Field, for example, referred to abstractions such as natural rights because, as a spokesman for vested interests, he could thereby defend these interests while avoiding real social problems.

Pragmatism did not develop specifically in response to Field and his judicial colleagues; however, in a general way its popular-ity can be viewed historically as a critical response to the widening divisions between the haves and the have nots in American society.[9] Or, stated differently, pragmatic philosophy developed partly in response to the increasing inequality of condition in America. This is not surprising. The crystallization of the demo-

8. John Dewey, *Reconstruction in Philosophy* (Boston, 1920), p. 26.
9. Thayer, *Meaning and Action*, p. 445. This is not intended as a socio-logical explanation of the origins of pragmatism. Once originated, however, its doctrines were very useful to partisans of the egalitarian political persuasion.

cratic philosophic method into a pragmatic school of philosophy might have been expected to occur at a time when the characteristic feature of the democracy, the equality of condition, was being eroded. Just as it was not necessary for the American colonies to develop a systematic philosophy until England was forced by events to make her presence known to the Americans in the 1760's,[10] it was unnecessary for the egalitarians to develop a systematic philosophy until economic factors, encouraged and endorsed by the state, called for such a response. Distrust of authority, whether that authority is the accumulated wisdom of the past, a particular social class, or simply habit and tradition, is, as Tocqueville pointed out, peculiar to the democratic socio-political environment. "The nearer people are drawn to the common level on an equal and similar condition, the less prone does each man become to place implicit faith in a certain man or a certain class of men."[11] Dewey's plea in *Reconstruction in Philosophy* is, in the terminology of the science he did so much to advance, that philosophy operationalize this distrust of authority, so that the abandonment of authority can become the first step toward the establishment of a new social order.

In this regard, Dewey assigned a function to philosophy reminiscent of Marx, "that of reconstituting the present stage of things instead of merely knowing it."[12] This left open the question whether meaningful and intelligent reconstruction is possible without "mere" knowledge. Dewey could avoid the question definitionally by maintaining that a transformation of the environment

10. This story is best told in Gordon Wood, *The Creation of the American Republic, 1776-1787* (Williamsburg, 1969), and Bernard Bailyn, *The Ideological Origins of the American Revolution* (Cambridge, 1967).

11. Tocqueville, *Democracy*, II, 11.

12. Dewey, *Philosophy and Civilization* (New York, 1963), p. 32. "In a profound sense," Dewey stated in *Reconstruction*, "knowing ceases to be contemplative and becomes practical." p. 116. According to H. S. Thayer, this constitutes the cardinal doctrine of Dewey's theory of knowledge. "Inquiry effects an existential transformation of subject matters inquired into; knowledge brings about a change in the thing known." Thayer, *Meaning and Action*, p. 198. Dewey's "instrumentalism" is a refinement of James's earlier description of what the pragmatist does. "He [the pragmatist] turns toward concreteness and adequacy, towards facts, towards action and towards power." William James, "Pragmatism," in *Pragmatism*, p. 25.

implies knowledge of the reconstructed situation. Ultimately, however, as Tocqueville suggested in his discussion of the American addiction to practical rather than theoretical science, traditional philosophy must give direction to practical science if we are to profit from the fruits of empirical inquiry. Tocqueville seemed to be saying that a balance must be struck between the "arrogant and sterile research for abstract truths" that characterizes the permanent inequality of conditions, and the exclusive reliance upon the "useful practical results of the sciences" that distinguishes inquiry during periods of equality.[13] Referring back once again to the Fieldian jurisprudence of the nineteenth century in order to anticipate the discussion of pragmatic constitutionalism, one should note the sterile application of abstract truths by the arch defenders of inequality, an application that stimulated the defenders of equality to adopt the opposite mode of inquiry. To anticipate further, an appropriate set of norms for constitutional decision making will somehow have to effect a reconciliation between these two contrary approaches. For the moment at least, it is important to appreciate the egalitarian basis for the view that philosophy must transform reality.

Related to this view, and to the narrower jurisprudential question, is Dewey's understanding of the sources and the elements of knowledge. Historically, he considered tradition, religion, and philosophy to have been the special preserve of the ruling elements in society, and facts to have been associated with the exploited classes. Equality was directly related to factual knowledge, and thus one measure of the equality of condition in any given society was the extent to which knowledge about the world rested upon an empirical foundation.[14]

Dewey did not suggest that reliance upon fact is totally absent from feudal societies. Like Tocqueville, however, he believed that democratic man is more likely than feudal man to seek guidance for his actions from his own analysis (or from those similarly

13. Tocqueville, *Democracy*, II, 47.
14. Indeed, reconstruction in all its myriad forms, involves "the substitution of a *democracy of individual facts* equal in rank for the feudal system of an ordered gradation of general classes of unequal rank." Dewey, *Reconstruction*, p. 66. Emphasis added.

situated) of all relevant factors than from the traditions and abstractions that have been handed down to him.[15] This individualism fascinated and alarmed Tocqueville, who saw within it the potential for great evil. He believed individualism to be of uniquely democratic origin, and a phenomenon whose influence varied directly with the equality of condition. Its problematic character resulted from its tendency to devolve into a selfishness that was destructive of the virtues of public life. These virtues are a barrier between freedom and despotism, and thus Tocqueville was concerned that "the vices which despotism produces are precisely those which equality fosters."[16] He concluded that the effects of individualism could best be combatted through local institutions. The courts were also important in this regard, and precisely for this reason, they ought to conduct their business in a manner distinguishable from the democratic ethic of individualism.

A most significant element of this democratic individualism is, according to Tocqueville, a depreciation of the contemporary significance of the past. The remembrance and study of one's ancestors had previously given one an insight into the future, into the probable situation of one's descendants. The orientation of pragmatic philosophy, on the other hand—and this can serve as a summary of Dewey's reconstruction—is directed almost exclusively toward the future. "It is not the origin of a concept," he wrote in *Philosophy and Civilization,* "it is its application which becomes the criterion of its value; and here we have the whole of pragmatism in embryo."[17] Dewey spoke in this connection of the law,

15. Religion had an interesting role in the development of this concern for independent factual analysis. Tocqueville indicated in several places that religion in America had been a mitigating factor in the application by ordinary men of data secured by their own observation. But there also seems to be some validity to the argument advanced by the pragmatist, Moore, that pragmatism was greatly aided by the existence of a social order which was, in part, premised on the protestant teaching of the right of the individual to seek the truth for himself. He saw as common to both pragmatism and protestantism "the right of the individual to insist that old truths be brought to terms with the thoughts of each new thinker." Moore, *American Pragmatism,* p. 7. These observations are not mutually exclusive; both have played a part in the shaping of American character and philosophy.

16. Tocqueville, *Democracy,* II, 109.

17. Dewey, *Philosophy and Civilization,* p. 29.

and maintained that legal rules and principles are "working hypotheses," whose validity is to be ascertained by the consequences of their application in concrete situations. The tradition of precedent, by which antecedent principles are accorded special respect, was consequently called into question by the pragmatists' futuristic orientation.[18] Law, like truth and language, is a process, continually redefining itself as it unravels, never fixed, always changing. For Dewey, and for the judicial pragmatists, this prospective outlook insures respect for law, because it maintains a congruence between social reality and the doctrines applied by the courts of law.

Not surprisingly, then, "[Francis] Bacon may be taken as the prophet of a pragmatic conception of knowledge." He realized that "a logic of discovery . . . looks to the future."[19] Tocqueville, in his discussion of the American philosophical method, noted that the philosophy and science of Bacon and Descartes, which "abolished received formulas, destroyed the empire of tradition, and overthrew the authority of the schools,"[20] had been adopted (though not studied) by the Americans. He went on to say that this new tradition could only be extensively applied when conditions in society had been sufficiently equalized. To Tocqueville, in other words, Bacon's philosophy was democratic; to Dewey it was pragmatic, which is to say, democratic. It liberated man and philosophy from the shackles of the past so that both could prove more effective in the contemporary world.[21] It looked to the future

---

18. James, for example, wrote that "just as pragmatism faces forward to the future, so does rationalism . . . face backward to a past eternity. True to her inveterate habit, rationalism reverts to 'principles,' and thinks that when an abstraction once is named, we own an oracular solution." James, "Pragmatism," p. 100. Note, also, Dewey's reference to precedent in *Philosophy and Civilization:* "Pragmatism . . . presents itself as an extension of historical empiricism, but with this fundamental difference, that it does not insist upon antecedent phenomena but upon consequent phenomena; not upon the precedents but upon the possibilities of action." p. 24.

19. Dewey, *Reconstruction*, pp. 38, 33.

20. Tocqueville, *Democracy*, II, 5.

21. Dewey, as Cushing Strout has remarked, "tended to be Jeffersonian in liking 'the dreams of the future better than the history of the past.'" Strout, "The Legacy of Pragmatism," in *Intellectual History in America,* ed. Strout (New York, 1968), II, 80.

for its definition of truth, but of course it never possessed the truth since it could never possess the future.[22]

Change

Excellence in the art of politics requires prudent mediation of the demands of stability and change. Perhaps no other political institution reflects the delicate workings of this process better than the Supreme Court, whose function is to evolve legal principles, the acceptance of which depends on the ability of the Court to mediate the pressures of public opinion and the pressures deriving from the inherently conservative nature of the law. For the advocates of pragmatic jurisprudence this mediation is accomplished by following the pragmatic position regarding change in human affairs.

The position follows logically from the premises underlying the reconstruction in philosophy. Once the notion of fixed standards derived from nature has been debunked, then "change rather than fixity is . . . a measure of 'reality' or energy of being; change is omnipresent."[23] The ultimate objective of the reconstruction in philosophy is to enable science to operate in the field of morals and human behavior as it has done in the physical world. Since one of the guiding principles behind science is change, change must also constitute the driving force in human affairs. Engineering is no longer related only to matters of physics and chemistry; instead a new character, the social engineer, is added to the roster of human types.

Dewey was extreme among pragmatists in adhering to these views. Nevertheless, the taste for change and the impatience with delay is a characteristic feature of pragmatic thought, and is, as Tocqueville observed, especially prevalent during periods dis-

22. Consider Michael Oakeshott's criticism: "Future as such is elected as a criterion of truth, and . . . when this criterion is considered it turns out to be no criterion at all. The problem has been postponed, not solved." Quoted in A. H. Somjee, *The Political Theory of John Dewey* (New York, 1968), p. 38.

23. Dewey, *Reconstruction*, p. 61. Dewey asserted and then inquired: "The theory of fixed ends inevitably leads thought into the bog of disputes that cannot be settled. If there is one summum bonum, one supreme end, what is it?" Ibid., p. 166.

tinguished by the equality of condition. There is a flux and dynamism connected with the ethos of such a society, just as an antithetic spirit often appears in social situations where everyone knows his place on the fixed hierarchy of ascribed status. But the major philosophical ingredient in the pragmatic idea of change remains to be discussed. For this crucial element one must look to the year 1859—the year of Tocqueville's death, of Dewey's birth, and of Darwin's *Origin of Species.*

Darwin teaches that change carries with it implications of perfection, that what will be ought to be.[24] In this process of endless change there are by definition no fixed ends, and therefore no idea of perfection. The application of this biological theory to other areas of inquiry is an oft-told tale. Earlier, for example, allusion was made to its social application by members of the Supreme Court. The pragmatists, and in particular, the judicial pragmatists, also availed themselves of the theory. The self-evident truths that Justice Field relied upon to defend property were reduced to the level of provisional rules by the onslaught of Darwinist thinking.[25] This was accomplished, as Richard Hofstadter has written, by looking upon "the environment as something that could be manipulated."[26] The environment was viewed as undergoing continual change; but unlike the Spencerian Darwinists, the pragmatists assumed that human endeavor would play a decisive role in the direction that change would take. Thus, the importance attributed to the interaction between man and the environment distinguished, on the theoretical level, the social Darwinists who defended property interests from the pragmatists who attacked these interests. By assuming the omnipresence of

24. This formulation is borrowed from Thayer, *Meaning and Action,* p. 62. Stow Persons ascribed to Darwin the primary responsibility for a major shift in American thought. "If we should ask how American culture today differs from that of a century ago, I think we might agree that in one respect we have lost any sense of an authoritative past. We accept change as a normal condition." "Darwinism and American Culture," in *Intellectual History in America,* II, ed. Strout, 8.

25. For a good discussion of this point see George H. Sabine, "The Pragmatic Approach to Politics," *American Political Science Review,* 24 (1930).

26. Hofstadter, *Social Darwinism in American Thought* (Boston, 1955), p. 124.

change, the pragmatists could then go about the business of judging actions and ideas according to their consequences. Thanks to the influence of Darwin, said Dewey, "philosophy forswears inquiry after absolute origins and absolute finalities in order to explore specific values and the specific conditions that generate them."[27]

Evaluation of consequences (to be considered later) may be, for some, one way of claiming that whatever works is best. In Darwinian terms, whatever proves successful in a certain situation is most fit. Since there are no immutable standards for judging success, this Darwinian notion, filtered through pragmatism, leads to Justice Holmes's "marketplace," where the idea that carries the day is identified, for political purposes, with truth. This is not an inevitable consequence of judicial pragmatism, and as we shall see, Holmes is an unusual sort of pragmatist. However, it is a very likely development because of pragmatism's innate relativism, and relativism is at the root of Holmesian indifference.[28] Before we address the issue of relativism, Tocqueville's brief reflections on the relationship between equality and the idea of indefinite perfectability warrant our attention.

The idea of perfectability and the condition of equality vary directly with one another. "In proportion as castes disappear and the classes of society draw together, as manners, customs, and laws vary, because of the tumultuous intercourse of men, as new facts arise, as new truths are brought to light, as ancient opinions are dissipated and others take their place, the image of an ideal but always fugitive perfection presents itself to the human mind." In contrast to an aristocratic world, where "they can conceive amelioration, but not change," democracy makes of change an object of reverence.[29]

27. Quoted in Persons, "Darwinism and American Culture," p. 9.

28. For a critical analysis of the meaning and implications of Holmes's judicial indifference see Walter Berns, "Oliver Wendell Holmes, Jr.," in *American Political Thought: The Philosophic Dimensions of American Statesmanship*, eds. Morton J. Frisch and Richard G. Stevens (New York, 1971).

29. Tocqueville, *Democracy*, II, 35, 34. Tocqueville concluded his discussion by maintaining that "aristocratic nations are naturally too liable to narrow the scope of perfectability; democratic nations, to expand it beyond reason." Ibid., p. 35.

Dewey, too, made explicit the connection between perfectability and equality. "Democracy has many meanings, but if it has a moral meaning, it is found in resolving that the supreme test of all political institutions and industrial arrangements shall be the contribution they make to the all-around growth of every member of society."[30] Growth constitutes pragmatic philosophy's principle of legitimacy, at least as originally formulated.[31] The evaluation of consequences is to be conducted using "growth" as the measure of performance and acceptability. Desirable growth is that which makes further growth possible, although as should be apparent, until one formulates a stable standard to measure growth itself (something Dewey was unwilling to do), it becomes difficult to speak of desirability in any meaningful way. In Chapter 4 will be a discussion of a book by Benjamin Cardozo entitled *The Growth of the Law*. To anticipate the analysis of that work, it should be noted that for legal development to be purposive, especially in the constitutional arena, reliance must be made upon certain abiding moral principles that give to purpose its meaning.

Such principles, however, must confront the relativism that is such an essential part of the philosophical legacy of the founders of pragmatism.[32] In particular, they must encounter the identification of philosophical absolutism with political authoritarianism that Dewey popularized in the course of developing his relativist theory of democracy.[33] This theory rested upon Dewey's claim that "growth itself is the only moral 'end,'" and that "how to live healthily or justly is a matter which differs with every person."[34]

30. Dewey, *Reconstruction*, p. 186.

31. In fact, it runs as a theme throughout all of Dewey's philosophy. As one Dewey student has remarked, "the idea of continuity [growth] is the inclusive category of Dewey's philosophy." Thayer, *Meaning and Action*, p. 174. For a good discussion of the concept of "growth" in Dewey's political philosophy see Robert Horwitz, "John Dewey," in *A History of Political Philosophy*, eds. Leo Strauss and Joseph Cropsey.

32. Philip P. Wiener, *Evolution and the Founders of Pragmatism* (Cambridge, 1949), p. 197.

33. Purcell, *Crisis in Democratic Theory*, p. 202.

34. Dewey, *Reconstruction*, pp. 177, 167. The statement must be distinguished from what the Declaration of Independence calls the "pursuit of happiness." For, unlike the Declaration, Dewey denied that there can be objective standards for different individuals.

As suggested by these statements, implicit in the underpinnings of the theory is a view that challenges the traditional conception of a philosophy of the Constitution prescribing immutable standards of justice, based upon an understanding of what is healthy for man. This understanding is embodied in constitutional principles, and these principles, it will be argued, ought to give direction to legal evolution. Change is indeed inevitable, but the exercise of judicial power must include a conscious awareness of what is unchanging beneath the change, of what remains constant in the midst of flux.

Experience

"By their fruits ye shall know them." The pragmatists cited this Biblical insight in order to clarify their theory of knowledge. Knowledge, of the physical as well as the moral, is obtained through experience. As Morton White said of Dewey, in a paraphrase of Holmes, the life of philosophy has not been logic, but experience.[35] Our knowledge of the world about us consists of the sum total of experiences with worldly phenomena. Or as James stated in *Pragmatism:* "Truth is *made,* just as health, wealth, and strength are made, in the course of experience."[36]

This understanding is implicit in what has been said about pragmatism and change. Truth resides in the future, and this "fallibilism," later to find expression on the Court in the "fighting faiths" dissent of Justice Holmes,[37] implies that man's knowledge of anything can only be incomplete. But consider further what James has said. Is the idea of health or wealth or strength only made through experience? Or is it the actualization of these ideals that is aided by experience? Does experience lead the medical researcher, for example, to know what health is, or does it lead him to a discovery of how to achieve human health? Similarly, does the judge make justice through experience, or rather is it the case that the judge, in judging, attempts to secure justice to the

35. Morton White, *Social Thought in America: The Revolt against Formalism* (Boston, 1947), p. 193.
36. James, "Pragmatism," p. 96.
37. *Abrams* v. *United States,* 250 U.S. 616 (1919).

individual litigants before him, and in that way to the polity as a whole? A question that has divided jurisprudence through the centuries is whether judges find the law or create it. The latter view is surely the pragmatic one; that is, judges create law through their experiences in rendering decisions. The acceptance of the Blackstonian view that judges discover the law and then apply it to the immediate case imputes a fixed character to the law, a character incompatible with the basic tenets of pragmatism. Applied to the interpretation of the Constitution, the question assumes the following form: Is justice to be found in the Constitution, in which case the judge, after having discerned its meaning, applies it to judicial controversies; or is justice (assuming its existence or possibility) developed incrementally through the judge's application of the words of the Constitution?

For example, John Dewey posited as one of his jurisprudential objectives the location and clarification of the appropriate sources of law. He sought to fix these sources in experience, pragmatically understood. This led him to reject the sovereignty doctrine of the source of law (law emanating from the command of the sovereign), for while it represented a transition from an external source (as had also been the case in natural law theories) to one that is to be found within social action, it concentrated exclusively on only one social factor. Instead, Dewey maintained, what was necessary was an understanding that the sources of law reside in custom, which, according to Dewey, "arises out of the interaction of environing conditions . . . with needs and interests of human beings.[38] Justice was not to be defined a priori; nor was it identifiable with the will of the sovereign. Rather, it was to be defined "transactionally," emerging out of social experience as an end to be juridically achieved. Such a recognition by jurists would make it unnecessary to appeal to an outside source, as, for example, an absolute standard of right conduct derived from the Constitution.[39]

38. John Dewey, "My Philosophy of Law," in *My Philosophy of Law, Credos of Sixteen American Scholars* (Boston, 1941), p. 80.
39. Such an absolute standard, Dewey made clear, does not exist. His evidence for its denial is the existence of a number of so-called absolutes that conflict with one another. "Their conflict is sufficient evidence that they were not derived from any *a priori* absolute standard." Ibid., pp. 83–84.

For Dewey, experience meant experimentation.[40] To suggest that learning is a function of experience means that learning comes about through science. The relevance of this view to jurisprudence was expressed by Dewey, quoting Holmes: "I have had in mind an ultimate dependence of law [upon science] because it is ultimately for science to determine, as far as it can, the relative worth of our different social ends."[41] Once again, Dewey was extreme among pragmatists; however, even James, much less scientifically oriented, maintained: *"True ideas are those that we can assimilate, validate, corroborate, and verify. False ideas are those that we can not."*[42] Accordingly, how would a judge interpret the Constitution so as to protect those "unalienable rights of man" that had become codified into constitutional rights? Indeed, the judge would have to prove scientifically that these rights are worthy social ends. First he would have to ascertain whether they lend themselves to assimilation, validation, corroboration, and verification. If not, he would have to conclude that such rights are false, and hence his judicial obligation would be clear. The point has been deliberately overstated for the purpose of suggesting a difficulty in the application of pragmatic philosophy to constitutional jurisprudence. That difficulty involves the attempt to interpret a natural rights document according to rules antithetical to the principles embodied in the document. If the Constitution it-

---

Dewey's legal theory has not attracted as much attention as have some of the other areas of his philosophy. The following studies have looked into aspects of his jurisprudence: Anton Donoso, "John Dewey's Philosophy of Law," *University of Detroit Law Journal*, 36 (1959); Jay Wesley Murray, "John Dewey—A Philosophy of Law for Democracy," *Vanderbilt Law Review*, 14 (1960–1961); Edwin W. Patterson, "John Dewey and the Law: Theories of Legal Reasoning and Valuation," *ABA Journal*, 36 (1950).

40. Thayer, *Meaning and Action*, p. 451.

41. Dewey, *Characters and Events: Popular Essays in Social and Political Philosophy*, ed. Joseph Ratner (New York, 1929), I, 105. The difficulty with this view is obvious, and the events of the twentieth century only emphasize its inadequacy. Morton White's criticism is quite appropriate: "Dewey's own philosophy might easily fall into the hands of those willing to cry 'science, science' in defense of the most obnoxious ends and means. Liberalism so construed supplies us with no particular or specific political position that can be acted on, only a plea for intelligence." White, *Social Thought*, p. 201.

42. James, "Pragmatism," pp. 88–89.

self implies certain social ends, ends based upon a judgment on the nature of man, then a scientific study that purported to demonstrate the superiority of different social ends would necessarily involve a judge in the unenviable position of having to decide between what is constitutionally required and what is scientifically understood to be desirable.[43]

In this context, three aspects of Dewey's complex ethical theory require special mention because of their relevance to jurisprudence: the grounding of ethics in desire, the transformation of traditional virtues into hypotheses for action, and the importance of problematic situations to the definition of morality.

"[Men living in democratic ages] commonly aspire to none but easy and present gratifications, they rush onward to the object of their desires, and the slightest delay exasperates them."[44] Tocqueville's observation was ultimately elevated to a theory of valuation by Dewey in the course of his development and refinement of pragmatism. For Dewey, desire is the source of morality.[45] There are no ultimate goods, but goods are suggested by the immediate problematic situation. Disturbances, or deficiencies in the environment, create a desire which in turn stimulates empirical inquiry, out of which a good is defined. Ethical judgments do not, then, derive from a fixed code of ethics, but rather from the objective situation, wherein desire emerges out of felt necessity. *"Moral goods and ends exist only when something has to be done."*[46]

43. For a good example of a case where the Court decided between the Constitution and scientifically derived social ends, see *Buck* v. *Bell,* 274 U.S. 200 (1927), dealing with the constitutionality of Virginia's compulsory sterilization program. The Court, speaking through Justice Holmes, chose science, and in the process rendered what Walter Berns has called "one of the most infamous decisions ever handed down by the Court." Berns, "Oliver Wendell Holmes, Jr.," p. 177. For a more extended analysis of the case, see his *"Buck* v. *Bell:* Due Process of Law?" *Western Political Quarterly,* 6 (1953).

44. Tocqueville, *Democracy,* II, 344.

45. See his "Theory of Valuation," *International Encyclopedia of Unified Science,* II (1939). Desire is viewed not in the abstract but is linked to existential situations. Dewey used the example of the desire for food, which will hardly be the same if one has eaten two hours or five days previously. Ibid., p. 16.

46. Dewey, *Reconstruction,* p. 169. Traditional virtues, as Professor Thayer notes, such as temperance and courage, function as hypotheses in the

Hypotheses are confirmed and thereby acquire validity if they successfully remove the defect or need involved in a problematic situation. Dewey's situational ethics thus suspend reliance upon antecedent principles ("rigid dogma"), since the truth or goodness of any idea can only be judged according to the consequences it produces. Every situation is unique, and therefore a hypothesis confirmed in one case will be rejected in another. All this rests, of course, on the assumption that a situation, viewed intelligently (i.e., scientifically), will indicate an objective need to the observer. When the need is either removed or not removed the hypothesis can surely be said to have been tested by experience. The desire created by the objective need thereby becomes objectively founded, distinguishable, in other words, from those desires which trace their origins to the irrationality of imperfect men.

Suppose Dewey was mistaken. Suppose that need and desire cannot be objectified. Suppose, further, that need and desire are related, as Tocqueville believed, to "easy and present gratifications." If this be the case, then do not those antecedent principles that have been dismissed as rigid dogma acquire additional significance? If the possibility exists that need can be wrongly ascertained and desire misdirected, what then is to be said of the hypotheses that have successfully satisfied the desire and eliminated the need? Are they true? Good? In contemplating these questions one should keep in mind the role of the Supreme Court in American public life. For it is an institution which can either apply constitutional (antecedent) principles or reject them. It can either present obstacles to desire or stimulate desire. And perhaps most importantly, the Court can either provide instruction in political morality or test hypotheses in the individual cases that present themselves for judgment.

---

ethics of pragmatism. Thayer, *Meaning and Action*, p. 400. Indeed, Deweyan ethics are best understood as a rejection of classical, Aristotelian ethics, which have absolutized moral virtues, not making them contingent upon particular problematic situations. In the first case the end, or good, emerges *out* of the individual situation; in the second, it is introduced *to* the particular situation. Compare, for example, Dewey's discussion of "health" in his "Theory of Valuation," with Aristotle's consideration of the same subject in *Nichomachean Ethics*.

Antiformalism

Morton White's excellent analysis of social thought in America is subtitled *The Revolt against Formalism*. Dewey in philosophy, Holmes in law, Veblen in economics, and Beard and Robinson in history, are descriptively linked by their repudiation of the formalism that characterized their respective disciplines in the nineteenth century. These men were identified in one way or another with the progressive movement in American history, a movement of reaction against the gross inequality associated with industrial capitalism. Their fight against abstractionism was calculated to expose this inequality as a step toward the development of a more egalitarian society.[47] Discussed in this context, the revolt against formalism receives much illumination from Tocqueville's analysis of the American "contempt for form."

In Tocqueville's day the philosophic posture toward formalism was related to the individualism of the equality of condition. "As it is on their [the Americans] own testimony that they are accustomed to reply, they like to discern the object which engages their attention with extreme clearness; they therefore strip off as much as possible all that covers it, they rid themselves of whatever separates them from it, they remove whatever conceals it from sight, in order to view it more closely and in the broad light of day. This disposition of mind leads them to condemn forms, which they regard as useless and inconvenient veils placed between them and the truth."[48]

After the discussion of reconstruction, change, and experience, it is not difficult to see in pragmatism a similar contempt for forms or abstractions, which impede the work of reconstruction, delay change, and limit experimentation. James's dichotomy between

47. Holmes is to be distinguished from the others in the above grouping by his personal lack of sympathy for the progressive cause.

48. Tocqueville, *Democracy*, II, 4–5. Much later Tocqueville returned to this theme. "Men living in democratic ages do not readily comprehend the utility of forms: they feel an instinctive contempt for them. . . . Forms excite their contempt, and often their hatred; as they commonly aspire to none but easy and present gratifications, they rush onwards to the object of their desires, and the slightest delay exasperates them. This same temper, carried with them into political life, renders them hostile to forms, which perpetually retard or arrest them in some of their projects." Ibid., p. 344.

"tender-minded" rationalists who are guided by "principles" and "tough-minded" empiricists who are guided by "facts" reflects the pragmatic attitude toward the utility of forms. The rationalists, those who deal in abstractions, see the world as fixed, already completed in form as well as content. On the other hand, pragmatism "has no dogmas and no doctrines save its method."[49] It represents enlightenment not faith, reason not emotion. It is not constrained by the demand of abstract principle, nor must it suffer very long the divergence between facts and doctrine. Thus pragmatism is timeless, never antiquated, never irrelevant. This makes it ideally appropriate for application to industrial America.[50] Pragmatic philosophy, because it is unprincipled, can resolve the problems engendered by a rapidly changing economy. Because it displays an "attitude of looking away from first things, principles, 'categories,' supposed necessities; and of looking towards last things, fruits, consequences, facts,"[51] it is capable of transforming the evils of industrialism into a foundation for a new and better social order. Man need not enter the world of the transempirical in order to realize the potentiality of the here and now. He needs no sustenance from without; he needs only himself and his method.

Forms, then, are indeed like veils separating man from the truth and preventing him from the easy gratification of his desires.

Yet this objection, which the men of democracies make to forms is the very thing which renders forms so useful to freedom; for their chief merit is to serve as a barrier between the strong and the weak, the ruler and the people, to retard the one and give the other time to look about him. Forms become more necessary in proportion as the government becomes more active and more powerful, while private persons are becoming more indolent and more feeble. Thus democratic nations naturally stand more in need of forms than other nations, and they naturally respect them less. . . .

49. James, "Pragmatism," p. 27.
50. "The social situation," wrote Dewey, "has been so changed by the factors of an industrial age that traditional general principles have little practical meaning. They persist as emotional cries rather than as reasoned ideas." Dewey, *The Public*, p. 133.
51. James, "Pragmatism," p. 27.

Nothing is more pitiful than the arrogant disdain of most of our contemporaries for questions of form.[52]

This is Tocqueville's harshest criticism of the American philosophic method (though, in this statement, he was referring to more than just philosophy). It deserves careful attention because its author is, in a very important sense, one of America's greatest admirers—and for this reason, one of her severest critics.

Political freedom, Tocqueville suggested, is intimately related to the capacity of a society to restrain its members in their single-minded pursuit of the object of their desires. Equality, while it increases desire and appetite, decreases each individual's ability to defend against the infringement of his rights by others similarly situated. As a result, the utility of forms ought to be perceived by those who wish to secure the benefits of democracy as well as the advantages of freedom. This does not call for blind adherence to forms, but rather intelligent, prudent application. "In aristocracies, the observance of forms was superstitious: amongst us they ought to be kept up with a deliberate and enlightened deference."[53] One might say that mastery over the uses of forms is a requisite for statesmanship in a democracy. A statesman will neither reject forms nor religiously adhere to them; rather he will display a conscious regard for the political advantage that is to be enjoyed through their judicious utilization. Forms will function in two ways and in two directions: as guidance for the formulation of intelligent public opinion and as filter for the reception of vigorous public demand.

This is one of several instances where Tocqueville cited a direct proportional relationship between the growth of democratic power and the necessity for something else to grow accordingly as a safeguard of freedom. Elsewhere Tocqueville referred to the courts as the most vital instrument for checking the expansion of the equality of condition.[54] He spoke of forms in the same manner. Surely it would not constitute an unwarranted extension of Tocqueville's argument to suggest a very close connection between these two

52. Tocqueville, *Democracy*, II, 344. Emphasis added.
53. Ibid., p. 344.
54. Ibid., p. 343.

checks. The Court, by virtue of its undemocratic structure and procedures, is the political institution whose reliance upon form is most clearly indicated. Thus the revolt against formalism, at least in the field of constitutional jurisprudence, merits special attention. For if forms, abstractions, and fixed principles are categorically rejected, an important defense of freedom and liberty may be rejected in the process.[55]

PRAGMATISM AND THE INSTITUTIONS OF DEMOCRATIC GOVERNMENT

The ethical neutrality of the pragmatic method renders it useful to a varied assortment of political regimes. In the writings of James and Dewey, however, special affinity exists between pragmatism and the democratic form of government. This affinity is implicit in what has been said regarding the pragmatic stance toward reconstruction, change, experience, and formalism. Democracy facilitates experimentation and change, and thus hastens the work of reconstruction.[56]

Democratic government was not favored, as by Jefferson, because it is likely to be successful in protecting the natural rights of man, but rather because it permits and encourages experimentation. Experimentation justifies the state; in fact, the very formation of states must be an experimental process. "And since," wrote Dewey, "conditions of action and of inquiry knowledge are always

55. Formalism can be abused; Justice Field, it will be argued, is an example of such abuse. The Supreme Court, however, can best fulfill its role in American political life if it studies Tocqueville's teaching and then develops appropriate norms for constitutional decision-making.

56. As one student of his political philosophy has commented, in Dewey "the only sanction for democracy lies in the fact that, like science, democracy has institutionalized the procedure of trial and error." Somjee, *John Dewey*, p. 3. Edward A. Purcell, Jr., in his historical survey of the development of American democratic theory, sees both Dewey and Holmes as the crucial figures in the formulation of a relativist theory of democracy, but argues that for those who were unwilling to accept the crucial role assigned to science by Dewey, Holmes's moral and intellectual skepticism provided a suitable alternative. As Purcell rightly points out, however, the arguments of Dewey and Holmes, and of their many followers, rest upon a number of common assumptions, and the differences between them are not very significant in point of substance. See Purcell, *Crisis in Democratic Theory*, pp. 197–217.

changing, the experiment must always be retried; the State must always be rediscovered."[57] Once again one is reminded of Justice Holmes in his *Abrams* dissent. "It [the Constitution] is an experiment, as all life is an experiment."[58]

In Dewey's political thought the work of the founding fathers is much less the object of reverence than had traditionally been the case. Indeed, the denigration of the founders is a theme frequently found in Dewey's writings. "The belief in political fixity, of the sanctity of some form of state consecrated by the efforts of our fathers and hallowed by tradition, is one of the stumbling-blocks in the way of orderly and directed change; it is an invitation to revolt and revolution."[59] Why is this the case? "The imagination of the founders did not travel far beyond what could be accomplished and understood in a congeries of self-governing communities."[60] In other words, while the founders may have devised a political solution to the practical needs of the eighteenth century, their work could not have anticipated the needs and demands of a postindustrial America. The political ideas of these early statesmen are therefore today of only antiquarian interest.[61] Dewey's deflation of the importance of institutional and constitutional arrangements means that extraconstitutional factors, prin-

57. Dewey, *The Public,* pp. 33, 34.
58. *Abrams* v. *United States,* 250 U.S. 616 (1919).
59. Dewey, *The Public,* p. 34. Elsewhere he expanded upon this theme, relating it specifically to developments in science. "The entrenched and stubborn institutions of the past stand in the way of our thinking scientifically about human relations and social issues. Our mental habits in these respects are dominated by institutions of family, state, church, and business that were formed long before men had an effective technique of inquiry and validation. It is this contradiction from which we suffer today." Dewey, *Philosophy and Civilization,* p. 328.
60. Dewey, *The Public,* p. 111.
61. Dewey's interpretation of the political ideas of the Revolutionary period reflected his belief in the sociological basis of all philosophy. Thus, "the development of political democracy represents the convergence of a great number of social movements, no one of which owed either its origin or its impetus to inspiration of democratic ideals or to planning for the eventual outcome." Ibid., p. 85. And later: "The American revolution was a rebellion against an established government, and it naturally borrowed and expanded [the] ideas [of democracy] as the ideological interpretation of the effort to obtain independence of the colonies." Ibid., p. 87.

cipally economic relationships, become more fundamental in explaining the American political experience.[62]

This is readily apparent in the field of history, where Charles Beard utilized many of the insights of the pragmatists in the course of his numerous works.[63] By ascribing to the Constitution's makers a single-minded economic purpose, Beard did much to eradicate the aura of reverence that had previously surrounded their achievement. Since history (pragmatically understood) was to be written from the perspective of the present and with a vision of the future, the relevance of the founders' work to contemporary society was diminished accordingly. Their political ideas constituted a response to economic problems. These problems are different today. Hence, we need new political ideas. Beard was not condemning the motives of the founders; he was only placing them in proper perspective. As such, his objective was to demonstrate the fundamental relativism of all political philosophy.[64]

These views did not go unanswered. In a powerful critique of pragmatic political thought, William Yandell Elliott addressed himself to the issues raised by Dewey and his school. Tocqueville, too, though obviously not in response to pragmatism, developed a view contrary to the one presented by the pragmatists (and related it specifically to the legal system). Both of these writers were concerned with the question of obligation, a question as absent from Dewey's political thought as it is from his ethical theory.[65]

The essence of Elliott's critique is that constitutional govern-

62. See Horwitz, "John Dewey," p. 761.
63. For excellent studies of the relation between Beard and the pragmatists see White, *Social Thought*, and Cushing Strout, *The Pragmatic Revolt in American History: Carl Becker and Charles Beard* (Ithaca, 1966).
64. Professor Strout's criticism of the pragmatic historians presents a reaction to this relativistic bias. He convincingly described the disillusionment of Beard and Becker during the crises of the twentieth century. "The search of Becker and Beard for orientation in the crisis of their age casts a harsh but revealing light on the plight of pragmatic relativism and antiformalism in a time of troubles." Ibid., p. 116. "Instead of saying with Jefferson that 'we hold these truths to be self-evident,' Becker could only say that these glittering generalities of liberal democracy were useful myths." Ibid., p. 123. The same critique is applicable to Dewey's thought and its relation to the convulsions of this century.
65. Somjee, *John Dewey*, p. 71.

ment, government based upon the consent of the governed, requires an element of shared purpose, by which the community is held together and by which legitimacy and justice can be achieved. This shared purpose embodies certain moral principles regarding the nature of man. By rejecting such a moral purpose, and placing in its stead a short-run, ad hoc evaluation of consequences, pragmatic philosophy in politics leads to the adoption of force, rather than consent, as the title to rule and as the adhesive element that holds the community together. Elliott, writing in the 1920's, anticipated the challenge to constitutional government that raised its ugly head in the succeeding decade. "If we eschew the pragmatic attitude toward values—i.e., that there is no rational basis for preferring some to others, except by pitting them like gamecocks for a test of consequences—we may escape the destruction of constitutional government and of the method of social settlement which it represents. Parliamentarianism rests upon the assumption of idealistic ethics that values achieve coherence and real meaning through criticism."[66]

In Dewey's philosophy, however, values achieve coherence and meaning only through scientific validation and replication. Thus laws, which embody the values of society, rest upon the same experimental foundation that justifies the existence of democratic institutions. Viewed in this light the precarious positions of these institutions is immediately obvious. For the nature of the law, procedural and substantive, reflects the nature and quality of the regime. Since democratic government, according to Dewey, is not an end in itself but rather a means toward the furtherance of scientific inquiry (and human growth), its continued existence is dependent upon the conclusions derived from this inquiry. There may, of course, be no explicit decision to dismantle democratic institutions, but since the laws will presumably reflect what is scientifically understood to be desirable, the perpetuation of democratic government rests upon faith—a faith that scientific inquiry will render conclusions that are compatible with the requisites of democracy. If it does not, then this failure will be reflected in the laws, and thus ultimately in the regime itself. Political obligation

66. Elliott, *Pragmatic Revolt*, p. 77.

and respect for laws are functions of this faith. The people must be educated in the values of pragmatism. Dewey's program of educational reform thus becomes the key to his political philosophy.

Tocqueville also relied upon faith, although it was faith of a different sort. "In order that society should exist, and, *a fortiori,* that a society should prosper, it is required that all the minds of the citizens should be rallied and held together by certain predominant ideas; and this cannot be the case unless each of them sometimes draws his opinions from the common source, and consents *to accept certain matters of belief already formed.*"[67] The acceptance of certain matters of belief is a very aristocratic notion. However, men living in a democracy must be taught to appreciate the utility of such an acceptance. The inevitability of democracy, in short, should not preclude intelligent application of ideas that may be, in principle, inconsistent with the ethos of equality.

To perform this crucial function Tocqueville looked, significantly, to the legal profession. "The lawyers do not, indeed, wish to overthrow the institutions of democracy, but they constantly endeavor to turn it away from its real direction by means that are foreign to its nature. Lawyers belong to the people by birth and interest, and to the aristocracy by habit and taste; they may be looked upon as the connecting link between the two great classes of society."[68] The "means that are foreign to its nature" include a taste for formalities, an instinctive love of public order, and perhaps most important, a "reverence for what is old." Deference to the opinions of one's forefathers, which in America means deference to the principles of the founding fathers, is the way to insure that a common source of predominant ideas exists to cement the bonds of political community.

In concluding this chapter it is perhaps worth emphasizing that Tocqueville was an important, if not uncritical, advocate of democracy. To be sure, he viewed with some sadness the passing of the aristocratic regime, but he was convinced that there was more

67. Tocqueville, *Democracy,* II, 9. Emphasis added.
68. Tocqueville, *Democracy,* I, 286. "Without this admixture of lawyer-like sobriety with the democratic principle, I question whether democratic institutions could long be maintained." Ibid., p. 286.

justice to be found in the best of democracies than in the best of aristocracies. And so he did not react to the inevitability of the democratic regime with resignation and grudging acquiescence, but welcomed the opportunity to establish freedom on a scale never before experienced. In this spirit, his observations and reflections demand careful scrutiny by students and practitioners of constitutional jurisprudence.

Tocqueville perceived that the egalitarian impulse was the most powerful force in democratic life. Equality, of course, was not simply an economic condition, but a way of life reflected in how people saw themselves in relation to their environment. The French observer's reflections on the American philosophical method were intended to demonstrate the influence of egalitarian beliefs upon epistemological assumptions. His insights into this question make it easier to explain the popularity of philosophical pragmatism as developed by Dewey, James, and others. For pragmatism represented the consummation of the egalitarian philosophical method, and thus gave expression to the deepest of democratic commitments.

As a sympathetic critic of democracy, Tocqueville understood that equality was not an unmitigated blessing. He shared this understanding with the founders of the regime, for they also believed that the egalitarian impulse needed to be harnessed to serve the ends of political justice. One of the institutional reflections of their concern was the Supreme Court, which was established not so much to frustrate the ends of democracy as to function in a manner that was distinctly undemocratic. The question we have raised in this chapter, and which will be pursued hereafter, is not whether pragmatism is a laudable philosophy, but whether its adoption by the Supreme Court should be viewed as a salutary development. If one accepts Tocqueville's concerns about democratic individualism, and his conclusion that in connection with these concerns law is a useful mitigating factor, then it becomes necessary to question the wisdom of employing a philosophy grounded upon egalitarian premises in the work of an essentially undemocratic institution whose responsibility is to interpret the nation's highest law, which is rooted in a tradition that is fundamentally nonpragmatic.

CHAPTER 4

The Pragmatic Method of Justice: The Judge as Democratic Fact Finder

The natural rights theory of law described in Chapter 2 did not bear the entire brunt of the pragmatic assault on American jurisprudence. Interestingly, the positivistic analytical school, though itself a rejection of traditional natural rights philosophy, was also, and for similar reasons, attacked by the pragmatic legal philosophers. The analytical positivists had denied the validity of any theory of law that was grounded in a priori speculation, and that posited the idea of a higher law transcending the world of empirical reality, from which objective, rational standards of justice could be derived. They insisted upon a strict separation of law from ethics and social policy, identifying and defining law as the official commands of a sovereign power. This led to an identification of positive law with justice, and to a conception of jurisprudence as a discipline, the function of which was to inquire into the network of norms, principles, and logical interrelationships that could be abstracted from actual legal systems.

The pragmatists were critical of the syllogistic process of legal reasoning that they found common to both the philosophical and the analytical schools. They also found, in the application of ethical considerations by the natural rights theorists, and in the abandonment of such considerations by the analytical positivists, a similar detachment from the realities of the social situation. In the first case ethics were not grounded in experience, and in the second, reality was distorted by the failure to understand the ethical imperatives implied in experience. The object of the pragmatists was thus to establish an empirical jurisprudence that included a consciousness of the moral basis of law. Their solution to this jurisprudential problem is the concern of the present chapter.

THE SEARCH FOR A MIDDLE ROAD

Our task is to inquire into the judicial role prescribed by pragmatic-juristic principles. The two thinkers who, perhaps more than anyone else, had been preoccupied with this problem were Benjamin Cardozo and Roscoe Pound; and their ideas will be critically discussed insofar as they relate to the pragmatic alternative.[1] In the development of pragmatic jurisprudence in America, these judicial philosophers were superseded by a generation of "legal realists," whose work enables one, in retrospect, to append the label "moderate" to the writings of Cardozo and Pound.[2] Although the work of these realists presents a much more graphic depiction of the logical extension of pragmatic principles, the concentration on Cardozo and Pound is justified by two related facts. First, they were thoughtful and sometimes profound men, whose rejection of the old jurisprudence included a recognition and understanding of the peculiar virtues associated with that jurisprudence. Second, their efforts to reform the law did not blind them to the demand for stability in the law; and indeed the

1. This chapter will not attempt to survey the genesis and growth of pragmatic jurisprudence. This account has been accomplished elsewhere in varying degrees of detail and comprehensiveness. Although Justice Holmes is commonly cited as the founder of the pragmatic tradition in American jurisprudence, Philip P. Wiener's research (*Evolution and the Founders of Pragmatism*) indicates that Holmes's lesser known colleague in the "Metaphysical Club," Nicholas St. John Green, was the actual "father" of the movement. The pragmatism of Holmes has received much attention, and can be found most readily in his famous article in the *Harvard Law Review*, "The Path of the Law," 10 (1897), as well as in his *The Common Law* (Boston, 1881). For good examples of the controversy engendered by Holmes's pragmatism see Paul L. Gregg, S.J., "The Pragmatism of Mr. Justice Holmes," *Georgetown Law Journal*, 31 (1943); and Burton F. Brody, "Pragmatic Naturalism of Mr. Justice Holmes," *Chicago-Kent Law Review*, 46 (1969). Both articles, the first critical, the second laudatory, shed little light on Holmes's pragmatism, but are good illustrations of the great polarization that appraisals of Holmes's work generally exhibit. The literature on Holmes is voluminous, and the present study does not seek to add appreciably to it.

2. For descriptive accounts of the relationship between the early pragmatists and the legal realists see Wilfred E. Rumble, Jr., *American Legal Realism* (Ithaca, 1968); Fred V. Cahill, *Judicial Legislation* (New York, 1952); and Edwin W. Patterson, *Jurisprudence: Men and Ideas of the Law* (Brooklyn, 1953).

explicit purpose of their thought was to effect a workable reconciliation of certainty and change in the legal system.

This concern for the certainty of legal rules was reflected in their critique of legal realism. "What is wrong in neo-realism," claimed Cardozo, "is a tendency manifest at times to exaggerate the indeterminacy, the entropy, the margin of error, to treat the random or chance element as a good in itself and as a good exceeding in value the elements of certainty and order and rational coherence—exceeding them in value, not merely in times and at places, but always and everywhere."[3] Pound, too, appreciated the desirability of certainty and order and the need for limits on judicial discretion. "If we must choose, if judicial administration of justice must of necessity be wholly mechanical or else wholly administrative, it was a sound instinct of lawyers in the maturity of law that led them to prefer the former."[4] The period of the "maturity of law" (according to Pound) was the nineteenth century, the century that had produced the mechanistic and formalistic jurisprudence against which the pragmatists were revolting. Cardozo and Pound attempted to develop a philosophy of law that not only would ensure that the growth of the law re-

3. Benjamin Cardozo, "Jurisprudence," New York State Bar Association Address, in *The Selected Writings of Benjamin Nathan Cardozo*, ed. Margaret E. Hall (New York, 1947), p. 30. Elsewhere he offered his views on the importance of constraints on judicial discretion. "The judge, even when he is free, is still not wholly free. He is not to innovate at pleasure. He is not a knight-errant roaming at will in pursuit of his own ideal of beauty or of goodness. He is to draw his inspiration from consecrated principles. He is not to yield to spasmodic sentiment, to vague and unregulated benevolence. He is to exercise a discretion informed by tradition, methodized by analogy, disciplined by system." Cardozo, *The Nature of the Judicial Process* (hereinafter cited as *NJP*) (New Haven, 1921), p. 141. In this, his most important book, Cardozo described four methods for rendering decisions in the judicial process. The first method, which he curiously titled the "method of philosophy," covers most of the cases decided by judges. It refers to the adherence to precedent which "must be the rule rather than the exception if litigants are to have faith in the even-handed administration of justice in the courts." Ibid., p. 34. The notion that *stare decisis* is to be the working rule in the law separates Cardozo from most of the realist movement.

4. Roscoe Pound, *An Introduction to the Philosophy of Law* (New Haven, 1922), p. 63. Pound, like Cardozo, also explicitly criticized the realists for their emphasis on rule and opinion-skepticism.

flected changes in society but also would secure the stability that makes meaningful change attainable. The older theories had achieved stability, but they had failed to realize that law was a social phenomenon, and that the judge, as creative actor within the legal system, had a special obligation to avoid any incongruence that might develop between existing law and the demands of society. Pragmatism provided the means by which they hoped to accomplish this judicial task.

As perceived by Cardozo and Pound, the attraction of pragmatic philosophy was its potential for steering a middle course between the extremes represented by John Austin's separation of is and ought and the natural rights fusion of is and ought according to standards derived outside of experience. Both extremes led to the protection of the status quo, the first by accepting the legitimacy of any existing legal arrangements, and the second by freezing the law into a mold formed by metaphysical abstractions.

For Pound, the notion that written constitutions were reflections of some "logically derivable super-constitution" prevented society from reaping the benefits of progress.[5] Indeed, earlier he had written: "We do not base institutions upon deduction from assumed principles of human nature; we require them to exhibit practical utility, and we rest them upon a foundation of policy and established adaptation to human needs. . . . We have . . . the same task in jurisprudence that has been achieved in philosophy, in the natural sciences and in politics. We have to rid ourselves of this sort of legality and to attain a pragmatic, a sociological legal science."[6]

The call for pragmatism to replace the jurisprudence based upon assumed first principles was echoed (though somewhat less emphatically) by Cardozo.[7] Because the judicial function involved

5. Ibid., p. 1. Pound, like Dewey, believed that natural law concepts were a convenient tool for those who possessed a vested interest in the status quo. "While it [natural law] professed to be ideal and universal, derived from universal reason, it was in fact . . . a positive, not a natural, natural law. It was an idealized version of the positive law of the time and place." *Social Control through Law* (New Haven, 1942), p. 4.

6. Pound, "Mechanical Jurisprudence," *Columbia Law Review,* 8 (1908), 609.

7. "The old Blackstonian theory of pre-existing rules of law which judges

more than finding the law, natural law, traditionally understood, could no longer serve as a major source for positive law.

Although he rejected the Blackstonian view of the judicial process, Cardozo did not, as others had, adopt the opposite approach. His objection to the Austinians was that their insistence upon the absolute separation of law from morals tended to breed distrust and contempt for law.[8] By assigning questions of what the law ought to be to the legislator and not the jurist, and by making the law into a self-contained and isolated system, they had removed from the political system its most crucial source of legal obligation—the capacity of the law to adapt to changing social circumstances.[9] There is in Cardozo's critique an argument reminiscent of the left-wing Hegelians' attack on their right-wing opponents. By identifying the real with the rational, these conservatives, like Cardozo's adversaries, had effectively precluded any possibility of reform in the political and social system.[10]

found, but did not make, fitted in with a theory still more ancient, the theory of a law of nature." Cardozo, *NJP,* p. 131. Cardozo quoted from Vander Eycken approvingly: "Law springs from the relations of fact which exist between things. Like those relations themselves, natural law is in perpetual travail. It is no longer in texts or in systems derived from reason that we must look for the source of law; it is in social utility, in the necessity that certain consequences shall be attached to given hypotheses." Ibid., p. 122.

8. Ibid., p. 134.

9. The best treatise on analytical jurisprudence is still the classic work by John Austin, *The Province of Jurisprudence Determined* (London, 1955). For a very good and succinct interpretation of the Austinian school see Edgar Bodenheimer, *Jurisprudence* (New York, 1940), Chapter 14. Bodenheimer made a useful distinction between "analytical positivism" and "social positivism." "Sociological positivism . . . undertakes to investigate and describe the various social factors which exercise an influence upon the development of the law. It analyzes, not the legal rules as such, but the factors by which they are brought about. With analytical positivism it shares a purely empirical attitude toward the law." Ibid., p. 268. See also, on this point, F. S. C. Northrop, "Ethical Relativism in the Light of Recent Legal Science," *Journal of Philosophy,* 52 (1955).

10. Pound was in complete agreement. "We are dealing with phenomena in the domain and under the control of the human will [and what-is does not tell] us the whole story. Here the ultimate question is always what ought to be." Pound, *Social Control,* p. 32. See also his "The Theory of Judicial Decision," *Harvard Law Review,* 36, (1923). Pound's reaction to analytical jurisprudence is discussed in Moses J. Aronson, "Roscoe Pound and the

Thus, the difficulty with the analytical school was that it sought too great an exclusion of the discretionary element from judicial decision-making. But there was more involved than this. It is noteworthy that one of the most important of the analytical positivists, John Chipman Gray, had argued that judge-made law was in fact the only legitimate law. Only those rules authoritatively handed down by the courts in the determination of legal rights and duties qualified as law.

In formulating and specifying society's legal rules, the judge, according to Gray, relied upon a variety of source materials, and, significantly, statutes, generally perceived as laws passed by the legislature, were placed under the rubric of sources. Thus the courts were not simply instrumental in the creation of law, they became, in Gray's theory, the actual embodiment of sovereignty. This implied an obvious creative role for the judge. Once the sources of law were introduced by Gray, consideration of that which "ought to be" became an integral part of jurisprudential theory. All of the sources—statutes, judicial precedents, opinions of experts, custom, and morality—are dependent upon men's notions of good and bad, right and wrong. A judge's interpretation of statutes, his selective application of judicial precedents, his discriminating reliance upon expert opinion, his understanding of the customs of the community, and his own ideas respecting the moral and the immoral, are all inextricably tied to a jurisprudence that conceives of law as expressions of general rules that ought to guide the actions of men. The problem with Gray's work is that, having opened the door to moral considerations, he then suggested that in practice it did not matter which test of morality was chosen, since men have no difficulty justifying their actions ac-

Resurgence of Juristic Idealism," *Journal of Social Philosophy*, 6 (1940). The debate surrounding the words "is" and "ought" is a familiar one in political philosophy. In the present context, Cardozo and Pound were reformists arguing for a pragmatic fusion of is and ought. Did Holmes, who was not a reformer but a skeptic, agree with this pragmatic critique of analytical positivism? For a provocative and informative debate on this subject see the exchange between Mark DeWolfe Howe, "The Positivism of Mr. Justice Holmes," and Henry M. Hart, Jr., "Holmes's Positivism—An Addendum," *Harvard Law Review*, 64 (1951).

cording to all the conceivable tests.[11] The danger of positivistic philosophy is thus nowhere better illustrated than in Gray—it encourages one to forget about justice. This deeply troubled Pound and Cardozo, who considered it imperative that justice once again be made central to the task of judging.

However, because justice was a word traditionally to be found in the vocabulary of natural law theorists, it was not a simple matter suddenly to remove it from these surroundings and place it in the pragmatic-empirical context. Both Pound and Cardozo saw the utility of retaining some notion of a natural law without accepting the absolutist connotations associated with it in the past. For example, in a defense of his philosophy of law against the charge that it constituted another natural law Pound wrote: "It is a natural law drawn from observation of the concrete civilization of the time and place and endeavour to ascertain the ideas of right which it presupposes, whereas the eighteenth century natural law was a deduction from the nature of the abstract man. Also it is a practical natural law and, as it has been put, a natural law with a changing or a growing content."[12]

This peculiar variety of "natural law" must provide the focus of our attention. Justice was identified with the end of law, and it is the end of law, in the view of the pragmatists, that must determine the direction of its growth. "The teleological conception of his function must be ever in the judge's mind."[13] To fulfill this teleological function, Cardozo offered the "method of sociology" and Pound, the "theory of social interests." Both are attempts to avoid the pitfalls of the natural law and analytical schools while accepting the teleological presuppositions of the first and the empirical foundations of the second. Cardozo and Pound developed a set of judicial norms in conformity with the thesis outlined in the last chapter; that is to say, the pragmatic basis of their philosophies of law is intimately connected with their essentially

11. John Chipman Gray, *The Nature and Sources of the Law* (Boston, 1963), p. 306.
12. Pound, *Interpretations of Legal History* (New York, 1923), p. 149. See also Cardozo, *The Paradoxes of Legal Science* (hereinafter cited as *PLS*) (New York, 1923), p. 149.
13. Cardozo, *NJP*, p. 102.

egalitarian theories of judicial decision making. Finally, both theories were developed for application to the private law world of torts and contracts as well as to the public law world of the Constitution.

THE EQUALITY OF INTERESTS

Roscoe Pound's reading of William James's essay, "The Moral Philosopher and the Moral Life," led him to remark that "this seems to me a statement of the problem of the legal order."[14] James had made no references to legal questions; however, his ethical theory had such a profound impact on Pound, the legal philosopher, that the latter constructed his philosophy of law upon the foundation set down by James's philosophical argument. It is, therefore, appropriate that the discussion of Pound's pragmatic jurisprudence begin with a brief consideration of the essay by James.

James was a pragmatist because he was a democrat, and he was a democrat because he was an individualist. The main purpose of his paper was to show that in ethics, as in physics, there is no final truth.[15] The value of anything, according to James, is determined by the individual—what is good in the world is what is good for him. This is not to say that James believed all values to be equal—he, after all, had his own preferences. Because his neighbor was of the same opinion, the only acceptable form of government was democracy, the one regime that was organized to respect the "sacredness of individuality."[16] Now this entails some significant political consequences. The claim of an individual or group upon government becomes an obligation for government by virtue of the very existence of the claim.[17] What some have called the "validity" of a claim is no more than the existence of the claim

14. Pound, *Interpretations of Legal History*, p. 157.
15. William James, "The Moral Philosopher and the Moral Life," in *The Will to Believe and Other Essays in Popular Philosophy* (New York, 1908), p. 184.
16. The phrase is Ralph Barton Perry's. *The Thought and Character of William James* (New York, 1954), p. 265.
17. James, "The Moral Philosopher," p. 194. "Claim and obligation are . . . co-extensive terms; they cover each other exactly."

as a matter of fact. Therefore, its obligatory character is not related to any external considerations. "Take any demand, however slight, which any creature, however weak, may make. Ought it not, for its own sake, to be satisfied? If not, prove why not. The only possible kind of proof you could adduce would be the exhibition of another creature who should make a demand that ran the other way. The only possible reason there can be why any phenomenon ought to exist is that such a phenomenon is actually desired. Any desire is imperative to the extent of its amount; it makes itself valid by the fact that it exists at all."[18] The relationship between imperativeness and "amount" must be understood in the context of James's "most universal principle"—*"that the essence of good is simply to satisfy demand."*[19] A regime, in other words, is good to the extent that it responds to the quantitative, not the qualitative, dimension of demand. The Jamesian ideal is Plato's democratic man, who satisfies all pleasures, the good and the bad, according to the principle of mathematical equality.[20] To secure the ideal, the Jamesian method became the method of pragmatism.

18. Ibid., p. 195. Notice that James demanded of his readers to "prove why not" all claims should not be treated on an equal basis. Aristotle was the first to point out that *inequalities* are in need of greater justification than equality. In other words, unless one can prove why there should be inequality, the assumption is that such inequality as exists is unjustified. The same does not necessarily hold for equality. Perhaps this explains why one can be pragmatic in the defense of equality, whereas more seems to be required to defend inequality. Aristotle, *Politics*, 1283a 2. For a recent discussion of these questions see Stanley Benn, "Egalitarianism and the Equal Consideration of Interests;" and Hugo Adam Bedau, "Egalitarianism and the Idea of Equality," both in *Nomos IX—Equality*, eds. J. Roland Pennock and John W. Chapman (New York, 1969).

19. Ibid., p. 201. "The demand may be for anything under the sun. . . . The elementary forces in ethics are probably as plural as those of physics are."

20. See Plato, *The Republic*, trans. Allan Bloom (New York, 1968). Socrates told his interlocutors: "He [the democratic man] doesn't admit true speech or let it pass into the guardhouse, if someone says that there are some pleasures belonging to fine and good desires and some belonging to bad desires, and that the ones must be practiced and honored and the others checked and enslaved. Rather, he shakes his head at all this and says that all are alike and must be honored on an equal basis." Ibid., p. 239. Book VIII/561b-c.

There is, of course, a practical need to place limits upon the satisfaction of demands. However, these limits do not derive from aristocratic standards or trans-empirical abstractions such as natural rights; rather, they inhere in a quantitative judgment concerning the consequences of any decision affecting the totality of claims and obligations. James stated this pragmatic calculus in the following way: "Since everything which is demanded is by that fact a good, must not the guiding principle for ethical philosophy (since all demands conjointly cannot be satisfied in this poor world) be simply to satisfy at all times *as many demands as we can?* That act must be the best act, accordingly, which makes for the *best whole,* in the sense of awakening the least sum of dissatisfactions. In the casuistic sense, therefore, those ideals must be written highest which *prevail at the least cost,* or by whose realizations the least possible number of other ideals are destroyed."[21]

At this point, one should notice the extent to which James's ethical prescriptions were translated into an understanding of law by Roscoe Pound. "For the purpose of understanding the law of today I am content with a picture of satisfying as much of the whole body of human wants as we may with the least sacrifice. I am content to think of law as a social institution to satisfy social wants—the claims and demands and expectations involved in the existence of civilized society—by giving effect to as much as we may with the least sacrifice, so far as such wants may be satisfied or such claims given effect by an ordering of human conduct through politically organized society."[22] This nicely states Pound's overriding commitment. Throughout his writings Pound, like James, insisted that the law, which is the organized expression of civil society, is not equipped to make distinctions between competing demands according to their intrinsic value. He was skeptical about the possibility of developing any absolute standard by which the law can determine the relative weight of the various claims that cry out for recognition. Yet in adopting the Jamesian argument, Pound committed the legal system to the most basic of political choices—the choice of a regime. We are thus confronted in prag-

21. James, "The Moral Philosopher," p. 205.
22. Pound, *An Introduction to the Philosophy of Law,* p. 47.

matic jurisprudence with the image of a judge who functions within a system dedicated to particular values—democracy and equality—but who despairs of any possibility of evaluation or discrimination according to fixed political principles.

Pound's egalitarian jurisprudence can be said to represent a commitment founded upon a lack of commitment. Consider, for example, what he had to say about justice, the end of law. "This is what we mean when we say that the end of law is justice. We do not mean justice as an individual virtue. We do not mean justice as the ideal relation among men. We mean a regime. We mean such an adjustment of relations and ordering of conduct as will make the goods of existence, the means of satisfying human claims to have things and do things, go round as far as possible with the least friction and waste."[23]

Without an explicit declaration, Pound was depicting equality as the definition of justice. Also important, he identified this definition with the regime itself. Further, he asked that the end of law be accomplished "with the least friction and waste." Elsewhere, however, he cautioned against the unlimited satisfaction of the desire to be equal, maintaining that when extended to its fullest development such satisfaction "would reduce all activity to the lowest possible attainment." Like Tocqueville, he believed that "men's desire to be equal and their desire to be free must be kept in balance."[24] How, it may be asked, is one to effect this balance? By positing the equal satisfaction of wants as the principle of the regime, and by denying an objective standard with which to evaluate these wants, did he not undermine the basis for such a balance? Tocqueville, of course, had discovered a solution to the problem in the denial, or at least the postponement, of certain desires or wants.[25] His solution, it might be added, did not come easily— indeed, it probably involved more than a minimum of friction and waste. In Pound's regime, unlike Tocqueville's, freedom is only a social want. It is not the end of law. Although equality may also be a

23. Pound, *Social Control*, pp. 64–65.
24. Pound, *An Introduction to the Philosophy of Law*, p. 168.
25. For a good discussion of the Tocquevillian solution see Marvin Zetterbaum, *Tocqueville and the Problem of Democracy* (Stanford, 1967), especially Chapter 3.

social want, its claim, in terms of the basic commitment of the regime (the equality of interests), would appear to carry with it an added presumption of urgency. The fact that the demand for equality, considered as a social want, corresponds to the organizing principle of the political-legal system, suggests, despite the frequent disclaimers about judicial valuation, that in a conflict of wants, the egalitarian claim is entitled to first consideration. Certainly, in terms of the legal reforms advocated by Pound, this suggestion is not unsupported by evidence.[26]

Pound's jurisprudence did not end with the Jamesian proposition. He was determined to proceed beyond the point where James had left off. Concerned as he was with the question of obligation, with establishing a basis for respect for law and stability of legal institutions, he was determined to limit the satisfaction of wants to those that would not disrupt the pattern of civilized society. His solution, developed in the "theory of social interests" and in its corollary, the "jural postulates of civilization," has received wide recognition and acclaim among students of jurisprudence.

At first glance the theory suggests a significant departure from James's thesis. Not all demands, it would seem, possess an equal claim to satisfaction, but only those that conform to the jural postulates or scheme of interests of a particular society. The judge, whom Pound liked to think of as a "social engineer," is to evaluate competing claims according to this established juristic standard.

Very briefly,[27] the jural postulates are, according to Pound, the rules required to secure the minimum level of general security necessary for civilized society to exist. He did not claim perma-

26. This is not intended as a criticism of Pound's reforms. His work in reforming the law has been justly praised by many students of our legal institutions. However, as his proposals in the fields of liability, property, and contracts illustrate, and as he freely admitted, the object of reform was to provide the institutions of government, and particularly the courts, with the capacity to insure the people of their general security through the equalization of social and economic conditions.

27. Pound's theory is distributed over a great number of books and articles. Perhaps the best explication is to be found in Patterson's book (quoted above), and especially in Julius Stone's *The Province and Function of Law* (Sydney, 1946). Both of these men, in addition to being major interpreters of Pound's work, were distinguished philosophers of law in their own right.

nence or universality for these postulates—that would undoubtedly smack too much of natural law. They may in fact differ from society ("civilization") to society; however, since all societies desire security, the potential internal variation of many of the postulates seems not to be of very great magnitude. For example, the postulate which holds that in civil society there must be an assumption that men will not commit intentional aggressions upon others,[28] is probably recognized (sometimes in the breach) by all regimes as a necessary condition for stable society. Even so, according to Pound, there is no basis in reason for this postulate, or for some of his less universally accepted postulates, such as the protection of private property. They are all theoretically subject to change, depending upon the general principles reflected in the society at any given point in time.

The theory of social interests is a compendium of interests that the courts are obliged to recognize as controlling in the judicial decision making process. An interest is defined as "a claim, a want, a demand, of a human being or group of human beings which the human being or group of human beings seeks to satisfy and of which social engineering in civil society must therefore take account."[29] For example, there are social interests in general security, including peace, order, health, and security of acquisitions; in general progress, including free speech, free trade, and free science; and so on for other interests such as general morals and conservation of resources. These "social interests represent what the members of a society expect of their legal order."[30] Unless in direct conflict with the jural postulates (which, strangely, appear to be derived according to the same process) the entire classification of interests will include all the claims actually made; in other words, all those in harmony with the jural postulates.[31] The task for the social engineer then becomes one of reconciling

28. Pound, *Outlines of Lectures on Jurisprudence* (Cambridge, 1928), p. 168.

29. Pound, "A Theory of Social Interests," in *Readings in Jurisprudence,* ed. Jerome Hall (Indianapolis, 1938), p. 241.

30. Edwin W. Patterson, "Pound's Theory of Social Interests," in *Interpretation of Modern Legal Philosophies,* ed. Paul Sayre (New York, 1947).

31. Stone, *Province and Function,* p. 361.

conflicting interests (as represented by the individual litigants in a case) and of adopting that solution which does least injury to the scheme of interests as a whole.

It should be clear that we have not advanced very far, if at all, beyond the point where James left off. When we ask how an individual claim becomes a social interest, the answer is to be found, once again, in the fact that it has been made. Of course, in practice, this requires not merely *a* demand, but a demand supported by sufficient resources—in most cases this refers to the power of numbers. The jural postulates do not constitute a significant limiting factor over demand; first, because their minimal character only extends to the point where the hard legal questions begin, and second, because they are only postulates, derived from essentially the same process as the social interests themselves. Relevant here is Pound's claim: "We are coming to study the legal order instead of debating as to the nature of law. We are thinking of interests, claims, demands, not of rights."[32] By not grounding his postulates in "rights," which would have entailed metamorphosing them into something *natural,* Pound failed to accomplish the purpose of his endeavor, which was to provide a stable basis for the law. A postulate produced by demand is only effective so long as that demand does not disappear. When the demand (for example, the demand for general security) has a variable content, one whose meaning is determined by changing circumstances and opinion, it becomes even less clear how the postulates serve to anchor the law to a stable foundation.

Pound's image of the "social engineer" is highly instructive. An engineer, say a civil engineer who is to build a dam, is not the person responsible for the decision to construct the dam. Rather, because of his unique skills, he has been given the task of constructing it. Part of his skill, of course, is to accomplish his task with a minimum of friction and waste. The ultimate decision, however, as to whether the dam is necessary, or whether it is of sufficient priority to warrant the allocation of scarce resources, is not for him to make. He is simply responding to a decision that has been made elsewhere. He can advise those who have made the decision that

32. Pound, *Interpretations of Legal History,* p. 152.

the dam might have the effect of disrupting the scheme of interests as a whole—by polluting the environment, for example. But this is a purely factual determination, not involving a judgment as to the relative worth of the competing interests.

Pound's engineer, though garbed in judicial robes, performs a similar task. He too is involved in exclusively factual determinations. The judgment as to which judicial solution will involve the least sacrifice to the totality of claims and interests is, after all, a judgment of fact, not value. Preceding this determination is yet another judgment of fact: what are the judicial postulates and social interests at this particular time and place? For it must be understood that this survey of interests is the product of an empirical study of claims and demands and carries no implications of moral worth.[33] The moral decision, as in the case of the civil engineer, has already been made, presumably by the individual or group raising the claim. By the time the demand reaches the judge it no longer is either good or bad; it simply *is*. It will be gratified, not because the judge has decided its intrinsic worth merits gratification, but because he has asked rhetorically: "Is the end of law anything less than to do whatever may be achieved . . . to satisfy human desires?"[34]

The judicial function is thus one of "keeping up with the times." The judge must insure that the law reflects the spirit of the day, and the burden of his task involves finding out what that spirit is. The judge, the social engineer, is, accordingly, the democratic fact finder. Aided by the social sciences, he is to discover where we are at any given time and then make sure that the law is not lagging behind. He is not equipped however, to ascertain whether where we are is where we ought to be.[35]

33. Jerome Hall, *Living Law of Democratic Society* (Indianapolis, 1949), p. 65.

34. Pound, *An Introduction to the Philosophy of Law*, p. 46.

35. In Pound, unlike (with rare exception) in Holmes, the Court, though deferential to the legislative will, need not accept its judgment of fact. The suggestion seems to be that the legislature and the executive can also be behind the times, and if so, the Court must lead the way. Thus pragmatism as a philosophy of law for the Supreme Court may be expressed through judicial restraint as well as through judicial activism. We will return to this question in Chapters 7 and 8.

Among critics of Pound the most frequent charge is that he offered no standard by which to evaluate the law.[36] This is only partly true and quite misleading. Unlike the analytical positivists, who identified justice with the will of those in power, Pound did provide a definition of justice alongside of which the law of the state could be measured. Justice, for Pound, was the inclusive good. It was a quantitative good, but it nevertheless suggested an "ought" against which the "is" of the law could be evaluated. The absence of a standard in Pound relates only to the inability to discriminate among competing interests. To accept such discrimination would mean that justice could no longer be defined as the inclusive good; rather, it would be identified with the common good. It would no longer accept the equality of interests, but would establish a hierarchy of interests, giving first priority to the common interest.[37] Pragmatic philosophy, of course, rejects the notion of a common good, a good that assumes a solidarity of interest among the constituent parts of society. This rejection, as we saw in James, inevitably leads to the acceptance of all "good," and this acceptance in turn leads to the evaluation of a legal system according to the number of goods included in the totality of demands.[38] A legal system that accommodates twelve demands with a minimum sacrifice to the system as a whole is more praiseworthy than if it accommodated only ten. The difficulty with this

36. For examples see Cahill, *Judicial Legislation,* p. 95 and Cohen, *American Thought,* p. 299.

37. As Jerome Hall observed, the legal system can be viewed not only in terms of the protection of interests, but also in terms of their limitation and rejection. Hall, *Living Law,* p. 66. For an excellent discussion of the relationship between legal authority and the common good see Yves Simon, *The Philosophy of Democratic Government,* Chapter 1. A persuasive argument for distinguishing among interests that today include "not merely life, liberty, and the pursuit of happiness, but motor cars, refrigerators, radio sets" is to be found in Carleton Kemp Allen, "Justice and Expediency," in *Interpretations of Modern Legal Philosophies,* p. 24.

38. Professor Patterson, a great admirer of Pound's theory, correctly stated what can and cannot be evaluated: "While Pound's theory of social interests provides a fairly objective set of criteria for evaluative judgments in the society from which its data are drawn, it offers much less for the comparative evolution of societies differently constituted. . . . Not even the Nationalist Socialist regime of Germany . . . can be objectively shown to be wrong." Patterson, "Pound's Theory of Social Interests," p. 565.

standard is as obvious as it is dangerous. The successor to Plato's democratic man stands ready for the arrival of the Poundian engineer.

THE MORALITY OF LAW

Benjamin Cardozo's writings on the nature of the judicial decision-making process are still the most thoughtful and sober account we have in the literature of that field. Many valuable insights, no doubt reflecting the author's intimate and highly successful involvement with the law, are distributed throughout the pages of his extrajudicial writings. Cardozo, in these writings, is as felicitous of phrase as he was, according to those who knew him, gentle of character. However, his teaching on the way the judge ought to proceed in the quest for justice, is in all essential respects similar to Pound's. The approach is somewhat different, but the conclusions are familiar.

Cardozo began by carefully limiting the scope of judicial law-making. In most cases where the directive force of a principle is to be judicially extended the judge is simply following a pattern already established by precedent, history, or the customs of the community. It is, according to Cardozo, only in a small number of cases that the judge breaks new ground. These are the cases where there is no pattern to follow or where the three methods of extension (i.e., precedent, history, and custom) will clearly lead to undesirable consequences. This the judge cannot permit to happen. "The final cause of law is the welfare of society. The rule that misses its aim cannot permanently justify its existence."[39] Accordingly, societal welfare must fix the path and direction of legal growth. For Cardozo, justice is to be equated with the welfare of society. But what is the welfare of society? Or as Cardozo himself put it: "If justice has this place in shaping the pathway of the law, it will profit us to know what justice means."[40]

Initially, we do not learn very much. "I hold it [justice] for my

39. Cardozo, *NJP*, p. 31, 66. "It is true . . . today in every department of the law that the social value of a rule has become a test of growing power and importance. This truth is powerfully driven home . . . in the writings of Dean Pound." Ibid., p. 73.
40. Cardozo, *PLS*, p. 31,

part to be so much of morality as juristic thought discovers to be wisely and efficiently enforcible by the aid of jural sanctions." Thus, the welfare of society is justice, and justice is a certain amount of morality, but what is morality? And more importantly, whose morality? The latter question is quickly answered. "Law accepts as the pattern of its justice the morality *of the community* whose conduct it assumes to regulate."[41] But the morality of the community must somehow be distinguished from the customs of the community, since the latter are not to be looked to for the creation of new rules but only for the application of established ones. This distinction was never made clear by Cardozo, who maintained only that the morality of the community involves "a slight extension of custom," and that this extension provides the "prevailing standard of right conduct."[42] This standard, which is to guide the jurist in the creative enterprise of adjudication, was referred to by Cardozo as the social mores.

Once again, however, the question occurs: what are the social mores? Do they refer to habits, traditions, opinions, behavior, or what? At one point he suggested that the method of sociology is an expression of Dewey's understanding of philosophy, as stated in *Reconstruction in Philosophy*.[43] A better source for the sociological meaning of the mores is ironically enough, the writing of William Graham Sumner. Sumner, of course, although he shared Dewey's contempt for traditional philosophy, adhered to a social philosophy antithetical to that represented by Dewey and Cardozo. Nevertheless, his analysis of the social mores, which was widely read at the time, sheds much light on an understanding of Cardozo's jurisprudence. Indeed, his sociological study renders intelligible Cardozo's quest for justice.

Sumner had pointed out that "morality" is derived from the mores, and he had contrasted this notion with "ethics," which he understood to be an attempt to systematize ideas of right and wrong according to some absolute, universal doctrine.[44] Here is the point

41. Ibid., pp. 35, 37. Emphasis added.
42. Cardozo, *NJP*, pp. 60, 63.
43. Cardozo, *GOL*, pp. 130–131.
44. William Graham Sumner, *Folkways* (Boston, 1907), p. 37. "They [the mores] are the ways of doing things which are current in a society to

of contact between Dewey's understanding of philosophy and Sumner's analysis of morality—both were grounded in experience; both were relative to the conditions of time and place. When Cardozo spoke of morality he was not referring to the ethics that Dewey had debunked or that Sumner had been careful to distinguish from morality. In the same manner as the validity of a claim, for James and Pound, inheres in its having been made, the validity of the social mores inheres in the fact of their existence.

One should note, for example, the similarity between James's discussion of individualism and Sumner's account of the mores. "They [the mores] are all equally worthy of attention from the fact that they existed and were used. The chief object of study in them is their adjustment to interests, their relation to welfare, and their coordination in a harmonious system of life policy. For the men of the time there are no 'bad' mores. What is traditional and current is the standard of what ought to be."[45] As this suggests, Sumner's description of the mores and James's prescription for ethical philosophy both lead to the equality of interests. Thus, for Cardozo's judge, the identification of justice with the social mores carries with it an obligation to translate the prevailing standards of right conduct, irrespective of their agreement or disagreement with an absolute ethical standard, into law.

It must be emphasized, however, that the mores do include, in addition to the opinions of the day, the traditions and historical aspirations of a nation and its people. While this may expand the sources of judicial decision, it does not alter the basic nature of the process. Because "each class or group in a society has its own mores,"[46] and because a survey of these groups will reveal conflicting and sometimes hostile purposes and goals, the judicial ac-

---

satisfy human needs and desires, together with the faiths, notions, codes, and standards of well living which inhere in those ways, having a genetic connection with them." Ibid., p. 59.

45. Ibid., p. 59. And further: "It is important to notice that, for a people of a time and place, their own mores are always good, or rather that for them there can be no question of the goodness or badness of their mores. The reason is because the standards of good and right are in the mores. . . . Everything in the mores of a time and place must be justified with regard to that time and place." Ibid., p. 58.

46. Ibid., p. 39.

commodation of the mores will still involve a posture of neutrality
with regard to the "scheme of interests as a whole."

For example, one of the traditions reflected in the mores of particular groups in this country is the exclusion of race as a factor in
the treatment of fellow citizens. But, of course, this is not a tradition shared by all groups in society. How then must a judge proceed in resolving a question concerning racial discrimination?
Must he accept the principle of equal consideration of interests or
mores and then fashion a pragmatic rule that will satisfy as many
interests as possible? This is the logic of Cardozo's jurisprudence.
An alternative approach (to be considered shortly) holds that
accommodation, while politically desirable, ought to proceed
within a framework of principle, derived from the judicial determination of common interest. It argues that the "mores" of the
Constitution are to be accorded special recognition, and that accommodation begins only after the first priority, which is constitutional principle, has been ascertained.

Before returning to this question, however, attention should be
drawn to the factual basis of the mores.[47] For the judge who is to
be guided by the social mores, the creative dimension of his
judicial function, as it was for Pound, is the accumulation of
empirical information. The facts to be accumulated describe the
details of the immediate social situation. As the philosopher
Morris Raphael Cohen put it: "The consequence of judicial recognition that the judges make law is the responsibility of making it
in accordance with existing conditions."[48] In this regard, Jerome
Frank's criticism of Cardozo, to the effect that the latter ignored
facts, is very misleading. While he was correct in charging Cardozo
with a neglect of the trial court stage of the judicial process and
the means by which these courts secure the facts related to judicial
disputes, he was incorrect in assuming that upper courts are not
concerned with facts, but only with legal rules and principles.[49]

47. "The mores contain embodied in them notions, doctrines and maxims,
but they are facts . . . They have nothing to do with what ought to be,
will be, may be, or once was, if it is not now." Ibid., p. 77.
48. Morris R. Cohen, *American Thought,* p. 166.
49. Jerome Frank, "Cardozo and the Upper-Court Myth," *Law and Contemporary Problems,* 13 (1948), 375.

The method of sociology (which, it is true, is involved in only a small percentage of cases) is almost exclusively a fact-finding decision making technique. Indeed, the judicial norm that it prescribes might serve very well for the lawmakers in the legislative branch of government; perhaps better, for doubtless their fact-finding resources are much more extensive than those available to the courts. Frank, however, performed a useful function (even if inadvertently) in indicating that Cardozo provided a less than complete account of the actual process by which the court was to amass the facts necessary to accomplish the tasks of a creative, pragmatic jurisprudence.[50]

Assuming the capacity of the courts to discern the content of the "social mind," the next step is to achieve what Cardozo calls the "goal of jurisprudence"—compromise. Compromise, or as he sometimes preferred, "concordance," represents a "balancing of interests, an appraisal of their value with reference to jural ends."[51] These jural ends, Cardozo pointed out, were to be understood pragmatically.[52] This means that the compromise spoken of

50. Two years later Frank continued his attack on the pragmatists, concentrating his fire on Dewey. He contrasted Dewey with Aristotle, whom Frank maintained was a superior pragmatist to Dewey. His rationale for calling Aristotle a pragmatist was that the Greek philosopher paid careful attention to facts and experience. The man of practical wisdom, he pointed out, was not concerned only with universals but also with particulars. But Frank only proved, in his reference to Aristotle, that one does not have to be a pragmatist to be concerned with facts. Aristotle was *not* a pragmatist, for while he was a careful student of particulars, he also recognized the importance of universals in political and moral life. In all fairness to Frank, he did admit: "I, a rank amateur in philosophy and no Greek scholar, may have misinterpreted Aristotle." "Modern and Ancient Legal Pragmatism— John Dewey and Co. vs. Aristotle," *Notre Dame Lawyer*, 25 (1950), 484.
51. Cardozo, *PLS*, pp. 5, 56.
52. Indeed, as Moses J. Aronson, one of Cardozo's followers, has written, pragmatism is "to serve as the underpinning of his conciliatory structure." Aronson, "Cardozo and Sociological Jurisprudence," *Journal of Social Philosophy*, 4 (1948), 20. Aronson went on to say: "The operation as performed by pragmatism is never perfectly successful, but the patient invariably survives. And this, after all, is the ultimate test of achievement in all matters human, including the law." Ibid., p. 20. Survival as "the ultimate test of achievement" does not, of course, constitute the answer given by all political philosophers. Some would say, and particularly with regard to questions of law, that mere survival is not good enough for man.

by Cardozo is of a different order from the compromise suggested by Blackstone, who argued, as we noted in Chapter 2, that absolute rights must be limited (or compromised) in political society. For Cardozo, there were no absolute rights, natural or otherwise,[53] and thus a compromise was not a prudent decision about principle, but rather a quantitative adjustment calculated to avoid, in a term he borrowed from Pound, "friction and waste." Since an absolute hierarchy of values or ends has been denied, Cardozo's compromise can only be justified pragmatically.[54]

The implications of this conception of the judicial function are quite revealing. In effect, they amount to juristic abnegation of the statesmanship role—a role that requires political and moral leadership. "If there is any law," Cardozo wrote, "which is back of the sovereignty of the state, and superior thereto, it is not law in such a sense as to concern the judge or lawyer, however much it concerns the statesman or the moralist."[55] Cardozo's distinction between judge and statesman is of more than semantic or rhetorical significance. The judge, for whom justice is synonymous with the social mores, and for whom compromise is determined without reference to fixed principles, cannot be a statesman. He might still be a very competent judge (in some areas of the law), but he cannot give to the judiciary what Lincoln gave to the executive, or indeed, what Marshall gave to the Supreme Court.

Statesmanship implies leadership. It also implies, in fact it requires, a due regard for public opinion. The statesman cannot presume to raise the level of public opinion if he ignores it in developing a strategy of action. Cardozo's jurisprudence is characterized by judicial concern for prevailing conduct and belief; however, it fails to rise significantly above the level that it finds. A judge must always subordinate his own views to the views of the

53. Cardozo's appraisal of Holmes revealed his views on this subject. "No one has labored more incessantly to demonstrate the truth that rights are never absolute, though they are ever struggling and tending to declare themselves as such." "Mr. Justice Holmes," in *Selected Writings*, p. 82.

54. Thus, the following statement by Cardozo is rendered almost meaningless by his pragmatic orientation. "In general we may say that where conflict [between values] exists, moral values are to be preferred to economic, and economic to aesthetic." *PLS*, p. 57.

55. Cardozo, *GOL*, p. 49.

community, both in those situations where the legislature has expressed these views and in those where it has not.[56] "The law will not hold the crowd to the morality of saints and seers. It will follow, or strive to follow, the principle and practice of the men and women of the community whom the social mind would rank as intelligent and virtuous."[57] The accepted standards of morality, the mores of the time, must always be his guide. As William James put it: "The presumption in cases of conflict (between values) must always be in favor of the conventionally recognized good."[58] This presumption rests upon another presumption, "that the vulgarly accepted opinions are true, and the right casuistic order that which public opinion believes in."[59] In short, Cardozo's judge, like James's ethical philosopher, "is on no essentially different level from the common man."[60]

In the final analysis, Cardozo's jurisprudence, like Dewey's philosophy, rests upon faith. The future, Cardozo informed us, will take care of the errors of the present. "In the endless process of testing and retesting, there is a constant rejection of the dross, and a constant retention of whatever is pure and sound and fine."[61] The enduring element of the judicial product is enduring because it is good, whereas the perishable part of the judge's output is perishable because it is bad. This may or may not be true; political history is filled with examples of the perishable bad bringing down with it what was thought to be enduringly good. Cardozo might have been on firmer ground had he based his faith on a certainty regarding political ends. When the morality of law resides in the morality of the community it seeks to govern, faith in the future must rest upon an assurance that the ends of the community are just.

The judicial pragmatists, we might say in summary, accomplished what they had set out to do. They managed to avoid the analytical positivist's identification of the law that is with the law

56. Ibid., p. 94.
57. Cardozo, *PLS*, p. 37.
58. James, "The Moral Philosopher," p. 206.
59. Ibid., p. 208.
60. Ibid., p. 214.
61. Cardozo, *NJP*, p. 179.

that ought to be. They also steered clear of the natural rights philosopher's fusion of the is and ought according to standards derived outside of immediate experience. They did not, however, avoid entirely the assumptions underlying Austinian jurisprudence. That is to say, after rejecting analytical positivism they adopted instead the jurisprudence of democratic positivism. The law that is was not what it ought to be if it did not reflect the "is" of popular behavior and opinion. To determine this latter "is" was to be the function of the jurist, and to establish a congruence between the law and the "is" was to achieve justice. Hence, the method of justice involved the judge as democratic fact finder.

The description and critique of pragmatic jurisprudence included in this chapter are prerequisites for the presentation of an alternative method of conceiving and adjudicating constitutional questions. That alternative involves three considerations—fact, doctrine, and principle—only the first two of which were emphasized by the pragmatists. They quite rightly attacked the mechanical jurisprudence of the late nineteenth century for its failure to adjust judicial doctrine to changing social realities. However, in denigrating principle they failed to indicate how doctrine should change in the face of new facts. The view that will be developed in the remaining chapters is that doctrine (or rule of law) consists of the application of principle to facts. Thus, if facts change, doctrine must also change, but constitutional principle remains unchanged. After the relevant facts have been determined, the Court then determines doctrine, and, in doing so, applies principle. In this way the desire for purposive legal growth can be fulfilled, because a meaningful standard has been developed with which to chart or prescribe this growth. The judge will consequently be concerned with the common (or public) interest of adjusting old principles of republican government to new social realities.

CHAPTER 5

Pragmatism in Action: The Paradox of "One Man, One Vote"

THE CONSTITUTION AS PUBLIC LAW

The reader of Cardozo and Pound will notice that the preponderance of examples used to illustrate their analyses and recommendations are taken from private law, primarily the law of torts and contracts. Only occasional reference was made to constitutional law, although both writers indicated that their prescriptions were intended to apply to public and private law. Cardozo, of course, wrote while sitting on a state court of appeals, and no doubt his selection of illustrations was influenced by that fact. A more persuasive explanation as to why he and Pound (and also Holmes) were attracted to these kinds of examples is simply that the pragmatic jurisprudence that each advocated is more at home in the environment of private law. This is not an observation that they would have been likely to accept. Cardozo, for example, maintained that his method of sociology was especially useful in the field of constitutional law.[1] It is, however, an understanding compelled by the logic of their jurisprudential arguments.

The most important difference between private law and the public law of the Constitution resides in the location of standards for adjudication. The Constitution provides an external standard or reference point according to which the facts of particular cases can be evaluated. This does not mean that a judge in a constitutional case is more restricted in his range of alternatives than in a private law case. Edward H. Levi, for example, has correctly

A slightly different version of part of this chapter appeared in *Polity* (Vol. 9, No. 3, Spring 1977). Permission to use this material is gratefully acknowledged.

1. Cardozo, *NJP*, pp. 76 and 150. See also B. H. Levy, *Cardozo and the Frontiers of Legal Thinking* (Port Washington, 1938), pp. 62–63.

argued that the Court has greater freedom when it interprets the Constitution than it has in the application of a statute or in case law. But he was also correct when he claimed that "there is an affirmative recognition in a constitutional case that the problem is the connection between what is sought to be done and the ideals of the community."[2] The ideals of the community (as opposed to the contemporary ideas of the community) are to be found, in large part, in the Constitution. The pragmatic jurist who denies the possibility of an external standard, a source derived outside of immediate experience, in effect denies the legitimacy of constitutional ideals. In a case not controlled by the words of the Constitution; that is to say, not involving a question relating to the nature of the regime, the pragmatic method of Cardozo and Pound is less problematic. In such a case, the argument for a "social engineer" (though the term would still be unfortunate) who decides according to the social mores of the time and place, does not necessarily imply a neutrality respecting the decisive political choice inscribed in the regime's fundamental legal charter.

The pragmatists did not believe that the distinction between public and private law demanded a corresponding distinction in the methods and sources used in judicial decision making. Cardozo and Pound attempted to effect a merger between private and public law by demonstrating that the process of adjudication is essentially the same in both.[3] This is perhaps best seen in the work of the political scientist, Arthur F. Bentley, who, not coincidentally, was the coauthor with John Dewey of a book on ethics. Bentley viewed the law as a product of group pressures and demands: "There is no law that is fundamentally more 'public,' none that is more private, than any other. . . . All law is social." Thus, the Constitution is "but a special form of law," differing in no important way from all other law. "The Constitution," he observed,

2. Edward H. Levi, *An Introduction to Legal Reasoning* (Chicago, 1948), pp. 7, 60.

3. See Moses J. Aronson, "Cardozo," p. 13. Professor Patterson wrote, in this regard, of Pound: "By extending the notion of public policy to the entire field of positive law, the theory of social interests tends to break down the division between private law, conceived as a set of rules of the game, and public law, conceived as expressions of the policy of the state or government. . . . The social interests are a synthesis of values for all law." *Interpretation of Modern Legal Philosophies*, p. 566.

"is always what is."[4] In other words, the judge, ever responsive to group pressures, interprets and creates law according to popular will. This failure to notice any significance in the distinction between public and private parallels the abandonment of the distinction between judicial and legislative modes of decision making. Bentley's analysis (shared in all essential respects by Cardozo and Pound) prescribed a resolution of judicial questions according to basically legislative criteria.

In the pragmatic view the Court is not to interpret the original will of the people but rather the present will, as revealed by the social wants and mores. For the founders, on the other hand, this kind of interpretation was to be left to the more representative institutions. They agreed that judges were to exercise a certain amount of discretion, but they saw no basis in republican principles for admitting such discretion under the terms later adopted by the pragmatic judicial philosophers. They drew an important distinction between momentary interests and enduring interests, realizing that in political life the two are often opposed to one another. The pragmatists recognized only momentary interests, and based their recognition upon the principle of equality. In so doing, they rejected the traditional sources associated with public law judicial interpretation.[5]

PRAGMATISM AND DOGMATISM

The purpose of this chapter is to illustrate the application of pragmatic principles of jurisprudence to the work of the Supreme

4. Arthur F. Bentley, *The Process of Government* (Chicago, 1908), pp. 277, 295, 296. "Law is activity, just as government is. It is a group process, just as government is. It is a forming, a systematization, a struggle, an adaptation, of group interests, just as government is." Ibid., p. 272.

5. According to the founders, the Constitution expresses the *original* will of the people. The Court, because of its uniquely undemocratic character, is the institution best suited to perform the role of interpreting this will. See the *Federalist Papers,* particularly Numbers 49 and 78. As Ralph Lerner has shown, the early judges of the national judiciary understood very well the implications of this function, and thus saw themselves as "teachers to the citizenry." Lerner, "The Supreme Court as Republican Schoolmaster," in *The Supreme Court Review, 1967,* ed. Philip B. Kurland (Chicago, 1967). During the pre-Marshall Court the vehicle of their instruction was the charge to the jury; with the rise of Marshall, it was the opinion of the Court. The importance of rhetoric was thus implied in the nature of the

Court and to suggest what may be involved in the abandonment of the distinction between public and private law. The specific focus is the reapportionment issue when the Warren Court forged the judicial doctrine of "one man, one vote." In the course of the discussion we will have an opportunity to examine the commonly held assumption concerning the mutually exclusive characters of pragmatism and dogmatism, or, in judicial terms, whether the judicial pragmatist is by definition nondogmatic. It will be argued that, at least in this area, pragmatism and dogmatism are not inconsistent, but on the contrary, are complementary. Moreover, this somewhat paradoxical conclusion derives from the relationship between pragmatism and equality described in the previous chapters.

We are accustomed in our society to hear praises sung to the pragmatic spirit that animates our actions and ideas. The accomplished politician, the successful businessman, the winning football coach have all "made it" because they are innovative, adaptable, flexible. In short, they are not wedded to the ideas of the past or to the dictates of unexamined authoritative doctrine. To be otherwise would make one dogmatic, which is to say, in the minds of many, arrogant, imperious, and arbitrary. The pragmatist, on the other hand, is likely to be thought modest, unpretentious, and tolerant—possessed, in other words, of all the qualities considered virtuous in a liberal society. Following Mill, we distinguish between "dead dogma" and "living truth," and quite naturally we choose life over death.

It is not only the uninformed layman who sees as mutually exclusive the respective spheres of pragmatism and dogma and who rejects the latter. Our nation, we are informed by learned authority, has escaped the dark and gloomy fates of other less fortunate societies precisely because we are antitheoretical, unburdened and unchained by rigid theoretical commitments. Indeed, it is the "genius of American politics" that we are so favored, and if anything is sure it is that "we are doomed to failure in any attempt to sum up our way of life in slogans and dogmas."[6]

---

judicial function, and the opinion of the Court was in many ways as significant as the decision it rendered.

6. Daniel J. Boorstin, *The Genius of American Politics* (Chicago, 1953), p. 1.

Although we frequently associate judicial dogmatism with the natural rights absolutism that was a hallmark of the old property Court, such natural rights references and applications are not a necessary element of dogmatic constitutional adjudication. One's fascination with equality, for example, may lead one to become dogmatic in its defense, and yet that defense need not be grounded in the philosophy of natural right. The case of Justice Holmes is illustrative here. No Supreme Court jurist ever fought harder to banish from the law the stultifying dogmas of natural rights. And no Supreme Court jurist has been as frequently identified with pragmatic jurisprudence as Justice Holmes. Holmes, it was, who claimed in his famous *Abrams* dissent, "that the best test of truth is the power of the thought to get itself accepted in the competition of the market."[7] Pragmatic? Antidogmatic? Surely in light of what we generally associate with pragmatism Holmes's statement appears pragmatic. Indeed, what could be more opposed to dogmatism than a pronouncement that explicitly denies the claims of immutability made in behalf of truth? If a dogmatic statement is one that makes an assertion of belief as if it were an established fact, and develops an argument based upon insufficiently examined premises (meaning that it was grounded in reason to the neglect of experience), then how is Holmes's statement to be evaluated? Can it be agreed that a successful trip through the marketplace will validate the claim of an idea to truth? Unless truth is defined as the will of the strongest, then there is no empirical support for Holmes's argument. It becomes a positive assertion of opinion elevated to the status of constitutional truth. It becomes, in a word, judicial dogma. This is not meant pejoratively or in any deprecatory way, but only to indicate what will later become relevant in the context of reapportionment, that the respective realms of pragmatism and dogmatism may not be as mutually exclusive as is sometimes thought.

THE WARREN COURT AND EQUAL POPULATION

Upon his retirement Chief Justice Warren made it known that in his opinion the most important decision handed down during

---

7. *Abrams* v. *United States,* 250 U.S. 616, 630 (1919).

his tenure on the Court was *Baker* v. *Carr*.[8] Certainly there were many candidates to choose from including the landmark *Brown* decision (which Warren ranked second in importance), but in retrospect it is altogether fitting that Warren should have selected the decision pronouncing the issue of malapportionment to be justiciable as the one with the greatest significance. For it was only a short time thereafter that the Court established the constitutional legitimacy of the equal-population principle, and applied it to various levels of government. The appropriateness of Warren's choice resides, however, only in part in the impact of the reapportionment decisions on American society.[9] Perhaps more important, these decisions typify the spirit of egalitarianism which was the dominant and most characteristic theme of the Warren Court era.[10] Critics and supporters of the Court tend to agree on one thing: the push for equality—whether between blacks and whites, accused and accuser, or urban voter and rural voter—was the distinctive feature of the Warren Court's work. The reapportionment decisions, more than any others, reveal the magnitude of its commitment to this end.

Perhaps the individual most troubled by the Court's decision in *Baker* was Justice Frankfurter, who sixteen years earlier had cautioned the Court against entering the "political thicket."[11] Un-

8. Quoted in the *New York Times,* July 6, 1968, p. 42, col. 1. Before his retirement Warren was quoted as saying that the most important opinion that he, personally, had written was *Reynolds* v. *Sims.* See Fred Rodell, "It is the Earl Warren Court." *The New York Times Magazine,* March 13, 1966, p. 94.

9. Although it has been questioned whether the measures used were appropriate, most of the early empirical evidence indicated that little had changed. See, in particular, Herbert Jacob, "The Consequences of Malapportionment: A note of Caution," *Social Forces,* 43 (1964); Thomas Dye, "Malapportionment and Public Policy in the States," *Journal of Politics,* 27 (1965); Richard Hofferbert, "The Relation between Public Policy and some Structural and Environmental Variables in the American States," *American Political Science Review,* 60 (1966). Of course, further research will be necessary to establish whether structural changes may now be producing new lines of policy.

10. For an elaboration see Alexander M. Bickel, *The Supreme Court and the Idea of Progress;* Philip B. Kurland, *Politics, the Constitution, and the Warren Court* (Chicago, 1970); and Archibald Cox, *The Warren Court: Constitutional Decision as an Instrument of Reform* (Cambridge, 1968).

11. *Colegrove* v. *Green,* 328 U.S. 549, 556 (1946).

like the supporters of the subsequent reapportionment rulings, who maintained that the only neutral principle was the one announced by the Court, "one man, one vote," Frankfurter's basic position was that neutrality could best be preserved by judicial avoidance of the issue. "What is actually asked of the Court in this case is to choose among competing bases of representation—ultimately, really among competing theories of political philosophy."[12] Although there was at the time nothing more than intimations as to which competing theory would receive judicial affirmation and thus constitutional sanctity, it was relatively clear in what direction the Court was headed. Or, if there was any doubt on this matter Chief Justice Warren decisively extinguished it two years later when, quoting from an earlier opinion of Justice William O. Douglas, he declared for the Court that "the conception of political equality from the Declaration of Independence, to Lincoln's Gettysburg Address, to the Fifteenth, Seventeenth, and Nineteenth Amendments can mean only one thing—'one person, one vote.' " Warren maintained "that the fundamental principle of representative government in this country is one of equal representation for equal numbers of people, without regard to race, sex, economic status, or place of residence within a state."[13]

The equal protection clause of the Fourteenth Amendment was the principal constitutional vehicle for the announcement of the equal-population principle. The question was not so much whether the clause had been intended to deal with nonracial matters of representation—most people agreed that it had not—but whether, in view of the importance assigned to the concept of equal treatment in the Fourteenth Amendment and other places, it should apply to the problem of malapportionment. This distinction is quite important. The extension of a constitutional principle or clause to a situation not originally anticipated by its

12. *Baker* v. *Carr,* 369 U.S. 186, 300 (1962). Justice Harlan, who carried the Frankfurter banner after the latter retired, echoed his colleague's sentiments. "In the last analysis, what lies at the core of this controversy is a difference of opinion as to the function of representative government." Ibid., at 333.

13. *Reynolds* v. *Sims,* 377 U.S. 533, 558, 560–561 (1964). The Douglas quote is from *Gray* v. *Sanders,* 372 U.S. 368, 381 (1963).

authors assumes that had the authors been aware of the problem they would have mentioned it, or at the very least, that the principle, in this case equality, must by the very nature of the particular problem, be considered applicable.[14] In other words, the case would require a judgment by the justices that equality was in fact a necessary element, or more accurately, *the* necessary element, of democratic representation. If it was, then the responsibility of the Court was to enforce it through the application of the equal protection clause.

Of course, to those not persuaded that numerical equality was implicit in the meaning of democratic representation, the "one man, one vote" rulings became a focal point for criticism. The Court, they claimed, was assuming the ground in dispute by, in effect, denying that there were legitimate forms of representative government founded on other than majoritarian principles. "My own understanding of the various theories of representative government," argued Justice Stewart, "is that no one theory has ever commanded unanimous assent among political scientists, historians, or others who have considered the problem."[15] If Justice Stewart had elaborated on his observation he would have mentioned that theorists on representation have differed on such fundamental questions as who is to be represented (the illiterate as well as the educated?), what is to be represented (just people or economic interests too?), and how representation is to occur (through elections every two years or through plebiscites?). Is accountability more important than governing? Should representatives reflect, without distortion, the characteristics of their constituencies, and if so, which of these characteristics are politically important for this purpose? And so on. The way such questions are answered will be decisive in the selection of a particular

14. Or, as one scholar has written: "The crucial issue in apportionment involves the . . . central question: Is the 'adaptable' Constitution sufficiently flexible to provide hospitable shelter for application of the equal protection clause to matters not before considered within its scope?" Robert B. McKay, *Reapportionment: The Law and Politics of Equal Representation* (New York, 1965), p. 167.

15. *Lucas et al.* v. *Forty-Fourth General Assembly of Colorado, et al.,* 377 U.S. 713, 748 (1964).

districting and apportionment scheme.[16] One need not go so far as to suggest that the equal-population principle implies an "acceptance by the Court of an unrestricted egalitarianism inconsistent with the concept of democracy expressed in the Constitution of the United States,"[17] to acknowledge that the Court's treatment of the issue did not recognize the complexities of the problem. To say that "citizens, not history or economic interests, cast votes," or that "legislators represent people, not trees or acres,"[18] does not leave one with a sense that the Court fully appreciated the many dimensions that define the problem of representation.

Frankfurterian avoidance was not the only alternative to the rather rigid majoritarianism of the Warren Court's later reapportionment decisions. The opinions of the various members of the

16. The literature on the subject of representation is, of course, enormous, and no effort will be made to cite all the relevant materials. The complexity of the issue, however, can best be appreciated by studying the work of philosophers such as Hobbes, Locke, Rousseau, and Mill. One of the most interesting recent studies on the subject that nicely presents and contrasts the range of representational possibilities is Hannah Pitkin, *The Concept of Representation* (Berkeley, 1967). Among the reapportionment studies that focus upon the broader issues of representation are Richard Claude, *The Supreme Court and the Electoral Process* (Baltimore, 1970); Richard C. Cortner, *The Apportionment Cases* (Knoxville, 1970); Alfred de Grazia, *Apportionment and Representative Government* (New York, 1962); Robert G. Dixon, Jr., *Democratic Representation: Reapportionment in Law and Politics* (New York, 1968); Ward E. Y. Elliott, *The Rise of Guardian Democracy: The Supreme Court's Role in Voting Rights Disputes, 1845–1969* (Cambridge, 1974); Robert A. Goldwin, ed., *Representation and Misrepresentation: Legislative Reapportionment in Theory and Practice* (Chicago, 1968); Andrew Hacker, *Congressional Districting: The Issue of Equal Representation* (Washington, D.C., 1964); William P. Irwin, "Representation and Election: The Reapportionment Cases in Retrospect," *Michigan Law Review*, 67 (1969).

17. Stuart M. Browne, Jr., "Black on Representation: A Question," *Representation—Nomos X*, eds. J. Roland Pennock and John W. Chapman (New York, 1968), pp. 148–149.

18. *Reynolds* v. *Sims*, at 580, 562. In this regard, it is perhaps worthwhile to quote from Justice Harlan's dissenting opinion. "But it is surely equally obvious, and in the context of elections, more meaningful to note that people are not ciphers and that legislators can represent their electors only by speaking for their interests—economic, social, political—many of which do reflect the place where the electors live." Ibid., at 623–624. Off the Court the criticism was sharper. "The new decisions fundamentally ignore all that we have learned about the group nature of politics." Martin Shapiro, *Law and Politics in The Supreme Court* (New York, 1964), p. 249.

Court suggest a spectrum of positions, represented on one extreme by Frankfurter's and Harlan's tacit acceptance of any system of apportionment (and definition of representation) and on the other extreme by an insistence on approximate numerical, mathematical equality (despite the disclaimers in the early cases) by Warren, William Brennan, Hugo Black, and Douglas. The middle position was taken by Stewart, Abe Fortas, and Tom Clark, who advocated flexibility within prescribed standards which, as we shall see later, involved a distinction between equal protection and equal population. The first position represents a judicial abdication of any responsibility in expounding the regime's political principles, the second represents a judicial choice regarding the precise nature of those principles, and the third represents a judicial decision regarding what those principles are not, without indicating what specifically they are. The fact that the Warren group prevailed meant that the Court chose to follow the egalitarian path in the absence of any clear requirement, in precedent or constitutional theory, to do so.[19] To what can we attribute this choice?

For an answer it is helpful to quote at some length from Warren's opinion for the Court in *Reynolds* v. *Sims*.

The fact that an individual lives here or there is not a legitimate reason for overweighting or diluting the efficacy of his vote. The complexion of societies and civilizations change, often with amazing rapidity. A nation once primarily rural in character becomes predominately urban. Representation schemes once fair and equitable become archaic and outdated. But the basic principle of representative government remains, and must remain, unchanged—the weight of a citizen's vote cannot be made to depend on where he lives. Population is, of necessity, the starting point for consideration and the controlling criterion for judgment in legislative apportionment controversies.[20]

One noted authority on reapportionment has written in criticism

---

19. For Professor Shapiro this choice indicated "that the Court has given up its role of reflecting the American balance between Madisonian and populistic democracy and has chosen to become a leader in the populistic faction." Ibid., p. 248. We might add that Frankfurter and Harlan also gave up this role, although they decided not to become a leader of any faction.

20. *Reynolds* v. *Sims,* at 567.

of Warren's opinion that it contains "no trace of pragmatism."[21] On the other hand, the Warren reapportionment majority has been celebrated for its "pragmatism," for having made "expedient the fulfillment of the historic ideal of equality."[22] This follows the usual pattern of commentary, in which the supporters of the opinions praise them for their pragmatism and the opponents criticize them for their lack of pragmatism. Nowhere is there to be found a detractor who is critical because of the pragmatism reflected in the opinions. The above excerpt seems to support both contentions. Those who see pragmatism are pleased with Warren's recognition of the changes that have occurred in American society over the years, of his appreciation of the tremendous problems confronted by the urban majority. Those who fail to see pragmatism can cite Warren's insistence on population as the controlling criterion in resolving apportionment controversies and his refusal to legitimate a deliberate policy of overweighting or diluting the vote.

There is, however, an interesting problem in this opinion that seems to have escaped the commentators, but which is relevant to our considerations. Warren, after mentioning the rural to urban transition in American society, indicates that the basic principle of representative government (one man, one vote) must remain unchanged. He also indicates that the old representation schemes were once "fair and equitable" but that they have become "archaic and outmoded." The suggestion seems to be that the reason they were fair and equitable was because they had been consistent with the basic principle of representative government as described by Warren. The principle, after all, is unchangeable, which presumably means that in our representative government it has always existed, even if it has not always been practiced. A system weighted in favor of rural interests at a time when the population was primarily rural was just, and obviously meant that "one man, one vote" had been the operative principle. It automatically fol-

21. Robert G. Dixon, Jr., *Democratic Representation*, p. 273. Professor Dixon was not only disappointed in the opinion but surprised by it, for he considered pragmatism to be Warren's "pre-eminent quality."

22. Alan P. Grimes, *Equality in America: Religion, Race, and the Urban Majority* (New York, 1964), p. x.

lows that a given state's representation scheme must change in proportion to the shift in population. But is it so obvious? Can we assume that a system that did in fact conform to the equal-population principle was based upon that principle? Logic certainly does not support the assumption and, as Justice Harlan's dissenting opinion suggests, history does not either.[23] Would it not be more consistent with what we know about legislative motives to assume that political considerations (the protection of rural interests) rather than principled, egalitarian considerations dictated the configuration of the old districting plan? The plan's apparent compliance with Warren's "basic principle" may have involved little more than coincidence. It would thus be inaccurate to attribute automatically the fairness and equity of the old scheme to the existence of Warren's unchangeable basic principle. Rather, it may be plausible to conclude, particularly in view of the long-standing disagreement on the principles of representation, that Warren's principle reflected this Court's understanding of what should be unchangeable and not what in fact has been unchangeable. The Court, like off-the-Court advocates of reapportionment, was motivated, at least in part, by the desire to see a more egalitarian society, to remove the inequities experienced by the urban poor.[24] These motives were doubtless well intentioned, but the reasoning, whereby a newly legitimated principle was interpreted retroactively

23. Harlan cited evidence to indicate that in the years following 1868 the actions of the states, in their adoption of apportionment procedures, was highly suggestive of the inapplicability of the Fourteenth Amendment to problems of legislative districting. *Reynolds* v. *Sims,* at 608. Harlan also examined the congressional debates concerning the Fourteenth Amendment to argue that the intentions of the framers render inappropriate the application of the amendment to problems of apportionment. The best response to Justice Harlan may be found in William W. Van Alstyne, "The Fourteenth Amendment, the 'Right' to Vote, and the Understanding of the Thirty-Ninth Congress," 1965 *The Supreme Court Review.*

24. For example, one of these advocates, Professor Grimes, commented in this regard: "In giving new meaning to the 'equal protection' clause of the Fourteenth Amendment, the Supreme Court has but taken cognizance of an urban majority which has been seeking to achieve that power in politics which it may democratically claim by virtue of its numbers." Grimes, *Equality in America,* p. 125. As we shall see, however, it is not clear that the jurisprudence of the Court, which lead to the adoption of the equal-population principle, would in turn lead to the advancement of the urban majority.

and designated unchanging, may leave disappointed those who value a reason-oriented jurisprudence.

PRAGMATIC ADJUDICATION

The reapportionment decisions of the 1960's can be viewed as a political analogue to the Supreme Court's earlier about-face in cases dealing with wages and hours, working conditions, and union organization. In both situations the Court moved with the onrushing egalitarian tide to wash away old precedents supportive of an entrenched social order. There are, to be sure, glaring differences in the two cases. In the earlier decisions the Court adopted a posture of judicial self-restraint, whereas in the later ones, the defense of equality required that it assume a more activist role vis-a-vis other governmental institutions. In the long history of the Court, activism and self-restraint, with few exceptions, have not represented firm, irrevocable jurisprudential commitment. Rather, their ascendence and decline have been associated quite closely with the larger political-constitutional beliefs of the judges.

It has, however, been forcefully argued that the reapportionment decisions bear a very close resemblance to the old Court's defense of inequality.[25] Not only did the Court reject judicial self-restraint in both situations, but it also based its judgments upon dogmatic reasoning and a refusal to adjudicate pragmatically.[26] The Court, so the argument goes, should have continued "the pragmatic treatment of apportionment statutes as political questions,"[27] which is to say it should have continued to avoid such issues rather than fall victim to the temptations of doctrinaire social theory.

25. See A. Spencer Hill, "The Reapportionment Decisions: A Return to Dogma," *Journal of Politics,* 31, No. 1 (1967).

26. "It is the author's contention that the Court's move from dogma to pragmatism in the wage and hours cases was more consistent with the Constitution and its philosophy, more in accord with the legal powers of the Court, better adapted to the difficult role the Court must play, and better related to the economic and social necessities of our time than was the earlier dependence upon dogma. He fears that the Court has unwisely reversed its position relative to pragmatism and dogmatism in the reapportionment cases and sees no compelling reason for the reversal." Ibid., p. 187.

27. Ibid., p. 190.

The problem with this argument is that entrapment in doctrinaire social theory, expressed here in an insistence on mathematical equality, was not an inevitable consequence of the Court's rejection of the "political question" doctrine, and with it, all of Justice Frankfurter's warnings against entering the political thicket. The impact of a Supreme Court decision may be consistent with a particular social theory, but this does not necessarily mean that the reasoning behind the decision must be consistent with the social theory. Most of us know cases of people who, as the expression goes, came to the right decision for all the wrong reasons. An apportionment plan may be found constitutionally infirm either because it fails to conform to the requirements of "one man, one vote," or, as the concurring opinions in *Reynolds* illustrate, because of an arbitrariness amounting to a lack of due process. We call a decision dogmatic if the supporting reasons (if there are any) are dogmatic. It is also true, however, that decisions are not pragmatic or unpragmatic; *reasons* are. Thus, to the extent that there is an affinity between pragmatism and equality we might expect to find pragmatism not so much in the decision or result (which may indeed be egalitarian) but in the opinions or reasons employed in support of a given decision. A ruling, say, that orders State X to reapportion according to specific guidelines laid down by the Court, may by its sweeping character appear unpragmatic, even though the reasoning leading up to the decision may actually have been grounded in pragmatic principles.

What, then, was pragmatic about the reapportionment opinions, particularly those that announced and extended the equal-population principle? To answer this query requires that one recall the characteristic tenets of pragmatic jurisprudence outlined in Chapters 3 and 4.

First, attention to empirical evidence is a necessary, if not sufficient, condition of pragmatic jurisprudence. Failure to examine relevant sociological data leads, as it did in an earlier day, to judicial validation of an unjust status quo. In the reapportionment cases the Court was meticulous in its analysis of census figures and population-variance ratios. This analysis largely supported the complaints of spokesmen for urban interests who maintained that over the years their people had been shortchanged in terms of legislative representation. The Court was familiarized with the findings and conclusions of political scientists and journalists, who attributed much of the urban crisis to the existence of malapportioned state legislatures dominated by political interests generally unsympathetic to the needs of the metropolitan areas. Its opinions in the various reapportionment cases make important references to the research of social scientists in both substantive (demonstrations of bias in malapportionment) and methodological (development of statistical measures of vote devaluation) areas. If, as Dewey maintained, one measurement of societal equality is the extent to which knowledge is grounded in empirical evidence, the egalitarian implications of the Court's extensive inquiry into social science data are abundantly clear.

Related to the emphasis upon empirical information is the pragmatic reliance upon post-hoc evaluation of the validity of an idea or principle in terms of the consequences it produces. In this respect the Court was limited by the fact that it could only predict what these consequences might be. The data, however, seemed to point convincingly to more equal access to political decision-making by all individuals in society if the equal-population principle became a constitutional requirement. Indeed, the majority opinion in *Reynolds* is grounded on the assumption, however erroneous, that the consequence of equal-population districting is equal representation. As Robert G. Dixon, Jr. has noted, this was "a classic example of moving from an objective concept to a highly subjective concept without noting the shift."[28] Looking back, however, to our observations concerning Deweyan pragmatism, we are able to perceive what may have been the unarticulated premises of this shift.

It was pointed out in Chapter 3 that for the pragmatists ethical judgments are not derivative from a fixed code of ethics; rather they derive from an objective, problematic situation that indicates

28. Dixon, *Democratic Representation,* p. 269. For Dixon, "This easy equating of the objective and the subjective is the central inadequacy of the majority's constitutional theory in the 1964 *Reapportionment Decisions.*" Ibid., p. 269.

an objective need to the observer. The desire for change stimulated by the deficiencies in the environment defines for that observer the particular "good" that is to constitute the goal of his actions. When, through these actions, the need is satisfied and the deficiencies are removed, the good will have been achieved; the consequences of the activity will have merited a positive evaluation. The situation of malapportionment clearly presented the Court with an objective deficiency (i.e., a measurable dilution in balloting strength) that could be remedied through the imposition of the "one man, one vote" principle. The resulting equal-population districts, brought about by this requirement, provided the Court with objective evidence that the immediate problematic situation had been rendered unproblematic, thus validating the principle of per capita representation. In the process equal representation, which Dixon and others have viewed as a subjective concept (by which they meant to imply that its presence is always a matter of controversy), had become objectified. By limiting itself to the specific context of legislative malapportionment, the Court's majority, in effect, forged a doctrine which, as a response to the particular needs presented in that context, became an objective principle of democratic representation.

Of course, when viewed from outside the immediate electoral setting, political access defined in terms of voter equality does not necessarily translate into substantive, representational equality. However, from a pragmatic point of view this does not render undesirable the "one man, one vote" solution. Analogous to Holmes's marketplace, the standard provides a framework within which political competition may occur, but it does not provide a measure by which to evaluate the results of the competition. This is consistent with another of the characteristic tenets of judicial pragmatism, that the law ought not to distinguish between competing demands according to their intrinsic worth. As one scholar has written, "the lack of a generally accepted standard for determining political superiority, whereby voters might be classified into inferior and superior constituents, leads to the equalitarian solution of giving equal votes to all voters."[29] "Inferior" and "superior" may refer to need as well as merit. Thus, it is the Court's responsibility to facilitate

29. Grimes, *Equality in America,* p. 126.

the political recognition of all societal demands as they are manifested in numerical terms, i.e., votes. The specific hope of a particular judge may be that in requiring such a system the group or interest that he feels warrants greater governmental attention will be advantaged. That hope is only incidental to the pragmatic jurisprudence that may bring about its fulfillment. In much the same manner as Justice Holmes may have wished certain ideas to emerge triumphant at the marketplace, the pragmatic judge can only hope that the interests he favors will benefit from a reapportionment of electoral districts.

It is still (and most likely will remain) a matter of controversy whether urbanites, whose votes had previously been devalued, and whose interests were uppermost in the minds of the reformers, have actually been the beneficiaries of reapportionment. Some have argued that the suburbanites have prospered under the equal-population principle, and that the interests of the most needy have, in many instances, been submerged by the majoritarian requirements established by the courts.[30] Leaving aside the practice of gerrymandering, which may or may not have been further stimulated by reapportionment, it requires but a moment's glance at the at-large election (which, because it abandons districting, avoids the problem of malapportionment) to realize that "one man, one vote" is not synonymous with effective representation.[31] Effective representation may, of course, emerge from such a system, just as truth may emerge from the marketplace of ideas. In both cases, however, pragmatic relativism precludes judicial intervention in behalf of certain interests or ideas beyond the point of establishing the conditions for formal equality.

Finally, most judicial pragmatists have accepted the teaching of

30. For an interesting and lively exchange of views on this subject see the articles included in Nelson Polsby, ed., *Reapportionment in the 1970s* (Berkeley, 1971).

31. Note Justice Stewart's comment in this regard: "The very fact of geographic districting, the constitutional validity of which the Court does not question, carries with it an acceptance of the idea of legislative representation of regional needs and interests. Yet if geographical residence is irrelevant, as the Court suggests, and the goal is solely that of equally 'weighted' votes, I do not understand why the Court's constitutional rule does not require the abolition of districts and the holding of all elections at large." *Lucas* v. *Colorado*, at 750.

Arthur F. Bentley that the Constitution is "but a special form of law, differing in no important way from all other law."[32] Earlier we noted that the primary conclusion to be derived from this observation was that, contrary to Blackstone, judges create law through their experiences in rendering decisions. Thus, the excerpt from Warren's opinion in *Reynolds*, quoted earlier, upon which it was suggested that the chief justice was in fact creating the principle of representative democracy, may be seen in a context of pragmatic jurisprudence. The pragmatic judge will not be swayed by the importuning of Justice Frankfurter to avoid the political thicket. The task of judging is by its very nature political, involving creation as well as interpretation. Those critics of the Court who charge it with judicial legislation are perhaps correct in their allegation, although they are clearly wrong from a pragmatic perspective in their assumption regarding the impropriety of such legislation.

DOGMATIC ADJUDICATION

The Warren Court has been accused of having applied a "doctrinaire jurisprudence" to its handling of the reapportionment cases, of having attempted to resolve complex political problems by resorting to "arithmetic absolutism."[33] Perhaps more to the point was this observation by a political scientist. "The 'one man, one vote' slogan, in equating the whole of democracy with majority-rule elections represents naive political philosophy, bad political theory, and no political science. It remains that the *Reapportionment Cases* are, in one important sense, imprudent political action."[34] The thrust of these remarks, and others like it, is that the Court's dogmatic insistence upon equal population as the operative criterion in legislative apportionment avoided the central issue of effective representation.

If, as we indicated earlier, judicial dogma involves the elevation to the status of constitutional truth of an opinion whose premises have not been sufficiently examined, then the dogmatic character

32. Bentley, *Process of Government*, p. 295.
33. Robert G. Dixon, Jr., "The Warren Court Crusade for the Holy Grail of 'One Man–One Vote,'" in 1969 *The Supreme Court Review*, p. 224.
34. Shapiro, *Law and Politics*, p. 250.

of the Warren Court's reapportionment decisions is explicable in
the following way. The equal-population principle may indeed be
necessary to operationalize equal representation, narrowly defined
in terms of voter equality. But the Fourteenth Amendment requires
equal protection, and this requirement may or may not be enforced through a districting scheme based upon equal population.
As Justice Fortas expressed it in his dissenting opinion in *Avery*
v. *Midland County:* " 'Equal protection' relates to the substance
of citizens' rights and interests. It demands protection adapted to
substance; it does not insist upon, or even permit, prescription by
arbitrary formula which wrongly assumes that the interests of all
citizens in the elected body are the same."[35] The electoral system
is only one part of the political process, which itself is only one
part of the entire social system. What contributes to equal protection in terms of voting strength will consequently vary from jurisdiction to jurisdiction. To the extent, then, that the Court's analysis
of representation relies upon the Fourteenth Amendment's equal
protection clause, the equal-population doctrine is dogmatic.

The paradox is that this dogma is related to the pragmatic
jurisprudence discussed above. What appears contradictory (if
only because of the way "pragmatism" is used in common par-
lance) and opposed to common sense is in fact quite consistent. A
pragmatic jurisprudence lacking in standards by which to evaluate
the substantive merits of individual claims requires that equal
protection be determined on the basis of the easily quantifiable
and seemingly non-arbitrary measure of population ratios. For
example, in *Kirkpatrick* v. *Preisler,* decided in 1969, Justice
Brennan, speaking for the Court, wrote: "Equal representation for
equal numbers of people is a principle designed to prevent debase-
ment of voting power and diminution of access to elected representatives. Toleration of even small deviations detracts from these
purposes."[36] "Diminution of access to elected representatives,"

---

35. *Avery* v. *Midland County,* 390 U.S. 474, 499 (1968). And elsewhere:
"In the circumstances of this case equal protection of the laws may be
achieved—and perhaps can only be achieved—by a system which takes into
account a complex of values and factors, and not merely the arithmetic
simplicity of one equals one." Ibid., at 496.

36. *Kirkpatrick* v. *Preisler,* 394 U.S. 526, 531 (1969).

when understood in conjunction with "voting power," tells only a part of a much larger story. It says nothing of the access to elected representatives that is a function of other factors (e.g., money, organization, history, geography), and which may be offset by unequal voting power, leading perhaps to substantially more equal protection.

By 1969 these other factors were not likely to deter the Warren Court from its pursuit of arithmetic equality. "Mathematical exactness or precision is hardly a workable constitutional requirement."[37] The distance the Court had traveled since 1964 when Chief Justice Warren made this assertion in *Reynolds* is illustrated by the majority's nullification of the congressional districting plans of Missouri and New York, in which the maximum deviations from the arithmetic mean were only 3.1 percent and 6.6 percent, respectively.[38] In the New York case the plan had actually been the bipartisan product of a divided legislative body. As Archibald Cox has observed, "once loosed, the idea of Equality is not easily cabined."[39] Moreover, an idea that becomes crystallized into judicial dogma proceeds with an inexorability requiring an intolerance for even small deviations, whether or not they reflect prudent public policy.

In *Reynolds*, Chief Justice Warren pointed out that "the Constitution forbids sophisticated as well as simple-minded modes of discrimination."[40] In the most obvious sense, of course, this is true. Clearly the Constitution forbids invidious discrimination, simple-minded or sophisticated, unrelated to a valid state purpose. But it is equally clear that the Constitution in no way forbids discrimination that is characterized by discernment and good judgment in distinguishing between different situations. Indeed, this is the art of politics, an art that the Constitution was meant to encourage. By developing the equal-population doctrine the Court was, in effect, acknowledging its inability to discriminate among

37. *Reynolds* v. *Sims*, at 577.
38. The Missouri case was *Kirkpatrick* v. *Preisler;* the New York case, *Wells* v. *Rockefeller*, 394 U.S. 542 (1969).
39. Cox, *Warren Court*, p. 6.
40. *Reynolds* v. *Sims*, at 563, paraphrasing Justice Frankfurter in *Lane* v. *Wilson*, 307 U.S. 268, 275 (1938).

discriminations. This inability, it is submitted, is at once an outgrowth of pragmatism and a cause of dogmatism.

How, then, might the Court have approached the issue of reapportionment so as to have avoided dogmatism as well as the acceptance of an unjust status quo insofar as many districting systems were concerned? "The question before us," wrote Justice Harlan in a 1969 reapportionment dissent, "is whether the Constitution requires that mathematics be a substitute for common sense in the art of statecraft."[41] Harlan's solution, judicial avoidance, was, as indicated earlier, not the only alternative to the prevailing majority view. The position that best reflected the art of judicial statecraft was espoused by Justices Stewart, Fortas, and Clark. It called for flexibility within prescribed standards, a recognition that equal protection may be compatible with a variety of representational schemes, only one of which involved the "one man, one vote" formula. However, unlike the position of Harlan and Frankfurter, this position held that the Court has a responsibility to invalidate those districting systems that were clearly incompatible with equal protection and due process requirements.

At the conclusion of the previous chapter we noted that judicial statesmanship involves the application of fixed constitutional principles to a set of facts for the purpose of deriving judicial doctrine. Facts and doctrine may change, but constitutional principles are unvarying. Justice Stewart's dissenting opinion in *Lucas* v. *Colorado,* decided on the same day as *Reynolds,* illustrates what is involved.

"Constitutional statecraft often involves a degree of protection for minorities which limits the principle of majority rule."[42] It must have given Justice Stewart some satisfaction to use these words, for he was quoting from the brief of Solicitor General Cox in *Baker* v. *Carr,* which had suggested that on occasion it might be reasonable, in terms of enlightened public policy, to give urban residents less voting power than they would be entitled by a strictly numerical apportionment scheme.[43] A majority of the

41. *Wells* v. *Rockefeller,* at 552.
42. *Lucas* v. *Colorado,* at 759.
43. Archibald Cox's important role in the reapportionment effort of the

Court never adopted Cox's early approach; however, Justice Stewart employed it in the formulation of the most prudent of the several constitutional solutions to the apportionment problem.

The solution began from the premise that "representative government is a process of accommodating group interests through democratic institutional arrangements."[44] The nature of the accommodation must, by virtue of the great diversity within the nation, vary in accordance with this diversity. Thus, what appears as a rational plan of apportionment in one state may be totally irrational in another. Rationality, however, is not exclusively a matter of intelligent accommodation of interests. "So long as a State's apportionment plan reasonably achieves, in the light of the State's own characteristics, effective and balanced representation of all substantial interests, *without sacrificing the principle of effective majority rule,* that plan cannot be considered irrational."[45] Presumably, then, an apportionment plan could provide a basis for effective representation of interests and still be constitutionally invalid if, in the process, it sacrificed the principle of effective majority rule. This standard received further elaboration in Stewart's opinion:

I think that the Equal Protection Clause demands but two basic attributes of any plan of state legislative apportionment. First, it demands that, in the light of the State's own characteristics and needs, the plan must be a rational one. Secondly, it demands that the plan must be such as not to permit the systematic frustration of the will of the majority of the electorate of the State. I think it is apparent that any plan of legislative apportionment which could be shown to reflect no policy but simply arbitrary and capricious action or inaction, and that any plan which could be shown systematically to prevent ultimate effective majority rule, would be invalid under accepted Equal Protection Clause Standards. But, beyond this, I think there is nothing in the Federal Constitution to prevent a State from choosing any electoral legislative

---

sixties has been described in Dixon, *Democratic Representation,* pp. 177–182, and Victor Navasky, *Kennedy Justice* (New York, 1971), Ch. 6. The latter work relates the intragovernmental maneuverings that influenced Cox's decision to intervene in all six of the 1964 reapportionment cases.

44. *Lucas* v. *Colorado,* at 749.
45. Ibid., at 751.

structure it thinks best suited to the interests, temper, and customs of its people.[46]

"These principles," Justice Stewart argued, "reflect an understanding respect for the unique values inherent in the Federal Union of States established by our Constitution."[47] They also reflect other inherent values, those embodied in the due process and equal protection clauses and the republican guarantee clause of Article IV, Section 4. A republican form of government, especially one that provides an explicit guarantee of equal protection under its laws, demands respect for the will of the majority. This respect, however, does not require that majority rule be reflected in all institutional arrangements connected with political decision-making. It means, and due process standards are particularly relevant here, that departures from the principle of majority rule in legislative apportionment require convincing justification that they constitute rational means toward implementing the goals of domestic representation. Stewart would require of any plan of legislative apportionment that it not systematically prevent ultimate effective majority rule. This suggests that while the immediate frustration of a state's numerical majority may result from a specific apportionment scheme, this frustration may still pass constitutional scrutiny if it can be demonstrated that the nonmajoritarian legislative result is consistent with the basic intent of the state to secure equal protection for all of its citizens, equal protection here defined in terms of the final political allocation of goods and services. Thus, equal protection, as defined by Stewart, is a statement of purpose, the realization of which will vary in accordance with the federal principle. His opinion projects an awareness of the nuances and complexities of democratic representation, but more importantly, it reveals how this awareness is itself a reflection of fixed constitutional principles, the fixed character of which does not preclude their prudent application. The specific facts in a given case are thus to be carefully reviewed by the courts but the

46. Ibid., at 753–754.
47. Ibid., at 752.

process of review proceeds in tandem with the elucidation and application of timeless principles of constitutional government.[48]

The pragmatic approach, on the other hand, begins with the facts of the case—population variance ratios—and then deduces the judicial finding that will, in the jargon of pragmatism, render the immediate problematic situation unproblematic. Reliance upon antecedent (fixed constitutional) principle is suspended in favor of satisfying the demand for equality that is reflected in the demographic data.[49] It is at this point that "one man, one vote" becomes "the basic principle of representative government," thus completing a process of dogmatization. Here, too, one can observe the pragmatic creation of law through the judicial experience of rendering decisions. As we have seen, the old question of whether judges find law or create it, when asked in a constitutional context, is really a question whether justice is to be found in the Constitution, in which case the judge, after having discerned its meaning, applies it to judicial controversies; or whether justice is to be developed incrementally through the judge's situational development of the law. By choosing the latter approach to adjudication in the reapportionment field, the Warren Court was led pragmatically to a dogmatic solution.

It has not, despite this conclusion, been the argument of this

48. For an analysis of Stewart's voting record in malapportionment cases see Elliott, *Guardian Democracy*, pp. 267–272, 375. Elliott summarizes the justice's Warren era record in this way: "His votes . . . suggest[ed] reasonable and comprehensible rules for intervention: gross malapportionment, low Dauer-Kelsay scores, large detrimental deviation of a few districts— courts should intervene; medium malapportionment, variance between largest and smallest districts—maybe intervene; mild malapportionment deriving from a constitutional plan, especially one approved by a majority of voters— no intervention." Ibid., p. 272.

49. One commentator, an outspoken admirer of Chief Justice Warren, has written in this regard: "The question asked by the chief justice in his opinion [in *Reynolds* v. *Sims*] really determined the answer. He did not ask whether the Constitution applied to the whole issue of apportionment, or if so what theories of representation ought to be considered. He began with the premise that the democratic norm was equal treatment of individual voters and then asked what departures from absolute population equality the Constitution would countenance." Anthony Lewis, "Earl Warren," in *The Warren Court: A Critical Analysis*, ed. Richard H. Sayler, Barry B. Boyer, and Robert E. Gooding, Jr. (New York, 1969), p. 31.

chapter that there is a necessary affiliation between pragmatic jurisprudence and dogmatic adjudication. Rather, in focusing upon one important constitutional issue, it has been the author's purpose to illustrate that the pragmatic jurist is not guaranteed that his work will avoid the pitfalls of dogmatism. To the extent that dogmatism stands in the way of statesmanlike constitutional and political judgment, there is no necessary affiliation between pragmatic jurisprudence and judicial statesmanship.

CHAPTER 6

Felix Frankfurter and the Ambiguities of Judicial Statesmanship

A student of American political institutions has suggested the unique role available to justices of the Supreme Court: "A judge in any other country may be a great judge; in few countries can he be at the same time a great exponent of statecraft."[1] He might have added that very few among this select group have actually taken advantage of the various opportunities afforded them for exercising statesmanship. Only a minority of our justices have possessed the character, intellect, and abilities necessary to pursue successfully the statesman's role. Furthermore, a smaller minority than commonly thought has actually performed the tasks associated with judicial statesmanship. The idea of judicial statesmanship has been applied by those who reflect upon the work of the Court not so much as a rigorous standard to measure excellence, but as a convenient label to indicate one's approval of a particular justice's performance.

THE RELEVANCE OF JUSTICE FRANKFURTER

The previous chapters have suggested that the logic of judicial pragmatism is incompatible with statesmanlike adjudication. This chapter and the next will examine the nature and scope of the frequently misunderstood concept of judicial statesmanship through an exploration of the constitutional philosophy of a frequently misunderstood jurist, Felix Frankfurter. The discussion will demonstrate how Frankfurter's extrajudicial writings and Court opinions reveal his conception of judicial statesmanship. It

1. B. K. Sandwell, as quoted in Samuel J. Konefsky, *The Legacy of Holmes and Brandeis* (New York, 1956), p. 302.

will indicate how these reflections help us to sketch the broad outlines of a constitutional jurisprudence that reflects the unique
role and character of the Supreme Court. Finally, it will measure
Frankfurter's performance on the Court against a standard derived
from both his own writings and the writings of others.

In 1923, Frankfurter received a letter from Justice Holmes ad-
vising "caution in the use of the word statesmanship with regard
to judges. . . . The word suggests a more political way of thinking than is desirable and also has become slightly *banal*."[2] Frankfurter had a high regard for the advice of the justice; however, in
this matter it appears that Holmes's words went unheeded.
Frankfurter continued to use the term in his writings on the
judicial process. Indeed, the frequency of its application in his
extrajudicial writings strikes the reader's eye. Perhaps no other
scholar in the field of constitutional law, and certainly no other
Supreme Court justice, has given such serious reflection to the
problem of statecraft in the judicial context.

In addition to his early writings, Frankfurter's importance in
the present context resides, first, in the fact that his career both
on and off the Court coincides with the high point of pragmatic
jurisprudential thought; and second, and more important, in the
simple fact of his stature as a major figure in American public law.
One may disagree with Alexander Bickel's view that "without
exaggeration . . . Felix Frankfurter has been in his time the
single most influential figure in American constitutional law,"[3]
and still recognize the profound impact that his work has had on
the development of American constitutional jurisprudence. By
focusing on a major figure in our constitutional history, who was
well versed in the teachings of the pragmatists, who provided a
rare introspective analysis of the role and function of the judge in

2. Quoted in Alexander M. Bickel, *The Supreme Court and the Idea of
Progress,* p. 22.
3. Alexander Bickel, "Applied Politics and the Science of Law: Writings
of the Harvard Period," *Felix Frankfurter: A Tribute,* ed. Wallace Mendelson (New York, 1964), p. 168. Bickel's admiration for his old mentor extended to Frankfurter's scholarly work as well as to his judicial career.
"There were great scholars of the Constitution before Mr. Frankfurter, but
he was the first scholar of the Supreme Court. The study he pursued was
not constitutional law, but institutional law." Ibid., p. 197.

a constitutional democracy, and who was persistently concerned with the hard problems of statecraft, we hope to gain a more complete understanding of pragmatic constitutional jurisprudence, as well as to locate the path that will enable us to proceed beyond it.

Finally, Frankfurter's relation to the Warren Court and his frequent dissent from its decisions deserve careful attention because the justices of that Court were, as we saw in the last chapter, "children of the Progressive realists;" that is to say, they were schooled in the jurisprudence of Pound and Cardozo, and "were much preached to about facts, human experience, the scientific method, change, and progress."[4] Frankfurter himself shared in this background, but nevertheless parted company with his colleagues on many important constitutional issues. This departure was also a break with the tradition in which he was raised.

REFLECTIONS ON STATESMANSHIP

Felix Frankfurter's appointment to the Supreme Court met with a typical public reaction. Since he was considered a liberal, liberals generally commended Roosevelt's decision, and conservatives recorded their disapproval. The liberal *Nation* commented that "Mr. Roosevelt gave the Court new vitality with the appointment of Justice Black; he gives it new and rich talents for conciliation, adjustment, and statesmanship in Frankfurter."[5]

Doubtless, little significance ought to be assigned the journal's choice of words. Nevertheless, it is possible that the editors' reference to Frankfurter's talent for statesmanship was an indication of their familiarity with the new justice's large body of scholarly work, in which the subject of statesmanship had been a recurring theme. Just as "vitality" had been characteristic of Justice Black's prejudicial career, the quest for a definition of judicial statecraft was, if not characteristic, at least a major concern of Frankfurter's early career.

Unfortunately, Frankfurter did not devote any one article or book entirely to an analysis of judicial statesmanship. One is thus

4. Bickel, *The Supreme Court and the Idea of Progress*, pp. 19, 20.
5. *Nation* editorial, January 14, 1939, p. 53.

required to assemble his views from numerous references to the subject that are made over a wide range of scholarly and journalistic writings. Despite the distortion that inevitably results from such an enterprise, one point is certain: Frankfurter attributed critical importance to the existence of a statesmanlike Court. "To the success of our scheme of government," he wrote, "an independent and statesmanlike Supreme Court is vital."[6]

We are, then, dealing with a crucial term in Frankfurter's vocabulary. Moreover, while he asserted that "the great problems of statesmanship have determined the character of the Court at different periods in our history,"[7] Frankfurter also emphasized that the statesmanship of individuals on the Court can determine the manner in which such problems are resolved. "The accents of statesmen are the recurring motif of Supreme Court opinions."[8] He felt that the well-being of the nation is enhanced by these accents, and that notions of "what is desirable and what is undesirable,"[9] when these notions are well founded, are capable of creating the demand for a good society.

Frankfurter's emphasis on judicial statecraft derived in large part from his understanding of the nature of the Supreme Court's business, and in particular in his recognition of the important distinction between public and private law. "It is a great pity," he remarked in 1923, "that the differences in the content of the material, the intellectual approach, and the technique of adjudication . . . are not indicated at least by recognizing the broad classification of 'private law' and 'public law.' "[10] Frankfurter's

6. Felix Frankfurter, "The Supreme Court and the Public," *Felix Frankfurter on the Supreme Court: Extrajudicial Essays on the Court and the Constitution*, ed. Philip B. Kurland (Cambridge, 1971), p. 221. This opinion is affirmed elsewhere when he claims that "the country's well-being depends upon a far-sighted and statesmanlike Court." Frankfurter, "The Appointment of a Justice," in ibid., p. 217.

7. Frankfurter, "The Nomination of Mr. Justice Brandeis," in ibid., pp. 43–44.

8. Felix Frankfurter and James M. Landis, *The Business of the Supreme Court* (New York, 1927), p. 318.

9. Felix Frankfurter, *The Public and its Government* (Boston, 1964), p. 5.

10. Frankfurter, "Twenty Years of Holmes' Constitutional Opinions," in *Felix Frankfurter on the Supreme Court*, p. 113.

views concerning the fundamental differences between the two areas of the law were well established, and thus it is not surprising that in 1954, after sitting on the Court for fifteen years, he had this to say about Cardozo's *The Nature of the Judicial Process:* "The book would give me very little help in deciding any of the difficult cases that come before the Court. Why should a book about the judicial process by one of the great judges of our time shed relatively little light on the actual process of the Supreme Court? For the simple reason that *The Nature of the Judicial Process* derived from Cardozo's reflections while in Albany, before he came to Washington. The judicial business out of which Cardozo's experience came when he wrote the book was the New York Court of Appeals, and that is very different business from the most important aspects of the litigation on which the Supreme Court must pass."[11]

Unlike the work of the state courts, the business of the Supreme Court involves decisions relating to the basic structure and purpose of the government. "Though formally the product of ordinary lawsuits, constitutional law differs profoundly from ordinary law. For constitutional law is the body of doctrines by which the Supreme Court marks the boundaries between national and state action and by means of which it mediates between citizen and government. The court thus exercises functions that determine vital arrangements in the government of the American people.[12] Since constitutional law cases deal with these fundamental relationships, Frankfurter maintained that they require "the members of the Court [to] move in the field of statesmanship."[13] Cardozo

11. Frankfurter, "The Judicial Process and the Supreme Court," in ibid., p. 497. After making this telling point, Frankfurter attempted to remove any doubts concerning Cardozo's awareness of the distinction. "No one was more keenly aware than he [Cardozo] of the differences between the two streams of litigations; no one more keenly aware than he of the resulting differences in the nature of the judicial process in which the two Courts were engaged." Ibid., p. 498. What he did not say was that Cardozo intended his book to be of assistance to Frankfurter in his work on the Supreme Court. So whether he admitted it or not, Frankfurter made a very important criticism of Cardozo's book.

12. Felix Frankfurter, *Mr. Justice Holmes and the Supreme Court* (New York, 1965), p. 19.

13. Frankfurter, "Twenty Years of Mr. Justice Holmes' Constitutional Opinions," *Felix Frankfurter on the Supreme Court,* pp. 113–14.

had distinguished between the roles of statesmen and judges because he did not see anything very special about public law adjudication.[14] Frankfurter, on the other hand, felt that statesmanship was a necessary part of the judge's role in resolving public-law questions.

Frankfurter's stand on the importance of judicial statesmanship is thus clear; his views on how a jurist might fulfill the statesman's role are considerably less so. His more general comments on the subject are sufficiently vague that they can be taken to apply to different judicial approaches to constitutional adjudication. They do, however, indicate that he was in basic agreement with the sentiment expressed in the famous letter of President Theodore Roosevelt to Henry Cabot Lodge on the subject of Justice Holmes's appointment to the Court, from which Frankfurter was fond of quoting. Roosevelt distinguished between two kinds of partisanship, the "ordinary and low," which a Supreme Court justice ought not to represent, and the "higher" understanding, which a justice should embody. If he does he will be "a party man, a constructive statesman, constantly keeping in mind his adherence to the principles and policies under which this nation has been built up and in accordance with which it must go on."[15] In other words, he is to be a partisan of principle.

There is much evidence showing Frankfurter's agreement with these views. He claimed, for example, that the significance of the Declaration of Independence "does not lie in the ideas which it expressed but in their realization and their continuing ferment." In the same vein, he wrote that the real import of the Bill of Rights "is the conception of man's dignity and destiny which underlies it, and which can effectively be vindicated only if it controls public feeling and inspires all measures of government." Furthermore, he noted that the statesman's calling is "to further in practice a better vision of society, to promote social arrangements more conformable to reason and justice." He is "to translate edifying precepts about the dignity of man into their progressive fulfillment."[16]

14. See Cardozo, *GOL*, p. 49.
15. Quoted in Frankfurter, *Mr. Justice Holmes*, pp. 52–53.
16. Felix Frankfurter, *Of Law and Men* (New York, 1956), pp. 231, 237,

The gist of these remarks is that a major element in the role of the statesman is to ensure that the view of man inscribed in the Declaration and the Constitution achieves practical fulfillment, which is to say, political realization. The Court, then, if it is to be a place for statesmen, must be involved in politics; but politics in its most noble and exalted sense.[17] To argue, as some have, that Frankfurter's refusal to permit the Court to become entangled in the "political thicket" meant that he saw the Court only as a court of law and not as a political institution reflects a very narrow understanding of the political.

Frankfurter's statements about the Court's political role might be read profitably in conjunction with his thoughts on the Judiciary Act of 1925: "Carefully framed findings by the lower courts should serve as the foundation for review, leaving for the Supreme Court the ascertainment of principles governing authenticated facts, the accommodation between conflicting principles, and the adaptation of old principles to new situations."[18] He did not elaborate upon the nature of these principles. However, the juxtaposition of this particular concern—especially the Court's obligation to adapt old principles to new situations—with the above-mentioned reflections on the "edifying precepts about the dignity of man" at least suggests that the task of the judicial statesman is to implement the goals of statesmanship through the application and adaptation of stable constitutional principles.

In other words, Frankfurter seems to have been suggesting that the Court applies enduring principles to the facts of a particular case in order to derive appropriate judicial doctrine. Facts and doctrine may change, but constitutional principle remains immutable. For those who failed to distinguish between public and private law, constitutional principle was mutable. Thus, when

232, 224. Elsewhere Frankfurter maintained that among the "indispensable qualifications for high statesmanship" is that one be a "man of vision who harness[es] his science to the achievement of his vision." Felix Frankfurter, *Of Law and Life and Other Things that Matter* (New York, 1969), p. 118.

17. Alexander M. Bickel, *The Supreme Court and the Idea of Progress*, p. 23.

18. Felix Frankfurter and James M. Landis, "The Judiciary Act of 1925," *Harvard Law Review*, 41 (1928), p. 23.

facts changed, so did the Constitution.[19] In effect, then, constitutional principle and judicial doctrine were indistinguishable. Judicial statesmanship, on the other hand, required that they be separate, that the adaptation of the Constitution to societal change be effected without the abandonment of fixed constitutional principle.

This is not to say that the Supreme Court is to live exclusively in the higher world of principle, never deigning to descend to the less exalted plane of facts. On the contrary, Frankfurter, like Louis Brandeis, was a strong advocate of the type of legal brief that the latter made famous in *Muller* v. *Oregon*,[20] the brief for which facts have been secured through much searching and painstaking effort. At one point, for example, Frankfurter quoted T. R. Powell on the commerce clause: "The Court has drawn its lines where it has drawn them because it has thought it wise to draw them there. The wisdom of its wisdom depends upon a judgment about practical matters and not upon a knowledge of the Constitution."[21] "In other words," Frankfurter observed, "these decisions are at bottom acts of statesmanship."[22] He was not suggesting here, although it might be tempting for some raised in certain "realist" circles to maintain the contrary, that judicial statesmanship does not require a knowledge of the Constitution. Knowledge of the Constitution is not a sufficient condition for statesmanship. Indeed, the statement by Powell is perfectly consistent with the earlier statement regarding the Supreme Court's relationship to principle. The application of old principles to new situations requires an understanding of the relevant principles and a knowledge of the facts of the new situation. It is necessary to make explicit this apparently obvious truth because of the tendency

---

19. Arthur F. Bentley, *Process of Government,* p. 296.

20. 208 U.S. 412 (1908). In fact, Frankfurter helped Brandeis to prepare a similar brief for *Bunting* v. *Oregon,* 243 U.S. 426 (1917).

21. Frankfurter, "The Supreme Court and the Public," *Felix Frankfurter on the Supreme Court,* p. 222, quoting T. R. Powell, "Supreme Court Decisions on the Commerce Clause and State Police Power, 1910–14," *Columbia Law Review,* 22 (1922), 48.

22. Frankfurter, "The Supreme Court and the Public," *Felix Frankfurter on the Supreme Court,* p. 222.

among some pragmatists to assume that only they are concerned with the empirical realities of the moment.

Elsewhere Frankfurter indicated that "the attitude of pragmatism which evolved the scope and methods of English judicature, and subsequently its American versions, was powerfully *reinforced by considerations of statecraft* in defining the sphere of authority for a tribunal of ultimate constitutional adjustments."[23] The implication seems to be that pragmatic considerations alone are incomplete or inadequate, that they require the guiding force of statesmanlike considerations in order to establish the correct ends or goals for the legal system.[24] Frankfurter's position is perhaps best represented in a quotation, discussing the figure of the statesman, that he borrowed from John Maynard Keynes: "He must contemplate the particular in terms of the general, and touch abstract and concrete in the same flight of thought. He must study the present in the light of the past for the purposes of the future."[25] Applied to the judicial process, these words indicate that the statesmanlike judge must accommodate and apply timeless principles of constitutional government to contemporary realities in order to guide the future in a manner consistent with the view of justice prescribed in the principles of the Constitution.

In light of the above discussion, it may seem a bit odd that Frankfurter also maintained that the "insight of statesmanship" is self-restraint.[26] Self-restraint, after all, is not the most obvious element of statesmanship. Indeed, the word "statesmanship" generally suggests action taken on behalf of the common good. How then can the assertion that judges must exercise self-restraint be reconciled with Frankfurter's picture of the judge as statesman? This, in fact, is the key question requiring an answer. We need, as

23. Felix Frankfurter, *Law and Politics* (New York, 1962), p. 24. Emphasis added.
24. For example, he wrote that "the attitude of pragmatism which evolved the scope and methods of English judicature, and subsequently its American versions, was powerfully 'reinforced by considerations of statecraft' in defining the sphere of authority for a tribunal of ultimate constitutional adjustments." Ibid., p. 24. Emphasis added.
25. Frankfurter and Landis, *The Business of the Supreme Court,* p. 318, quoting John Maynard Keynes.
26. Frankfurter, *Law and Politics,* p. 27.

it were, to capture the insight of Frankfurter's insight. One way to do so is to examine Frankfurter's writings about various justices of the Supreme Court, where explications of his ideas of statesmanship frequently appeared. Through an analysis of Frankfurter's views of these jurists, we can perhaps understand how he struck the balance between the statesman's application of constitutional principle and his exercise of self-restraint.

FRANKFURTER AND HOLMES

Most writers on Frankfurter find it necessary at some point to introduce Justice Holmes into their discussions. This necessity has not escaped the present writer. Generally, Holmes is used as the model according to which Frankfurter's constitutional philosophy is rendered intelligible. However, the purpose of including Holmes in the present discussion is quite different. It is to suggest that the opposite is true; if not rendering Frankfurter's philosophy unintelligible, the Holmesian model at least complicates the task of discerning a consistent, coherent philosophy in Frankfurter's writings.

Frankfurter's admiration for Holmes is well known. Indeed, it is hardly an exercise in hyperbole to agree with Max Lerner that at times Frankfurter sought the deification of his old friend and mentor.[27] Yet Frankfurter's commitment to certain liberal political principles was not shared by Holmes, whose skepticism precluded commitment to any political cause. For the liberals, of course, Holmes's skepticism (and the constitutional philosophy that it entailed) was an important weapon in the fight against the Spencerian interpretation of the Constitution. This happy alignment of skepticism on the side of liberalism greatly attracted Frankfurter to Holmes. Beyond this political attraction to the man lay a deep and abiding personal affection, and these two factors must be remembered in considering the numerous accolades to Holmes that are found throughout Frankfurter's writings. Among the many worshippers at the temple of Holmes none was more extravagant and generous in his adulation than Frankfurter.

27. Max Lerner, "Holmes and Frankfurter," *The Nation,* November 19, 1938, p. 537.

Psychological analysis can be left to others; but the ambiguity in Frankfurter's reflections on statesmanship is at least in part attributable to the complex nature of his relationship with Holmes.[28]

Much of the praise that Frankfurter lavished upon Holmes was given by comparing him with Chief Justice John Marshall.[29] He claimed that Holmes was at least the equal of Marshall in the statesmanship that he brought to the Court.[30] More specifically, Frankfurter saw Holmes as carrying on the tradition embodied in Marshall's warning: "We must never forget that it is a *constitution* we are expounding."[31] Frankfurter included Justice Brandeis in the same tradition, associating both him and Holmes with Marshall's famous statement. He argued that according to this tradition, the Constitution is "not a detached document inviting scholastic dialectics," but rather "a way of ordering society, adequate for imaginative statesmanship, if judges have imagination for statesmanship."[32] Frankfurter perceived two related political considerations as common themes in the opinions of these three

28. Though the latter part of this sentence may itself appear to reflect psychological analysis, what is suggested here is somewhat less ambitious— that the difficulty of making sense out of Frankfurter's reflections on statesmanship is caused by the fact that sometimes he was clearly writing with Holmes in mind and other times he was not. Moreover, what he said on these latter occasions at times appeared to contradict his remarks when he was discussing Holmes. Although it is possible that he misunderstood Holmes, it seems more likely that his perception was merely clouded by personal affinity when Holmes was his subject. The paradox of the politically and socially committed Frankfurter's frequent invocation of the Olympian Holmes is noted by Joseph P. Lash in his essay introducing Frankfurter's diaries. To Lash, Holmes as a model for Frankfurter "seems a little forced." Joseph P. Lash, ed., *From the Diaries of Felix Frankfurter* (New York, 1974). See also Sanford V. Levinson, "The Democratic Faith of Felix Frankfurter," *Stanford Law Review*, 25 (1973).

29. "The tradition of Marshall is best expressed for our days by Mr. Justice Holmes." Frankfurter, *The Public*, p. 76. The specific tradition that Frankfurter was referring to was deference to legislative action so as not to foreclose the future.

30. Although Holmes "did not bring to the Court the experience of great affairs, not even Marshall exceeded him in judicial statesmanship." Frankfurter, *Law and Politics*, p. 68.

31. *McCulloch* v. *Maryland*, 17 U.S. (4 Wheat.) 316, 407 (1819). Emphasis added.

32. Frankfurter, *Law and Politics*, p. 117. Felix Frankfurter, "The Constitutional Opinions of Justice Holmes," *Harvard Law Review*, 29 (1916), 685.

great justices. First was the promotion of expanded national power adequate to meet the needs of a changing society; second was the willingness not to use the judicial power as a means of foreclosing the future. Thus, Marshall's statesmanship in *McCulloch* v. *Maryland*[33] was similar to that of Holmes's dissent in *Hammer* v. *Dagenhart*,[34] the case that overturned Congress' efforts to deal with the child-labor problem. Both opinions called for deference to a legislative decision that sought to assert the power of the national government in order to respond to problems of national dimension.

Frankfurter's belief in the necessity for keeping open all channels for the solution of national problems in time became a cornerstone of his own judicial philosophy when the opportunities for statesmanship were thrust upon him in 1939.[35] While the defense of the national power against attempts to "foreclose the future" may reflect the wisdom of the Founders, not all those who partake in such a defense do so for the same reasons. Just as the agreement between Justices Black and Douglas on civil liberties questions often disguised differing premises for similar conclusions,[36] Frankfurter's discussion of Holmes and Marshall may

33. 17 U.S. (4 Wheat.) 316 (1819).
34. 247 U.S. 251, 277 (1918).
35. See, for example, *Youngstown Sheet & Tube Co.* v. *Sawyer*, 343 U.S. 579, 593 (1952) (concurring opinion): "Not the least characteristic of great statesmanship which the Framers manifested was the extent to which they did not attempt to bind the future. It is no less incumbent upon this Court to avoid putting fetters upon the future by needless pronouncements today." Ibid., at 596.
36. In the latter years of Justice Black's tenure on the Court, he and Justice Douglas increasingly parted company on a number of civil liberties issues that had linked them in common dissent for many years. The cases arousing the most attention, and the ones that prompted Court-watchers to wonder if Justice Black had "turned conservative," were those relating to the right of protest in the context of the civil rights movement in the South. A careful study of those opinions [e.g. *Adderley* v. *Florida*, 385 U.S. 39 (1966); *Brown* v. *Louisiana*, 383 U.S. 131 (1966); *Cameron* v. *Johnson*, 381 U.S. 741 (1965); *Cox* v. *Louisiana* 379 U.S. 536 (1965); *Bell* v. *Maryland*, 378 U.S. 226 (1964); and *Edwards* v. *South Carolina*, 372 U.S. 229 (1963)] has convinced this Court-watcher that Black's "change" was more apparent than real and that the protest issues of the sixties only succeeded in highlighting those points of disagreement between the two justices which had previously been glossed over by the coincidence of Black's literalism and Douglas' conception of social justice.

have masked the great distance that separated their respective judicial philosophies.

The basis of this difference was suggested in an oblique way by Frankfurter himself. In a passage describing the characteristic qualities of statesmanship on the Court, he observed: "Throughout its history the Supreme Court has called for statesmanship—the gifts of mind and character fit to rule nations. The capacity to transcend one's own limitations, the imagination to see society as a whole, come, except in the rarest instance, from wide experience. Only the poetic insight of the philosopher can replace seasoned contact with affairs."[37]

Frankfurter's reference to "the poetic insight of the philosopher" was clearly written with Justice Holmes in mind. He had to explain how a man who not only lacked "seasoned contact with affairs" but also refused even to read the newspapers, still possessed "the gifts of mind and character fit to rule nations." "Other great judges," he wrote in another place, "have been guided by the wisdom distilled from an active life; Mr. Justice Holmes was led by the divination of the philosopher and the imagination of the poet."[38]

Elsewhere he indicated that Holmes's claim to preeminence—"philosophic skepticism"—was different from Marshall's.[39] The inference that one is entitled to extract, although unintended by Frankfurter, is that Marshall and Holmes should be viewed as representatives of the same tradition in constitutional jurisprudence on only superficial levels. Consider, for example, the following lines: "In his resolute insistence on keeping open the channels of free though heretical inquiry, Mr. Justice Holmes was a traditionalist. He found Constitutional confirmation for the tradition in which he was bred—the tradition of Emerson and Thoreau and Garrison."[40]

Now, whatever else one may say of these men, they were not individuals whose careers or whose contribution to American polit-

37. Frankfurter and Landis, *The Business of the Supreme Court*, p. 317.
38. Frankfurter, *Mr. Justice Holmes*, p. 55.
39. Frankfurter, *Of Law and Men*, p. 182.
40. Frankfurter, *Mr. Justice Holmes*, p. 82.

ical thought were characterized by a special allegiance to, or reverence for, the Constitution. The fact that Marshall doubtless would have felt politically uncomfortable in the company of this group speaks both to the different basis of the constitutional philosophies of Holmes and Marshall, and to the difficulties inhering in Frankfurter's discussion. Philosophical skepticism, which, as has been said, is a major element of pragmatic philosophy, was antithetical to everything that Marshall's jurisprudence represented.[41] Frankfurter's praise for Holmes's freedom from any commitments that would compel him to translate his own views into constitutional commands overlooked the fact that Holmes's greatest commitment, "his loyal adherence in judicial practice to his philosophical skepticism,"[42] was consistently translated into constitutional imperatives. Unlike Marshall, Holmes's reluctance to foreclose the future was not derived from a tolerance for the legislative decision on the particular means to accomplish certain constitutional ends. Rather, Holmes was skeptical about the existence of absolute principles in constitutional adjudication and, assuming they did exist, about the ability of judges to derive them independent of their personal predilections.

Another difference between Holmes and Marshall that seems relevant to the definition of statesmanship is Holmes's detachment from the issues he faced as a justice.[43] Consider this comment by

41. For an excellent comparison of Marshall and Holmes see Faulkner, *John Marshall*. Faulkner has argued convincingly that the "Holmesian victory . . . came at the expense of the older jurisprudence, and it is not unreasonable to take Marshall's thought as symbol of the old legal understanding," Ibid., p. 228.

42. Frankfurter, *Mr. Justice Holmes*, p. 31. Frankfurter was correct in saying of Holmes that more than any other judge in the history of the Supreme Court "the host of public controversies in which he participated was subdued to reason by relatively few guiding considerations." Frankfurter, *Law and Politics*, p. 69.

43. Professor Faulkner's consideration of Holmes's detachment warrants extended quotation. Responding to Holmes's view that a judge's thinking ought to be detached and cosmopolitan, he said: "This is plainly fallacious with respect to any statesman, however true it might be for some philosopher not engaged in governing. Clearly the thoughts of the statesman engaged in his tasks must be fixed on his tasks, and thus circumscribed by the peculiar customs and conditions of his particular nation. Else the man will be a thoughtless practitioner, perhaps a judge who conceives of his task as just

Max Lerner, one of Holmes's greatest admirers: "[Holmes] was not the greatest judge we have had on the Supreme Court. Marshall was greater, and Taney. He had too much skepticism and too little fighting faith, was too little part of the emerging forces of our economic life, to be able to shape those forces with an unquenchable will."[44] The quality of deep commitment may not make a difference in the outcome of an individual case, but over the course of time it may very well influence how events unfold. If what and how judges write is important, and if by their arguments they shape the opinions of their readers, then the difference between a detached justice and one who feels deeply about the decisions he makes is of decisive importance.

Thus, recognizing that a judge does not read the Constitution so as to foreclose the future or that he is a proponent of self-restraint does not reveal whether or not he is a judicial statesman. Whenever Frankfurter placed Holmes in the same tradition as Marshall, it is evident that his inquiry was either incomplete or inadequate, depending on the subject of his concern. When he wrote of Holmes he spoke of two great statesmen, yet when Marshall was the focus of his interest, only one judge earned that distinction.[45] Marshall's "supremacy lay in his recognition of the practical

---

playing the game according to the rules (as if rules didn't need politic and fair application), or an impractical doctrinaire. Holmes' jurisprudence encouraged both extremes while discouraging the statesmanlike mean." *John Marshall,* pp. 266–67.

44. Max Lerner, "Holmes and Frankfurter," p. 538. This evaluation is shared by another scholar and admirer of Holmes, Samuel J. Konefsky, who, in his excellent study of Holmes and Brandeis, concluded that Brandeis, precisely because he was less detached than Holmes, was by far the more statesmanlike of the two. "Because decisions on constitutional questions necessarily have far-reaching effects, it is of the utmost importance that those who make them not only understand the problems they have been asked to resolve but that they care deeply about the fruits of their labors." Konefsky, *Legacy,* p. 306.

45. "The decisive claim to John Marshall's distinction as a great statesman is as a judge. And he is the only judge who has that distinction." Felix Frankfurter, "John Marshall and the Judicial Function," *Harvard Law Review,* 69 (1955), 218. Interestingly, this appears in an article that never mentions Holmes. This recognition led Frankfurter to the conclusion that we observed earlier when the subject was Holmes. "He [Marshall] had too much of an instinct for the practical to attempt rigidities which could not possibly bind the future. He wished to promote the national power, but he left open the choice of doctrine for the attainment of his purpose." Felix

needs of government."[46] Since this statement could be applied to Holmes as well, wherein then does Marshall's supremacy lie? Although Frankfurter didn't explicitly answer this question, perhaps the explanation is contained in these remarks: "But while [Marshall] had *rooted principles,* he was pragmatic in their application. No less characteristic than the realization of the opportunities presented by the commerce clause to restrain local legislatures from hampering the free play of commerce among the states, was his empiricism is not tying the Court to rigid formulas for accomplishing such restrictions."[47] That Marshall was not simply pragmatic, but pragmatic in the application of rooted principles, is important. These principles circumscribed Marshall's deference to the legislative choice of means and shaped his approach to constitutional adjudication. By contrast, Holmes's skepticism precluded his recognition of similar principles.

The origins of the rooted principles applied by Marshall were not traced by Frankfurter, who perhaps did not wish to admit that they were essentially derived from the writings of natural law theorists—in particular, from the political writings of John Locke.[48] Frankfurter denied that natural law considerations were an important guide for Marshall.[49] His denial, as we shall see later, was very much like his assertion that he did not resort to principles of natural right in his own judicial opinions. In both cases, he discouraged use of the term while nevertheless recognizing the importance of what the term represented. When one remembers the time in which he wrote and the judicial depredations that had been made under the banner of natural right,[50] Frankfurter's reluctance to acknowledge his own and Marshall's reliance on these principles is understandable.

Frankfurter, *The Commerce Clause under Marshall, Taney, and Waite* (Chicago, 1964), p. 44.

46. Felix Frankfurter, *The Public,* p. 75.

47. Frankfurter, *The Commerce Clause,* p. 14. Emphasis added. In short, Marshall was prudent, and prudence (practical wisdom) is the statesman's virtue.

48. See Edward S. Corwin, "The 'Higher Law' Background of American Constitutional Law," *Harvard Law Review,* 42 (1929).

49. "While [Marshall] occasionally referred to 'natural law,' it was not much more than literary garniture, even as in our own day, and not a guiding means for adjudication." Frankfurter, "John Marshall," p. 225.

50. See, for example, *Lochner* v. *New York,* 198 U.S. 45 (1905).

Ironically, one can derive further support for the conclusion that Frankfurter, like Marshall, adhered to fixed principles of natural right by returning to his reflections on Holmes. Among these reflections Frankfurter wrote that "while fully aware of the clash of interests in society and of law's mediating function, Holmes had nothing in common with the crude notion according to which law is merely the verbalization of prevailing force and appetites."[51] Frankfurter's denial of Holmes's positivism is interesting because it probably is incorrect. It suggests that Frankfurter himself believed that apart from "prevailing force and appetites," a fixed standard existed by which these forces and appetites could be evaluated. In other words, he believed that, as Faulkner has said of Marshall, "the federal judiciary [must be] responsible for enforcing upon the country the public law and private law implicit in the Constitution—the natural constitution behind the written law."[52]

Frankfurter's comments on the work of two other major figures in constitutional history, Chief Justices Taney and Waite, afford further insight into his concept of judicial statesmanship. "Taney, like Marshall," Frankfurter wrote, "had the consciousness of statesmanship. Waite, on the other hand, was predominately the lawyer." He praised Waite, but not for the same reasons that he praised Marshall and Taney. The impressive feature of Waite's work was not his statesmanship but his adherence to "traditional canons of constitutional adjudication," which for Frankfurter meant the doctrine of self-restraint.[53]

51. Frankfurter, *Of Law and Men*, pp. 166–167.
52. Faulkner, *John Marshall*, p. 254. It is interesting also to compare Frankfurter's evaluation of Marshall with Holmes's. Holmes denigrates the idea of statesmanship, and, specifically in regard to Marshall, he commented that "I should feel a greater doubt whether, after Hamilton and the Constitution itself, Marshall's work proved more than a strong intellect, a good style, personal ascendancy in his court, courage, justice and the convictions of his party." Oliver Wendell Holmes, "John Marshall," in *James Bradley Thayer, Oliver Wendell Holmes, and Felix Frankfurter on John Marshall*, ed. Mark DeWolfe Howe (Chicago, 1967), p. 132.
53. Frankfurter, *The Commerce Clause*, pp. 81–82. "Waite is not in the tradition of Marshall and Taney, who often set out beyond the requirements of the specific controversy, to chart new constitutional directions." Ibid., p.

Taney's self-restraint was also praised by Frankfurter, who pointed out, however, that its basis was very different from the self-restraint exercised by Waite. Waite, he said, applied his self-restraint "in the main as he did any other legal doctrine—as a requirement of the judge's art in constitutional adjudication." In contrast, Taney's restriction of the area of judicial discretion was related to policy considerations, specifically to the need to redress the balance between the public interest and property interests. Taney "was alert against an application of the Constitution which would foster an economic development regarded by him as mischievous." The Constitution and the Lockean principles upon which it rests envisage a balance between the public interest and property interests that coincided with Taney's view. To the extent that economic development had upset the proper balance of these interests, that development was mischievous, and consequently the task of judicial statesmanship required a constitutional interpretation that rendered the expectations of the founding fathers a reality. In many of Taney's decisions, judicial self-restraint accomplished this result.[54]

In the last analysis, we can derive only a vague understanding of Frankfurter's views on judicial statesmanship from his writings. We do know that Frankfurter's statesman must be a politician in the high sense of the word, an active participant in the effort to achieve political realization of constitutional principle. Yet, his cardinal virtue is self-restraint—the willingness to defer to legislative determinations so as not to foreclose the future. There is an

---

81. Frankfurter also said that Waite "brought to the Court no emotional commitments compelling him to translate his own economic or political convictions into constitutional commands." Ibid., p. 111. In *Of Law and Men*, Frankfurter made a similar statement about Holmes (p. 175). Yet he described Holmes as a statesman while Waite was referred to only as a very competent lawyer.

54. Felix Frankfurter, *The Commerce Clause*, pp. 82, 69. Elsewhere Frankfurter perceptively cited Taney's opinion in *Proprietors of the Charles River Bridge* v. *Proprietors of the Warren Bridge*, 36 U.S. (11 Pet.) 420 (1837), as an act of statesmanship. But Story's dissent in that case "proves that even vast erudition is no substitute for creative imagination." Felix Frankfurter, "Twenty Years of Mr. Justice Holmes' Constitutional Opinions," *Harvard Law Review*, 36 (1923), 918.

inevitable tension between these two precepts, and the true challenge of statesmanship lies in reconciling them. Thus, the crucial question is: when does the exercise of self-restraint become the "insight of statesmanship?"[55]

Unfortunately, Frankfurter's extrajudicial writings give us no clear answer to this question. He had high praise for Marshall, for whom principles of natural law marked the outer limits of deference to legislative judgment. Nonetheless, Holmes, whose deference was virtually unbounded, was elevated to the same pedestal as a model of self-restraint. In this apparent contradiction lies the ultimate ambiguity of Frankfurter's extrajudicial reflections on statesmanship. For further clarification one must therefore turn to his opinions on the Court.

55. "It is a commonplace of constitutional law," Frankfurter said on the occasion of the nomination of Louis D. Brandeis to be associate justice of the Supreme Court, "that justices of the Supreme Court must be lawyers, of course, but above all, lawyers who are statesmen," Felix Frankfurter, "The Nomination of Mr. Justice Brandeis," in *Felix Frankfurter on the Supreme Court*, p. 44.

CHAPTER 7

Justice Frankfurter:
Statesman or Pragmatist?

THE PREVAILING VIEW: THE JUSTICE AS PRAGMATIST

Justice Frankfurter's crucial importance in the history of the twentieth-century Court has not passed unnoticed. The scholar's pen continues to dance across page after page, moving sometimes gracefully but often blindly, seeking to master the peculiar rhythms of the Frankfurter record. Many of these writings fall beyond the scope of the present inquiry. However, even those that do often present conclusions relevant to our considerations. One that is particularly relevant holds that Frankfurter was a judicial pragmatist. An examination of this conclusion follows, based upon the discussion of the previous chapters and directed toward further clarification of the concept of judicial statesmanship.

Perhaps the best way to present the view of Frankfurter as pragmatist is to quote from some of the leading studies of the justice. Thus, Clyde E. Jacobs has called him "the Court's authentic spokesman for the pragmatic jurisprudence pioneered by Justice Holmes," and has maintained that "from the time of his appointment, [he] has been the Court's principal exponent of the pragmatic approach."[1] Helen Shirley Thomas, who has written the most comprehensive analysis of Frankfurter's judicial philosophy, suggested that "while other members of the Court either approve or disapprove absolutely of power conceptions and their implications, Justice Frankfurter pursues a pragmatic path to the decision of a case at hand."[2] Wallace Mendelson, the most sympathetic of the

1. Clyde E. Jacobs, *Justice Frankfurter and Civil Liberties* (Berkeley, 1961), pp. 212, 211.
2. Helen Shirley Thomas, *Felix Frankfurter: Scholar on the Bench* (Baltimore, 1960), p. 263.

Frankfurter scholars, found that in contrast to Justice Black's idealism, Justice Frankfurter is a "pragmatist."[3]

Not all of these studies attribute the same importance to Frankfurter's pragmatism. Jacobs, for example, was the most emphatic whereas Thomas mentioned it in passing. All are united in the belief that Frankfurter belonged to the school of pragmatism.

More specifically, Frankfurter is viewed by critics and admirers alike as a follower of Holmes.[4] Although Holmes's influence, in one form or another, can be discovered in the work of most of the justices of this century, Frankfurter's opinions are said to represent applications of the Holmesian philosophy in its most pristine and unadulterated form. It is said, for example, that Frankfurter and Holmes took similar stances on the existence and applicability of absolutes in constitutional decision making. "Frankfurter, like Holmes and in common with philosophers of pragmatism such as William James and John Dewey, rejects all absolutes, all finished

3. Wallace Mendelson, *Justices Black and Frankfurter: Conflict in the Court* (Chicago, 1961), p. 13. In addition, Moses J. Aronson, writing during the very early part of Frankfurter's judicial career, indicated that the latter is "motivated by his underlying philosophy of pragmatic experimentalism." "The Juristic Thought of Mr. Justice Frankfurter," *Journal of Social Philosophy*, 5 (1940), 171.

4. Jacobs explicitly linked Frankfurter to Holmes's *pragmatism*. "This [Frankfurter's pragmatism] probably more than any other aspect of his judicial work, marks him as a disciple of Holmes, whose opinions were instrumental in fostering a pragmatic jurisprudence." Jacobs, *Justice Frankfurter*, p. 211. For Mendelson, Frankfurter pursued a "Holmesian middle way," steering a course between "the willfullness of the old regime" and Justice Black's "mechanical jurisprudence." Wallace Mendelson, "Mr. Justice Frankfurter and the Process of Judicial Review," *University of Pennsylvania Law Review*, 103 (1954), 300. Aronson saw Frankfurter as a "disciple of Holmes and Brandeis," which, according to Aronson, meant that he subscribed to the sociological jurisprudence of Roscoe Pound. Aronson, "Juristic Thought," p. 159. Another scholar wrote of Frankfurter as the third in a "trio of pragmatic justices," his predecessors being Holmes and Brandeis. W. Robert Goedecke, *Change and the Law* (Tallahassee, 1969), p. 165. Thomas was much more cautious, refusing to assign him to the sociological school. "If Frankfurter thinks of himself as the heir of Holmes and Brandeis, the mere identification has meaning regardless of its validity." Thomas, *Felix Frankfurter*, p. 39. Unfortunately, she did not pursue the very interesting possibilities raised by her statement. And finally, Richard G. Stevens, a respectful critic of Frankfurter, concluded that "ultimately Frankfurter's problem goes back to Holmes." Stevens, "Felix Frankfurter," in *American Political Thought: The Philosophical Dimensions of Statesmanship*, p. 259.

systems."[5] Frankfurter's wisdom is said to be derived from experience, not from any preconceived, a priori, noble design that is brought down from the heavens through the magic of judicial divination. Mendelson formulated this position very well: "In his pragmatic view, ultimates—whether economic or libertarian—are not for judges. He sees the Constitution as largely open-ended. Its essence is not an embodiment of final substantive truths but an allocation of powers and processes. Let the community by these *devices* choose its own ends."[6] The important word here is the last word. It appears to contradict the view of John Marshall in a statement that Frankfurter cited as the most important ever written in "the literature of constitutional law."[7] In *McCulloch* v. *Maryland,* Marshall measured the end sought by legislative action against the Constitution, while leaving the means to accomplish it to be selected by the community, through its chosen representatives. Marshall explicitly rejected the view that the Constitution was but a list of "devices" available to the community to use for any purpose it decided upon. He believed that the ends of government were themselves suggested in the Constitution; they were not, as in the pragmatic calculus, brought into being through ad hoc interaction of community and environment. Frankfurter, it is submitted, although differing from Marshall in many important respects, was in agreement with him on this fundamental point.

Furthermore, Frankfurter's agreement with Marshall in this instance indicates a basic way in which he differed from the judicial pragmatists. Like Marshall, Frankfurter perceived that the Constitution incorporates rooted principles which do not change with the passage of generations. To the pragmatists, such a view was untenable. Yet, one can understand why Jacobs and other commentators were misled into concluding that Frankfurter "rejects all absolutes." While Frankfurter adhered to rooted constitutional

5. Jacobs, *Justice Frankfurter,* p. 211.
6. Wallace Mendelson, *Justice Black and Frankfurter: Conflict in the Court,* p. 47.
7. Frankfurter, "John Marshall," p. 219. "Let the end be legitimate, let it be within the scope of the constitution, and all means which are appropriate, which are plainly adapted to that end, which are not prohibited, but consist with the letter and spirit of the constitution, are constitutional." *McCulloch* v. *Maryland,* 17 U.S. (4 Wheat.) 316, 421 (1819).

principles, he did not contend that any of those principles was so absolute as to override all others. This perception becomes obvious when we consider Frankfurter's judicial opinions.

THE OPINIONS
The First Amendment

Those seeking to portray Frankfurter as a judicial pragmatist often comment on his opinions in the field of civil liberties. His well-known debate with his libertarian colleagues over the question of First Amendment absolutes may suggest to some an analogy with Justice Holmes's earlier stand against economic absolutes. Opposition to Fieldian absolutes, as we saw in Chapter 2, was expressed from two different perspectives, represented at one time by Holmes and by the first Justice Harlan. The latter did not reject the objectivity of natural rights principles, but merely recognized that their absolute quality had to be "civilized" (that is, transformed from natural to civil rights) and compromised when enforced through the judicial process. A distinction was drawn between this sort of compromise, where the principle, though limited, is still retained, and the pragmatic compromise, where principles change over time and may succumb to temporary, pressing needs. Frankfurter's opposition to uncompromising adherence to absolute principles must not be mistaken for complete abandonment of such principles. Indeed, his attitude may demonstrate more concern with preserving them and more respect for their legitimacy.

First Amendment cases generally involve a conflict between governmental and individual claims. Frankfurter is said to have resolved this conflict by a pragmatic and balancing assessment of the particular interests competing for judicial recognition.[8] Were it not for the frequent references to pragmatic philosophy, it would be easy to account for, and to accept, the use of the word "pragmatic" in this context. The layman, for example, unencumbered by esoteric philosophical notions, uses the word as a synonym for "realistic." However, as Richard G. Stevens has pointed out: "It is one thing to say that the resolution of certain problems involves

8. See, for example, Jacobs, *Justice Frankfurter*, pp. 56, 70, 95, 111–112; and Thomas, *Felix Frankfurter*, pp. 224–225, 364.

'pragmatic considerations;' it is quite another thing to call someone a 'pragmatic jurist.' "[9] Frankfurter's First Amendment opinions demonstrate a healthy respect for the vitality of basic principles, but a reluctance to afford them absolute priority, without regard to other interests. One of his earliest cases, *Bridges* v. *California*,[10] involved a conflict between the right to a free press and the right to a fair trial. Frankfurter, dissenting from a decision upholding the right of the press to publish, wrote: "Free speech is not so absolute or irrational a conception as to imply paralysis of the means for effective protection of all the freedoms secured by the Bill of Rights."[11] His purpose was to indicate that justice is not always achieved when First Amendment freedoms supersede other rights.

Five years later, Frankfurter concurred in a decision upholding the press in a similar case, and in so doing, elaborated upon the theme of his earlier dissent. "Without a free press there can be no free society. Freedom of the press, however, is not an end in itself but a means to the end of a free society. The scope and nature of the constitutional protection of freedom of speech must be viewed in that light and in that light applied."[12]

Freedom of the press is therefore a necessary but not a sufficient condition of a free society. Its limitation may be necessary to advance the conditions for its realization in civil society. Notice the order in which Frankfurter states his proposition. The first sentence affirms, in absolute terms, the relationship between a free press and a free society. The next two sentences suggest an awareness that rights are always exercised in a social context, and that the common good (a free society) takes precedence over the individual good that is achieved by the absolute protection of a particular right. Frankfurter's attack on absolutes in constitutional adjudication was

9. Richard G. Stevens, "Reason and History in Judicial Judgment: Mr. Justice Frankfurter's Treatment of Due Process" (1963) (unpublished doctoral dissertation, Department of Political Science, University of Chicago) p. 191. Stevens' remark was intended as a criticism of Thomas' "loose" usage of the term.
10. 314 U.S. 252 (1941).
11. *Bridges* v. *California*, 314 U.S. 252, 282 (1941).
12. *Pennekamp* v. *Florida*, 328 U.S. 331, 354–355 (1946).

not so much a pragmatic assault on the existence of absolutes as it was a recognition of one of the primary requisites of civil society. "No institution in a democracy," he went on to say, "either governmental or private, can have absolute power. Nor can the limits of power which enforce responsibility be finally determined by the limited power itself."[13] It is significant that this lesson on the limits of power should appear in an opinion upholding the exercise of power. Clearly Frankfurter saw an important educational function in his judicial role.[14]

What is "pragmatic" about judicial recognition of an old Madisonian theme—that freedom can be endangered by unlimited power in private as well as in public hands? The same concern underlay Frankfurter's opinions in other First Amendment issues— for example, the loudspeaker cases. His dissent in *Saia* v. *New York* from the Court's decision to overturn an ordinance that allowed local officials to determine when licenses would be issued for the use of sound trucks has been said to be "based upon a pragmatic assessment of competing interests."[15] In fact, Frankfurter did not weigh the interest of the public in peace and quiet against the interests of those who wanted to convey messages by loudspeaker. He merely showed his customary deference to decisions validly made by those authorized to make them: the locality's decision to pass an ordinance; the official's decision, under that ordinance, to deny a license to the petitioner.

In another loudspeaker case, *Kovacs* v. *Cooper,* Frankfurter delivered his well-known attack upon the "preferred position" doctrine, which holds that speech is entitled to greater protection than other constitutional guarantees. His basic point was that "such a formula makes for mechanical jurisprudence."[16] It is mechanical for the same reasons that Field's decisions were mechanical. Both decisions attempt to safeguard a liberty by subjecting it to a judicial

13. Ibid., at 355–356.
14. The reader can decide for himself whether the conclusion extracted by Thomas from Frankfurter's position on absolutes is valid or not. "The judiciary demands tough-minded relativists, not soft-hearted absolutists." Thomas, *Felix Frankfurter,* p. 225.
15. Jacobs, *Justice Frankfurter,* p. 86. *Saia* v. *New York,* 334 U.S. 558 (1948).
16. *Kovacs* v. *Cooper,* 336 U.S. 77 (1949), at 96.

formula that prevents one from appreciating the conditions required for its fulfillment. Frankfurter was saying that a judge can arrive at justice only by placing reasonable limits upon the exercise of any right.[17] Once again, he argued that limiting an individual's freedom is consistent with the goal of a free society.[18]

This same concern for the conditions of a free society is reflected in other areas where Frankfurter has been called a pragmatist—in the field of obscenity, for example.[19] Indeed, it could be argued that Frankfurter's willingness to limit freedom of expression revealed a higher form of respect for that freedom than did the reluctance of his absolutist brethren to permit qualitative discrimination among forms of individual expression. Frankfurter himself did not ordinarily engage in this discrimination; generally, he deferred to others whose function was to make such judgments. This judicial deference is a separable issue, related to his view of the judiciary in a constitutional democracy and not to a pragmatic orientation toward First Amendment absolutes.

Indeed, Frankfurter may have been correct with respect to the propriety of enforcing absolutes, but wrong about which branch of government should bear ultimate responsibility for deciding how to limit them. His concurring opinion in the celebrated *Dennis* case, upholding the convictions of members of the Communist Party for violations of the Smith Act, illustrates the problem. The opinion consists of two interwoven essays, one having to do with the need for judicial deference to the will of the more representative legislative branch, and the other with the need to assess competing societal interests in a dogma-free atmosphere. Thus, we find an eloquent argument that acknowledges the decisive importance of free speech

17. Recall, from Chapter 2, Blackstone's argument that in civil society the regulation of rights is necessary for their maintenance.
18. "So long as a legislature does not prescribe what ideas may be noisily expressed and what may not be, nor discriminate among those who would make inroads upon the public peace, it is not for us to supervise the limits the legislature may impose in safeguarding the steadily narrowing opportunities for serenity and reflection. Without such opportunities freedom of thought becomes a mocking phrase, and without freedom of thought there can be no free society." *Kovacs* v. *Cooper*, 336 U.S. 77, 97 (1949) (concurring opinion).
19. See, his opinions in *Winters* v. *New York*, 333 U.S. 507 (1948) and *Kingsley Books Inc.* v. *Brown*, 354 U.S. 436 (1957).

to civilized society by recognizing that the mark of such a society is its capacity to impose discriminating restraints upon expression. "Such are the paradoxes of life."[20] While weighing the competing interests—free speech and national security—the courts must respect the will of the people as voiced through their representatives. Frankfurter thus compounded the paradox by conferring upon the source of these necessary restraints the principal role in evaluating their necessity.

The balancing approach of Frankfurter in *Dennis* is not, then, suggestive of a commitment to a pragmatic view of the First Amendment, in which the interest in free expression is to be understood as one of several equal and competing claims seeking recognition through judicial accommodation. Rather, the balancing is a necessary strategy intended to support freedom in a civil society (the goal of the First Amendment), where "non-Euclidian problems"[21] prevent the adoption of absolutist, dogmatic solutions. Frankfurter's deference to the legislature in this regard does not alter this picture, although it may raise questions about the wisdom of such deference. Had Frankfurter opposed application of absolute principles on philosophical grounds—if he had been a moral and political relativist—there would have been a more natural connection between his beliefs and his posture of judicial restraint. He could have adopted a neutral position respecting the ends to which legislative or administrative action could be directed. But this perspective was more that of Justice Holmes than that of Justice Frankfurter.[22] We can perceive once again the tension between Frankfurter's adherence to fundamental principles and his policy of self-restraint.

Due Process

Frankfurter's due process decisions present in a different manner the question of whether he was a judicial pragmatist. The justice rejected as overly formalistic the view that all of the guarantees of the first eight amendments were "incorporated" into the due process

20. *Dennis* v. *United States,* 321 U.S. 494, 550 (1951).
21. Ibid., at 525.
22. For comparison, see Holmes's dissenting opinions in *Abrams* v. *United States,* 250 U.S. 616 and *Gitlow* v. *New York,* 268 U.S. 652.

clause of the Fourteenth Amendment. He advocated a case-by-case, selective approach, which extended due process protection to interests according to standards other than their inclusion in the Bill of Rights.[23] Deweyan pragmatists to the contrary notwithstanding, cases "cannot be judged on their own merits," since no case can have merits without the introduction of external standards of judgment. The only question is: what standards did Frankfurter apply to decide these cases? Were they derived from some natural rights philosophy or from the mores of the community? The portrait drawn by Stevens, in which Frankfurter is represented as a servant of the prevailing views of the community, is a convincing one.[24] However, it suffers from a defect characteristic of many accounts of Frankfurter's philosophy—it depends too heavily upon the justice's words. Frankfurter's actions may not have been entirely consistent with his explanations.

Early in his academic career Frankfurter had written that "the due process clauses ought to go."[25] Late in his judicial career his opinion seems to have changed: "Due process is perhaps the most majestic concept in our whole constitutional system."[26] It is important, of course, that in the first instance he was reacting to the "old" Court's interpretation of *substantive* due process, whereas in the second he was writing an opinion involving a question of *procedural* due process. This might account for his reluctance in the latter cases to use language similar to that used by the discredited laissez faire Court of a previous generation. That Court referred to principles of natural right; he spoke of "notions of justice," of "civilized canons of decency," and of the "concept of ordered liberty." But in point of fact, their respective standards were not too dissimilar.[27]

23. Felix Frankfurter, "Memorandum on 'Incorporation' of the Bill of Rights into the Due Process Clause of the Fourteenth Amendment," *Harvard Law Review,* 78 (1965) 748–749.
24. See Stevens, "Felix Frankfurter," in *American Political Thought,* pp. 255–260.
25. Frankfurter, *Law and Politics,* p. 16.
26. *Joint Anti-Fascist Refugee Committee* v. *McGrath,* 341 U.S. 123, 174 (1951).
27. For those who see Frankfurter as a pragmatist, these references mean as little as do his explicit rejections of natural law to this author. "Language of this kind," wrote Clyde E. Jacobs, "accounts, no doubt, for the mistaken

The classic confrontation between the total incorporationists, represented by Justice Black, and those who preferred a more flexible approach, represented by Justice Frankfurter, occurred in *Adamson* v. *California*. Unlike the earlier absolutists, Justice Black repudiated natural law as a source of judicial standards, preferring to base his judgment on the text of the Constitution as he read it. Frankfurter rejected Black's approach as no less subjective than the test he advocated—determining which rights are " 'of the very essence of a scheme of ordered liberty.' " Frankfurter did not advocate adoption of standards derived from natural law, but did acknowledge a certain respect for that tradition. "In the history of thought 'natural law' has a much longer and much better founded meaning and justification than such subjective selection of the first eight Amendments for incorporation into the Fourteenth."[28]

The specific issue in Adamson was whether the state could draw to the attention of the jurors the fact that a defendant had failed to testify on his own behalf; the Court assumed that such action would violate the Fifth Amendment privilege against self-incrimination were the case tried in federal court. Frankfurter contended that finding the state's conduct to be restricted by the Constitution in such a case would "trivialize the importance of 'due process.' "[29] If we accept the assertion that Frankfurter was a judicial pragmatist, this claim would not reflect his personal opinion, but only the views of contemporary civilized people—in this case, the people of California—about the nature of their scheme of ordered liberty. In short, Frankfurter would have been implementing Cardozo's "method of sociology" by translating the mores of society into the law of the land.

---

view that he resorts to natural law doctrines in his interpretations of the Fourteenth Amendment. Throughout his opinions, however, there is practically no suggestion that such norms have a cognitive validity for him." Jacobs, *Justice Frankfurter,* p. 208. For those who do *not* see him as a pragmatist, "it is ironic that Justice Frankfurter, in attempting to implement the policy of judicial restraint which had been pioneered by the positivist Oliver Wendell Holmes, sometimes found it necessary to use legal reasoning which savors of a natural law background." John P. Foley, *Natural Law, Natural Right and the "Warren Court"* (Rome, Italy, 1965), p. 30.

28. 332 U.S. 46 (1947), at 75 (dissenting opinion), at 65 (concurring opinion), quoting *Palko* v. *Connecticut,* 302 U.S. 319, 325 (1936).

29. Ibid., at 50 (opinion of the Court), and at 60 (concurring opinion).

Are we being misled? Might it not be that Frankfurter seemed to adopt the tenets of pragmatic jurisprudence only because in this particular case his perception happened to coincide with the mores of the people as reflected in the laws of California? Did he really believe, as Mendelson, among others, said he did, in "an external standard for the guidance of a hard-pressed court; a standard rooted in what Holmes called the only sound basis for any legal system—'the actual feelings and demands of the community, whether right or wrong?' "[30]

When Frankfurter's views did not coincide with the views of the community, the basis of his decision-making became even less clear. In *Haley* v. *Ohio*, Frankfurter concluded that a confession made by a fifteen-year old had been coerced, so that its admission into evidence violated due process.[31] But he did not reach that conclusion before writing a tortuous opinion that one observer has described as "perhaps the most remarkably frank and courageous analysis of the personal basis of judicial decisions ever included in a Supreme Court opinion."[32] In fact, the opinion exposes the shallowness of Frankfurter's professed dependence on the will of the people. He indicated that the question presented required judicial dissection of the deep, inarticulate feelings of our society. "Judges must divine that feeling as best they can."[33] Although he described the available tests as inherently vague and unsatisfactory, Frankfurter maintained that they had to be applied.

Frankfurter's introspection reveals how little he relied upon the consensus of society in deciding the hard questions of due process. He admitted that the tests were deficient—no polls had been taken, no vote had been recorded—and yet expected his readers to believe that he had succeeded in divining the feelings of the society. With all due respect to the considerable talents of the justice, is it not more than likely that his determination, despite the disclaimers, was in fact his own individual view—a view expressing not necessarily his personal emotional commitments, but rather his reading in historical context of the substantive natural rights content of due

30. Wallace Mendelson, *Justices Black and Frankfurter,* p. 48.
31. 332 U.S. 596 (1948), at 607 (concurring opinion).
32. C. Herman Pritchett, *The Roosevelt Court* (Chicago, 1969), p. 160.
33. 332 U.S. at 603 (concurring opinion).

process of law?[34] Even if we admit that due process, as Frankfurter understood it, is a generative principle, that it is not frozen
in meaning at any point in time, is it still not probable that his conception of the principle establishing an attitude of fairness in the
criminal process was derived from notions of natural right?

When Frankfurter claimed that certain conduct "shocks the con-
science," thus violating due process, and at the same time denied
a "resort to a revival of 'natural law,' " either he was being dis-
ingenuous or he was interjecting his own emotional biases into his
judgment.[35] Without ruling out the latter possibility, it is possible
to agree with John P. Foley that "Justice Frankfurter's fear of the
term 'natural law' does not preclude his use of reasoning which
would appeal to those men, bred in the natural law tradition, who
framed the fundamental documents of the United States."[36] The
difference, of course, is that these men would have explicitly
acknowledged that governmental conduct which "shocked the con-
science," or that offended "those standards of decency in our
civilization against which due process is a barrier,"[37] is conduct
repugnant to the principles of natural right. Frankfurter's position
was regrettably ambiguous and one learns little from it. Be this
as it may, a pragmatist he was not. He was simply a perceptive man
forced to distort the nature of his own beliefs to accommodate the
legacy of an earlier Court, whose misuse of natural rights principles
had given to those principles a bad name.

The Importance of Consensus

Before returning to the theme of judicial statesmanship, it is
important to take notice of an interesting element in Frankfurter's
constitutional philosophy, one that has been recognized by others,

34. See e.g., *Louisiana ex rel. Francis* v. *Resweber*, 329 U.S. 459, 466–
472 (1947) (concurring opinion), where Frankfurter explicitly ignored his
emotional commitments because of his interpretation of due process.
35. *Rochin* v. *California*, 342 U.S. 165, 171–172 (1952). In this case,
the police had used a pump to extract evidence from a suspect's stomach.
36. Foley, *Natural Law*, p. 31.
37. *United States* v. *Kahriger*, 345 U.S. 22, 40 (1953) (Frankfurter
dissenting).

but never fully appreciated. He placed special emphasis on the importance of a common core of belief to unite the citizens of a liberal democracy. "The ultimate foundation of a free society," he wrote in the first flag-salute case, "is the binding tie of cohesive sentiment."[38] The corollary of this understanding was a fear of divisions on fundamental questions, or, as Louis L. Jaffe aptly stated, a concern about the "balefulness of pressure."[39] Before coming to the Court, Frankfurter had expressed this concern by suggesting that "in a democracy, politics is a process of popular education—the task of adjusting the conflicting interests of diverse groups in the community, and bending the hostility and suspicion and ignorance engendered by group interests toward a comprehension of mutual understanding."[40] Much of his work on the Court constituted an effort to advance this goal in practice.

Frankfurter's opinion in *Illinois ex rel. McCollum* v. *Board of Education,* the first of the released-time cases, illustrates very well the consistency between his judicial work and his earlier views on the importance of avoiding public conflicts: "The sharp confinement of the public schools to secular education was a recognition of the need of a democratic society to educate its children, insofar as the State undertook to do so, in an atmosphere free from pressures in a realm in which pressures are most resisted and where conflicts are most easily and most bitterly engendered. Designed to serve as perhaps the most powerful agency for promoting cohesion among a heterogeneous democratic people, the public school must keep scrupulously free from entanglement in the strife of sects."[41]

A measure of the importance attached to these views by Frankfurter is the fact that in order to support them he occasionally had to ignore two fundamental tenets of his judicial philosophy—respect for federalism and judicial self-restraint. In the flag-salute cases, however, he was able to maintain consistency between those commitments and his preeminent concern with creating the basis

38. *Minersville School District* v. *Gobitis,* 310 U.S. 586, 596 (1940).
39. Louis L. Jaffe, "The Judicial Universe of Mr. Justice Frankfurter," *Harvard Law Review,* 62 (1949), 409.
40. Frankfurter, *The Public,* p. 161.
41. *McCollum* v. *Board of Education,* 333 U.S. 203 (1948) at 216.

for agreement on fundamental beliefs.[42] He did not necessarily subscribe to the means chosen to inculcate these beliefs—a salute to the flag—but this personal disagreement was not sufficient to overcome his fear of group disruptiveness. "Jefferson and the others . . . knew that minorities may disrupt societies. It never would have occurred to them to write into the Constitution the subordination of the general civil authority of the state to sectarian scruples."[43]

Frankfurter's defensiveness toward group pressure was, of course, most manifest in his opinions involving issues relating to the public schools; however, it also found expression in other areas such as censorship, interstate commerce and fair trial versus free press.[44] Indeed, this posture, in conjunction with his great deference to the decisions of other branches of government, has exposed Frankfurter to charges of insensitivity and neglect of minority rights. The merits of these charges are of less concern to us, however, than the appreciation that Frankfurter viewed group conflict and group assertiveness with great suspicion and distrust. Instead of recognizing them as a particular virtue of the political system, he regarded them as potential threats to the stability of society, to be watched with special care and vigilance.

The relevance of these views to the present inquiry requires some explanation. In Chapter 4 we noted, principally in the work

42. Professor Thomas' perception of the underlying unity between the flag-salute cases and the released-time case is worth quoting: "In the flag-salute cases Justice Frankfurter's main concern seemed to be that sects should not be able forcibly to infuse their divisiveness into the public school system. In the McCollom case almost the reverse preoccupation became apparent in that the Justice seemed to fear the public schools' voluntarily opening themselves to sectarian schools' differences through their liaison with various religious groups." Thomas, *Felix Frankfurter*, p. 61.

43. *West Virginia State Board of Education* v. *Barnette*, 319 U.S. 624, 653 (1942).

44. "The public school is at once the symbol of our democracy and the most pervasive means for promoting our common destiny. In no activity of the State is it more vital to keep out devisive forces than in its schools." *McCollum* v. *Board of Education*, 333 U.S. 203, 231 (1948). See, generally, Frankfurter's concurring opinion in *Burstyn* v. *Wilson*, 343 U.S. 495 (1952); his dissenting opinion in *Youngstown Sheet and Tube Co.* v. *Bowers*, 358 U.S. 534 (1958); and the dissent in *Bridges* v. *California*, 314 U.S. 252 (1941).

of Pound and Bentley, an intimate connection between pragmatic jurisprudence and group interests. The judge was to be a "social engineer," whose task was to accommodate as many interests as possible with the least amount of friction and waste. As should be apparent, this was not the way in which Justice Frankfurter viewed his judicial duties. That is to say, for Frankfurter, the accommodation of group interests was not necessarily a desirable judicial or political end if it meant that in the recognition and satisfaction of group wants and claims, social unity would be undermined. For Frankfurter, unlike the pragmatists, the common good was not to be determined quantitatively as a function of the number of claims that could be accommodated by the legal system at any given time. While he was occasionally influenced by pragmatic considerations, Frankfurter was not, as he has been mistakenly classified, a member of the school of pragmatic jurisprudence.

Second, and perhaps more important, Frankfurter's preoccupation with the problem of divisiveness permits one to distinguish more clearly between his constitutional philosophy and that of Justice Holmes. For the latter, group conflict and the clash of opposing ideas presupposed by that conflict constituted the essence of democracy. This view does not portray very well the sentiments of Frankfurter, whose conception of democracy placed a greater emphasis upon consensus than upon conflict. Frankfurter's judicial efforts to minimize the influence of divisive and disruptive groups suggests why in free speech cases he, unlike Holmes, was not to be found in the marketplace shopping for the truth.

Finally, this difference is suggestive, though admittedly not conclusive, of an important distinction to be made between the respective bases of judicial self-restraint in Frankfurter and Holmes. Both men were decisively influenced by a profound respect for popular government. For Holmes, the essence of popular government was philosophic skepticism, whereas for Frankfurter, its precondition, if not its essence, was a common core of belief. Thus, Holmesian self-restraint reflected his neutrality, or better, his indifference, with respect to the particular political decisions to which he deferred. However, Frankfurter's self-restraint, because it assumed the existence of shared fundamental beliefs, was an expression of faith in the people and their representatives. Holmes also had faith, a faith in the future.[45] Because the pillars of this faith were fastened less securely to a solid foundation than were Frankfurter's, the entire structure of popular self-government was to that degree rendered less secure.

EVALUATING THE STATESMANSHIP OF JUSTICE FRANKFURTER

In Justice Frankfurter's extrajudicial writings on statesmanship, viewed through the filter of his own record on the Court, we can discern the rough outlines of a statesmanlike approach to constitutional adjudication. The statesman must combine judicial restraint with a vigilant regard for the principles underlying the Constitution. Frankfurter's regard for those principles rendered his approach distinct from the pragmatic jurisprudence with which it was frequently and mistakenly identified. But the willingness to recognize in theory the validity of underlying principle does not in itself make one a judicial statesman; philosophy must be translated into practice. Thus, Frankfurter's record must be evaluated according to the standards of judicial statesmanship.

Many, of course, have written of statesmen and their art, but the most thoughtful treatment is also the oldest—Plato's *Statesman*. The following discussion will create the setting and framework for the analysis of the contribution made by Justice Frankfurter to the field of constitutional jurisprudence.[46]

The *Statesman* is as much a demonstration of the art of dialectical reasoning as it is a discourse on statesmanship. Throughout the dialogue, Plato painstakingly proceeds to his definition by the method of division, whereby he isolates those elements or characteristics that ultimately define the object of his inquiry. One of the final divisions, or distinctions, that he makes is between the art of statesmanship and the art of judging. Speaking through the Stranger from Elea, Plato says of the latter:

45. Faulkner, *John Marshall*, p. 264.
46. This author does not pretend to speak with authority in the area of Platonic philosophy, particularly when the subject is as complex and difficult a dialogue as the *Statesman*. Fortunately, other scholars have reflected on Plato's teaching in this dialogue. Of primary assistance to the author have been A. E. Taylor, *Plato: The Sophist and the Statesman* (London, 1961) and Leo Strauss, "Plato," in *A History of Political Philosophy*.

Does its province extend beyond the sphere of mutual contractual obligations? It has to act in this sphere by judging what is just or unjust according to the standards set up for it and embodied in the legal rules *which it has received from the kingly lawgiver.* It shows its peculiar virtue by coming to an impartial decision on the conflicting claims it examines, *by refusing to pervert the lawgiver's ordinance* through yielding to bribery or threats or sentimental appeals, and by rising above all considerations of personal friendship or enmity.[47]

The judge, then, like the orator and the general (the other examples used in this context), is distinguished from the statesman by virtue of the fact that the statesman, and only the statesman, possesses the science of determining when, how, and where these other actors are to use their special knowledge and expertise. Only he "knows the right and wrong moment for initiating and setting in motion the most important matters in the state. The other sciences must do what they are bidden."[48]

Plato makes it quite clear that the statesman, the person possessing scientific knowledge of the art of ruling, is not likely to be found. The one genuine constitution, which is the rule of the statesman (with or without law), is in fact only an ideal to be approached but never fully realized.[49] The "second-best" constitution is the rule of law, which, because "it cannot prescribe with accuracy what is best and just for each member of the community at any one time," falls short of excellence, but nevertheless avoids the baneful consequences associated with the lawless rule of non-statesmen.[50] Of course, the true statesman, were he suddenly to emerge, might, consistent with the common good, transgress the law; but barring this exceedingly improbable eventuality, the best practical situation is one in which all men are bound by the law. As A. E. Taylor has commented: "We . . . shall fare best if we do the very thing which . . . would not be in place if we could count on the presence of a living scientific statesman among us; that is to say, if

47. Plato, *Statesman*, J. B. Kemp (Indianapolis, 1957), 305c, p. 88. Emphasis added.
48. Ibid., 305d, p. 88.
49. As Professor Strauss put it: "The *Statesman* may be said to bring into the open what the *Republic* had left unsaid, namely, the impossibility of the best regime presented in *The Republic*." Strauss, "Plato," in *A History of Political Philosophy*, p. 45.
50. *Statesman*, 294b, p. 66.

we strictly follow the second-best practice of adhering to such traces of statesmanlike insight as are embodied in our codes of law and permitting no infringement of them."[51]

Let us now return to the judges. It is Plato's view that in the best regime these figures would not be statesmen, but rather would perform a subordinate, if not unimportant, role.[52] What would their role be in the second-best regime, where strictly speaking, the statesman is not in control of the affairs of state? In the first place, it seems apparent that they would have a special responsibility to make the authority of the law paramount. The old precept that "ours is a government of law not men," is, despite the criticism of "realists" in jurisprudence and much recent work in modern political science, a much more profound idea than the casual manner in which it is often uttered suggests. Second, since the best practical regime is doubtless the one that embodies statesmanlike wisdom in its laws, the judge who interprets these laws should insure that this wisdom is preserved intact.[53] This entails essentially the same function as that prescribed by Plato for the judge when the latter is subordinate to the statesman. That is to say, the judge in the best practical regime would refuse to pervert the intentions and meaning of the original (or fundamental) law, and he would adjudicate according to standards received from that law.

If we move, for a moment, from Athens to the United States, the relevance of this particular point is immediately obvious. For the founders of this regime, as has been convincingly argued, intended to create a system of government that would survive and prosper after the period of the founding, when statesmanlike wisdom no

51. Taylor, *Plato*, p. 232. Professor Strauss commented in this regard: "In the absence of the true king, the stranger [from Elea] would probably be satisfied if the city were ruled by a code of laws framed by a wise man, one which can be changed by the unwise rulers only in extreme cases." Strauss, "Plato," in *A History of Political Philosophy*, p. 50.

52. Actually, they *could* be statesmen *if* they possess scientific knowledge of ruling. But this knowledge does not inhere in their position as judges. The statesman, in other words, need not, in Plato's view (perhaps thinking of Socrates) be in a position to direct affairs of state.

53. Something like this function is suggested by Plato in *The Laws* when the Athenian describes the Nocturnal Council. Among its duties is the important one of insuring that later amendments in the laws are made in the same spirit as the original laws.

longer prevailed.[54] If, then, we are permitted to speak of "statesmanship" in this context without distorting Plato's teaching, it makes sense to append the label of judicial statesmanship to the judge whose efforts are directed towards, and whose work is characterized by, the enhancement of respect for law and the furtherance and preservation of the vision of society embodied in the fundamental law of the land.

Perceived in this light, the judicial statesman will be part educator and part judge. "Novelty of ideas," Justice Frankfurter once said, "is not the special function of a statesman."[55] The education of citizens in the ideas that give the regime its special character *is* a part of his function. Indeed, Frankfurter was well aware of the educative dimension of the Court's work, and his opinions often reflected the importance that he ascribed to that function. He knew, for example, of the role performed by the early circuit-riding justices, who "carried out . . . hopes . . . as inculcators of national patriotism . . . [and] utilized charges to the grand juries as opportunities for popular education."[56] He also knew that the habit of law-abiding was particularly important in a democracy and that the courts were instrumental in fostering this habit. "Broadly speaking, the chief reliance of law in a democracy is the habit of popular respect for law."[57] "The standards of what is fair and just set by courts in controversies appropriate for their adjudication are perhaps the single most powerful influence in promoting the spirit of law throughout government."[58]

Frankfurter's judicial opinions, more so than anyone else's on the modern Court, were intended to imbue the habits and sentiments of the people with a reverence and awe of the law and the

54. Martin Diamond, "Democracy and *The Federalist:* A Reconsideration of the Framers' Intent," *American Political Science Review,* 53 (1959). "The reason of the Founders constructs the system within which the passions of the men who come after may be relied upon." Ibid., p. 67.

55. Frankfurter, *Of Law and Men,* p. 232.

56. Frankfurter and Landis, *The Business of the Supreme Court,* p. 20.

57. Frankfurter, "The Judicial Process and the Supreme Court," in *Felix Frankfurter on the Supreme Court,* p. 496.

58. Felix Frankfurter, "John Marshall," p. 238. "What matters most is whether the standards of reason and fair dealing are bred in the bones of the people" p. 235.

judicial process. Yet this noble effort suffered in part because Frankfurter was reluctant to extend his views on the role of law to their ultimate logical conclusion. In perhaps the most important opinion of his lengthy judicial career, he wrote that "law is concerned with external behavior and not with the inner life of man."[59]

This suggests that the guidance or education that the Court provides terminates at the point of obedience. In other words, the assumption seems to be that it is sufficient to have men obey the law even if the law to which they have become obligated makes no lasting impact upon their character or goodness. Why, then, obey the law? The answer provided by Frankfurter is that we cannot live together without obedience, and, of course, he was correct. Nonetheless, he would have been more persuasive if he had demonstrated that the very act of obedience in a regime dedicated to the principles of popular self-government is likely to influence the "inner life of man." As Judge Learned Hand, whose judicial philosophy was comparable to that of Frankfurter, claimed: "The subject matter of science is recorded observation of the external world; the subject matter of . . . statecraft is the soul of man."[60]

Many years later, in one of his finest judicial utterances, Frankfurter came close to an explicit appreciation of this legal understanding. In *Cooper* v. *Aaron,* the famous Little Rock school segregation case, he wrote a concurring opinion in which he reflected upon questions of legal obligation and respect for law. Its importance warrants extended quotation.

The Constitution is not the formulation of the merely personal view of the members of this Court, nor can its authority be reduced to the claim that state officials are its controlling interpreters. Local customs, however hardened by time, are not decreed in heaven. Habits and feelings they engender may be counteracted and moderated. Experience attests that such local habits and feelings will yield, gradually though this be, to law and education. *And educational influences are exerted not only by explicit teaching.* They vigorously flow from the fruitful exercise of the responsibility of those charged with political official power and from *the almost unconsciously transforming actualities of living under law.*[61]

59. *West Virginia State Board of Education* v. *Barnette,* at 655.
60. Learned Hand, *The Spirit of Liberty* (New York, 1953), p. 283.
61. *Cooper* v. *Aaron,* 358 U.S. 1 (1958), at 25. Emphasis added.

He went on to speak of the pedagogic potential of elected officials in words that are certainly applicable to the work of the Court and, indeed, that characterize his own opinions. "That the responsibility of those who exercise power in a democratic government is not to reflect inflamed public feeling but to help form its understanding, is especially true when they are confronted with a problem like a racially discriminating public school system."[62]

It is interesting that Frankfurter chose to emphasize that education need not be accomplished through "explicit teaching." For despite his opportunity to emulate Marshall by using his position on the Court to engage in powerful rhetoric that might move his readers, Frankfurter for the most part chose rather to convey his message of respect for the law by acting out his role as a justice with self-restraint and deference to the coordinate branches of government.[63]

One of the most effective methods used by Frankfurter to demonstrate the wisdom of self-restraint was to apply with care the rules determining justiciable controversies. Although strict application of the doctrines of ripeness, mootness, standing, and political question might have seemed overly formalistic to the pragmatists, Frankfurter saw these rules as essential tools for maintaining the Court's proper role in our system of government. He was influenced in his viewpoint by Brandeis' rules for avoiding unnecessary adjudication of constitutional issues.[64] In addition, he believed that the rules

62. Ibid., at 26.
63. See, for example, Frankfurter's opinion in *American Communications Association* v. *Douds*, 339 U.S. 382 (1950), where he spoke of the "unrhetorical manner of opinion-writing." For a revealing look at Frankfurter's general view of education see his concurring opinion in *Wieman* v. *Updegraff*, 344 U.S. 183 (1952). "To regard teachers—in our entire education system, from the primary grades to the university—as the priests of our democracy is . . . not to indulge in hyperbole." Ibid., at 196. Frankfurter was capable of delivering eloquent and powerful lectures on the subject of law-abiding. See, in particular, his concurring opinion in *United States* v. *United Mine Workers of America*, 330 U.S. 258, 307 (1947), where his intention was to show how "the historic phrase 'a government of laws and not of men' epitomizes the distinguishing character of our political society."
64. See e.g., *Baker* v. *Carr*, 369 U.S. 196, 266 (1962) (dissenting opinion) (political question); *Adler* v. *Board of Education*, 342 U.S. 485, 497 (1952) (dissenting opinion) (ripeness); *Joint Anti-Fascist Refugee Committee* v. *McGrath*, 341 U.S. 123, 149 (1951) (concurring opinion) (standing). See Felix Frankfurter and Adrian S. Fisher, "The Business of the Supreme

governing justiciability provided the Court with greater flexibility. "Not least of the arts of statesmanship," he noted, "is that of correct timing, of knowing what to say and when."[65] Finally, the justiciability doctrines ensured that the Court would consider only those controversies with issues sufficiently defined and parties sufficiently concerned so that the decisions reached would be just. These doctrines thus promoted careful adjudication and, as a result, respect for the law. In a sense, they became a substitute for rhetoric as the pedagogical instrument of Frankfurter's educational mission.

Before coming to the Court, Frankfurter had written that "the formalities and modes of doing business, which we characterize as procedure, though lacking in dramatic manifestations, may, like the subtle creeping in of the tide, be a powerful force in the dynamic process of government."[66] These formalities make the legal profession a force for constructive conservatism. Tocqueville, who had depicted this formalism as the principal virtue of the American legal system, would doubtless have approved of Frankfurter's emphasis on such factors as ripeness, standing, and *stare decisis,* and his appreciation of the peculiar political import of the rigorous observance of such rules. Indeed, he would have been less reluctant than Frankfurter to exalt the undemocratic basis of this formalism. As the discussion of Chapter 3 pointed out, democracy is in greater need of such auxiliary protection than other forms of government. Frankfurter's high regard for these devices is in significant contrast to the pragmatic "revolt against formalism."

Many commentators have focused on the most obvious element

Court of the October Terms, 1935 and 1936," *Harvard Law Review,* 51 (1938), 620–626, 637. See *Adler* v. *Board of Education,* 342 U.S. 485, 505 (1952) (Frankfurter dissenting), citing *Ashwander* v. *TVA,* 297 U.S. 288, 346 (1936) (Brandeis concurring). See also Paul A. Freund, "Mr. Justice Brandeis," in *Mr. Justice,* eds. Allison Dunham and Philip B. Kurland (Chicago, 1964); and Gerald Gunther, "The Subtle Vices of the 'Passive Virtues'—A Comment on Principle and Expediency in Judicial Review," *Columbia Law Review,* 64 (1964), 16–17.

65. Frankfurter, *Of Law and Men,* p. 362.

66. Frankfurter and Landis, *The Business of the Supreme Court,* p. vi. It is significant that this thought should appear immediately after he indicates that "the essentially political significance of the Supreme Court's share in the operations of the Union can hardly be overemphasized."

of Frankfurter's cautious approach to the exercise of judicial power, his Jeffersonian majoritarianism, and have either praised his respect for the democratic process or have been critical of his neglect of the auxiliary precautions that make popular government free government.[67] Their emphasis has not been misplaced. Frankfurter consistently maintained the belief that judicial invalidation of laws debilitated popular democratic government. "The Court," he informed us, "is not saved from being oligarchic because it professes to act in the service of humane ends." Thus, he tolerated what he believed to be unwise legislation, arguing that "the indispensable judicial requisite is intellectual humility, and such humility presupposes complete disinterestedness."[68] It already has been observed that there were limits to his toleration, just as his humility did not force him to become a completely detached judicial automaton. What needs to be noted at this point is the relationship between Frankfurter's self-restraint and his unique manner of instruction in the habit of law-abiding.

This should be prefaced by noting that such instruction as can be observed is a by-product, or indirect effect, of his principal concern, which was to limit the impact of an oligarchic, unrepresentative branch of government. While limiting the scope of the Court's authority Frankfurter provided a splendid example of the moderation and restraint that must be the basis of the popular government to which he deferred. His judicial example can serve as a model, which, if imitated on a wide scale, would make it less necessary for the Court to intervene on behalf of the precious individual liberties of a free people. Such liberties have been threatened at times from within and without government by persons and groups who have

67. Mendelson's work is typical of the admirers of Frankfurter's deference to majority decisions. Alpheus Thomas Mason, *The Supreme Court from Taft to Warren* (New York, 1964), is representative of Frankfurter's critics. "Frankfurter thinks of judicial review as limiting popular government. True enough; but the point is irrelevant since the Constitution establishes . . . not popular government (Frankfurter's expression) but free government." Ibid., p. 140.

68. *AFL* v. *American Sash & Door Co.,* 335 U.S. 538, 555–556, 557 (1949) (concurring opinion). Or, as he said on another occasion: "Holding democracy in judicial tutelage is not the most promising way to foster disciplined responsibility in a people." Felix Frankfurter, "John Marshall," p. 229.

not learned this lesson: for a people to govern itself successfully, individuals must first demonstrate the capability of governing themselves. As Learned Hand remarked: "This much I think I do know—that a society so riven that the spirit of moderation is gone, no court *can* save; that a society where that spirit flourishes, no court *need* save; that in a society which evades its responsibility by thrusting upon the courts the nurture of that spirit, that spirit in the end will perish."[69]

It is not clear whether Judge Hand meant to suggest that the Court is to have no responsibility in nurturing the spirit of moderation. If he did, then his otherwise excellent insight is seriously flawed. For, as Justice Frankfurter noted, the Court is in a preferred position to nurture, if not be entirely responsible for, the spirit of moderation. Said Frankfurter: "The Court has no reason for existence if it merely reflects the pressures of the day. Our system is built on the faith that men set apart for this special function, freed from the influences of immediacy and from the deflections of worldly ambition, will become able to take a view of longer range than the period of responsibility entrusted to Congress and legislatures."[70] This argument, written in the context of a defense of judicial self-restraint, is perhaps more persuasive as an argument against that posture, and some of the critics of judicial self-restraint have made telling points by applying just such an argument.[71]

Charles L. Black, Jr., who has written at great length of the "legitimating" function performed by the Court when it refuses to strike down an action of a coordinate branch of government,[72] has

69. Hand, *Spirit of Liberty*, p. 164. Emphasis in original.
70. *West Virginia State Board of Education* v. *Barnette*, at 665 (dissenting opinion).
71. See, for example, Alfred A. North, S. J., *The Supreme Court: Judicial Process and Judicial Politics* (New York, 1966), pp. 189–203; C. Herman Pritchett, "The Limits on Judicial Self-Restraint," in *Courts, Judges and Politics: An Introduction to the Judicial Process*, eds. Walter F. Murphy and C. Herman Pritchett (New York, 1961), p. 691; Alpheus Thomas Mason, "The Supreme Court: Temple and Forum," *Yale Review*, 48 (1959), p. 540; Fred Rodell, "Judicial Activists, Judicial Self-Deniers, Judicial Review and the First Amendment—Or, How to Hide the Melody of what You Mean behind the Words of what You Say," *Georgetown Law Journal*, 47 (1959); Eugene V. Rostow, "The Democratic Character of Judicial Review," *Harvard Law Review*, 66 (1952).
72. Charles L. Black, Jr., *The People and the Court* (Englewood Cliffs, 1960), pp. 48–86.

made a similar point: when a justice of the Supreme Court, with great eloquence and restrained intensity, refuses to exercise his authority to invalidate a measure despite his strong personal convictions, an impressive lesson in moderation and self-discipline may be learned. Of course, such a point of view may be dismissed, even ridiculed by those who denigrate the importance of judicial opinions. However, people do read Supreme Court opinions; perhaps not those whose reactions are sought by sample surveys, but lawyers, teachers and others whose influence may have an important impact upon segments of the body politic. At a time when public officials at the highest levels of government have displayed contempt for the rule of law, who is to say that such judicial pronouncements on behalf of moderation and restraint are simply vacuous exercises in the art of judicial pedantry and obscurantism?

But there is also a danger in such judicial moderation. The two dimensions of judicial statesmanship previously discussed included a role for the judge that requires him to recall and preserve the statesmanlike wisdom embodied in the Constitution. This demands restraint, self-imposed by the judge, but also imposed by the judge upon others who choose to innovate upon the statesmanship of the founders. Taylor's interpretation of Plato's *Statesman* indicates why this is the case: "In the state which is ruled by laws, the party who tries to innovate on the law is trying to imitate a feature of the conduct of the genuine scientific statesman. If he attempts to do so without any scientific understanding of statesmanship of his own, we may be sure that his imitation will be a bad one (if he were acting with scientific understanding, his conduct would, of course, not be an *imitation* at all; it would *be* scientific statesmanship)."[73]

Notice the special burden of statesmanship that is thrust upon the shoulders of Supreme Court justices if the logic of this view is applied in the judicial process. Not only must they restrain themselves—that is, their personal predilections; but they also must see to it that the statesmanship of the founders is not perverted through the actions of those possessing only unenlightened knowledge. This may require the imposition of restraints upon others, which is to

73. Taylor, *Plato,* p. 234. Emphasis in original.

say, vigorous judicial assertiveness. A very fine line separates a judge's restraint of his personal prejudices from his assertions in defense of constitutional wisdom. This, after all, is the line that separates judicial statesmen from ordinary judges. It is no mean task to become the impersonal voice of the Constitution.

Before coming to the Court, Frankfurter had written that "the constitutionality of a policy does not determine its wisdom."[74] This was a line that was to appear, in one form or another, in a number of his judicial opinions.[75] If all that was intended by this remark was the observation that unwise policies may not expressly offend the Constitution, then there is not very much of interest one can say about it one way or the other. If the distinction between constitutionality and wisdom succeeds in obscuring the fact that in a broader sense there is a convergence of constitutionality and wisdom, that a wise public policy will reflect constitutional intent, then the statement is no longer as innocuous as at first glance it may have appeared. One student of the Court has commented: "No one expects the Supreme Court to stamp out every silly law which the majestic representatives of the people pass, but it is questionable whether it is either possible or wise to separate constitutionality and wisdom."[76]

Unfortunately, Frankfurter's attempt to separate them did force him to neglect this vital component of judicial statesmanship. In *United States* v. *Lovett,* he suggested that "it is not for us to find unconstitutionality in what Congress enacted although it may imply notions that are abhorrent to us as individuals or policies we deem harmful to the country's well-being."[77] When viewed merely as a sign that a justice has successfully overcome his personal biases, this statement commands respect and admiration. However, if the "policies we deem harmful to the country's well-being" are harmful by virtue of the fact that they innovate upon the statesmanlike

74. Frankfurter, *The Public,* p. 79.
75. See, e.g., *Polish Nat'l Alliance* v. *NLRB,* 322 U.S. 643, 650 (1944); *West Virginia State Bd. of Educ.* v. *Barnette,* at 646–650 (dissenting opinion); *Osborn* v. *Ozlin,* 310 U.S. 53, 62 (1940).
76. Walter F. Berns, *Freedom, Virtue, and the First Amendment* (Chicago, 1965), p. 183.
77. *United States* v. *Lovett,* 328 U.S. 303 (1946), at 319 (concurring opinion).

wisdom embodied in the Constitution, should a justice not find them unconstitutional? Frankfurter would not accept this contention. He stated: "Inadmissible is the claim to strike down legislation because to us as individuals it seems opposed to the 'plan and purpose' of the Constitution. That is too tempting a basis for finding in one's personal views the purposes of the Founders."[78] In other words, Frankfurter was unable or unwilling to draw the fine line between restraint of his personal views and defense of the Constitution.[79] A good example of Frankfurter's reluctance to engage in this inquiry was observed in Chapter 5 in regard to the reapportionment issue. For the ordinary judge, the fear expressed by Frankfurter is certainly a legitimate one. However, for the judicial statesman, the purposes of the founders can be explicated at the same time that the temptation to inject his personal views into these purposes is avoided. Once again, this is not a simple task to accomplish. The burden of statesmanship would not be a burden if it were.

We may recall, in this regard, Frankfurter's own words, written before he had taken a seat on the Court. Among the "indispensable qualifications for high statesmanship," he had argued, is that one be able, and prepared, to translate into practical fulfillment the noble vision of society that was implicit in the "edifying precepts about the dignity of man" that had inspired the nation's founders. Judicial statesmen were thus to be involved in the politics of high purpose, which is to say, in the interpretation and judicial enforcement of those early political principles that were made legally enforceable through the Constitution. It was this crucial duty of statesmanship that Frankfurter, though eminently qualified by scholarship and experience, was reluctant to perform. Recall, too, in this context, Frankfurter's comparison of Chief Justice Waite with Chief Justices Taney and Marshall. Taney and Marshall possessed the "consciousness of statesmanship," whereas Waite was "predominately

78. *West Virginia State Bd. of Educ.* v. *Barnette,* at 666 (dissenting opinion).
79. Frankfurter did not always refuse to engage in the practice of discerning the "plan and purpose" of the Constitution. See, for example, Stevens's discussion of Frankfurter's opinion in *San Diego Building Trades Council* v. *Garmon,* 359 U.S. 236 (1959), "Felix Frankfurter," in *American Political Thought,* pp. 240–241.

the lawyer." Frankfurter praised Waite for his judicial self-restraint and for his adherence to "traditional canons of constitutional adjudication," but he suggested very strongly that these attributes, taken alone, do not a judicial statesman make. By the same token, Justice Frankfurter appears to have been more in the tradition of Waite than in the tradition of Marshall and Taney. He was far less a judicial statesman than a superb judicial craftsman.

Perhaps it is less important that we evaluate the statesmanship of Justice Frankfurter than that we understand the criteria according to which such evaluations are made. Frankfurter's career, taken as a whole, can teach us much about statesmanship. His extrajudicial writings, despite their ambiguity, often illuminated the thorny problems of statesmanship. His judicial work, while reflecting some attributes of statesmanship, was deficient in others. On balance, he was an unusually talented judge, but not a judicial statesman. It is, however, one of Frankfurter's enduring achievements that evaluations of this kind can be made through the application of his own insights and contributions to our constitutional jurisprudence. Finally, Frankfurter's writings, both on and off the Court, provide further support for the observation that adjudication and statesmanship must be distinguished when the former is grounded upon a philosophy of pragmatism.

CHAPTER 8

Toward Judicial Statesmanship

The development of standards for judges engaged in constitutional decision making must overcome a common tendency among many students of the Court to find in prevailing behavior the criteria by which to distinguish degrees of judicial excellence. For decades now, "realists" have taught us that it is naive and unrealistic for us to expect of judges much more than we are able to demand of ourselves. The politically involved layman, it is often maintained, like the activist judge, will do all that he can to advance what he conceives to be desirable social policy. Similarly, the modest judge parading behind the banner of judicial self-restraint defers in his judgments to others, since for him deference will generally lead to the fulfillment of his political objectives. As an empirical statement, of course, there is some truth to this observation. But truth does not always lead to progress, and especially if, as with the realists, it prevents us from advancing beyond the common level of experience. To do so, however, requires an understanding of statesmanship that conceives of the "political" as something considerably broader than what is usually assumed in discussions of the Court as a "political institution." To call into question the utility of principles of statesmanship based upon the broader definition suggested in the previous two chapters because they focus less attention upon the narrow definition, misses the point. Judges, after all need not act according to the expectations of presidents who nominate them, senators who confirm them, pressure groups who support them, or scholars who write about them. That they usually do so is beside the point. What is important is that they *may* come to appreciate that their role possesses the unique potential for leadership in political education.[1]

1. Or as Judge Charles E. Wyzanski, Jr. has nicely put it, they may see

The objective of this chapter is to proceed beyond judicial pragmatism toward an understanding of the factors which, taken together, define judicial statesmanship. What follows is in the nature
of a preliminary analysis, suggesting directions rather than providing detailed answers. Though we make a claim to go beyond
pragmatism, it should be pointed out at the outset that it is not the
intention of this endeavor to create out of whole cloth a bright,
shiny, new jurisprudence. History has recorded a number of examples of prudent judicial judgment, and they require only a
demonstration of their continuing vitality; in particular, they suggest
a method of responding to some of the legitimate pragmatic griev-
ances engendered by the late nineteenth-century jurisprudence—
without opting for the pragmatic solution. The effort will consist
of three parts. They are, first, a critical examination of two well-
known attempts to reach a viable alternative to pragmatic jurisprudence; second, an inquiry into, and reinterpretation of, Jefferson's reflections on constitutional development and construction;
and finally, a detailed analysis of a modern Supreme Court opinion
that provides important insight into the art of judicial statesmanship.

ACTIVIST RESTRAINT

The history of political thought is replete with examples of thinkers whose followers and intellectual descendants fail to agree on
much of anything. Indeed, the intellectual offspring of a great mind
are often in agreement only in their designation of a common source
of inspiration.[2] These remarks possess a special relevance to
twentieth-century constitutional jurisprudence, which is, among

---

that the Court, like other institutions "engaged in spreading knowledge, in
dealing concretely with cases, enhance[s] political morality and [may] in
fact preserve the state in its ultimate purpose." Wyzanski, "Comment," in
Government Under Law, ed. Arthur E. Sutherland (New York, 1968), p.
493.
   2. For example, the students of Hegel divided into Left and Right, as did
the followers of Jefferson. In both cases, the divergence among the suc-
cessors can be traced to the views of the common source, views that may
have been consistent as originally formulated, but which contained the
seeds of conflicting political traditions. Thus, the individualism and egalitarianism of Jeffersonian political thought inevitably produced antithetical
Jeffersonians.

other things, American political thought reflected in the opinions of the Supreme Court. Two opposing jurisprudential traditions, enunciated both on and off of the Court, refer to common origins. Judicial "activists" and judicial "self-restrainers" are fond of laying claim to Justice Holmes as the guiding light for their approaches to the exercise of judicial power. Justice Holmes was himself a practitioner of judicial self-restraint—thus, it is not his view of the role of the Court in American political life that provides the common basis for the traditions which honor his name. Rather, his philosophical association with pragmatism often finds its way into the opposing theories of judicial power. Pragmatic principles of jurisprudence are perfectly compatible with an approach that defers to the judgment of a coordinate branch of government as well as one that assumes a supremacy of the judicial branch in matters of substantive policy. That is to say, the judge who performs the role described in Chapter 4, that of "democratic fact finder," may do so either by passively accepting the judgments of the more representative branch of government or by taking it upon himself to engage in the delicate process of balancing competing social interests according to his judgment of the prevailing community standards.[3]

Now, to be sure, the activists of today profess allegiance to certain absolutes—a seemingly unpragmatic point of view, analogous to the Fieldian defense of an absolute right to private property. But there is a difference. The latter-day absolutists do not find support for their view in any philosophy of natural rights.[4] The absolute stand taken with respect to First Amendment questions leads directly to what appears at first paradoxical—the extreme relativism that is asserted in defense of any speech that seeks First Amendment protection.[5] This relativism, however, is the true legacy of Holmes,

3. Many activists reject the view that the review of legislative judgments makes the Court an undemocratic institution. The best explication of this position is in Rostow, "The Democratic Character of Judicial Review." See also Rodell, "Judicial Activists, Judicial Self-Deniers."
4. Indeed, Justice Black, the most important of the First Amendment absolutists, explicitly rejected natural right as a source for judicial judgment. See his dissenting opinion in *Adamson* v. *California*, 332 U.S. 46 (1947).
5. Justice Douglas' dissenting opinion in *Ginzburg* v. *United States*, 383 U.S. 463, 491–492 (1966), is especially revealing in this regard: "The First Amendment allows all ideas to be expressed—whether orthodox, popular,

and it unites many of those who march under the different banners of judicial power. Wallace Mendelson, for example, writing on judicial self-restraint, refers at one point to a remark made by Abraham Lincoln to "cut short the ranting of a northern extremist." "Mr. ———, haven't you lived long enough to know that two men may honestly differ about a question and both be right?" Mendelson then comments: "In this paradox lies the genius of our system."[6] Of course, Mendelson did not do justice to Lincoln even if he did capture the essence of a certain posture of judicial self-restraint. On the question whether slavery was morally defensible Lincoln was absolutely clear that only one point of view was right. He was, in other words, convinced—and acted upon his conviction—that the genius of our system would not permit disagreement as to the *ends* of the regime. What Mendelson (and he is not unique) described as both the "genius of our system" and the essence of judicial modesty and humility can also characterize much of the philosophy associated with the prevailing activist position on the Court. We have already seen how pragmatic jurisprudence fostered such a view of the polity. We have observed how statesmanship on the Court is radically inconsistent with that view. Both activism and self-restraint are empty words when each is defended against the other on the basis of a philosophy that serves, in a crucial sense, to unite rather than to differentiate them. What was said in the previous chapter of Justice Frankfurter's self-restraint can also be said of much activist thinking. Unless that activism is used to preserve and recall the statesmanlike wisdom embodied in the Constitution; that is to say, unless judges act so as to impose restraints upon whoever chooses to innovate on that wisdom, they are not performing the high tasks of judicial statesmanship.

There have been a number of attempts to break out of the simple molds cast by the representatives of these opposing schools.[7] Two of

---

offbeat, or repulsive. I do not think it permissible to draw lines between the 'good' and the 'bad' and be true to the constitutional mandate to let all ideas alone . . . Government does not sit to reveal where the 'truth' is."

6. Wallace Mendelson, *Justices Black and Frankfurter,* p. 130.

7. A point of clarification may be in order here. In referring to these two approaches I am not arguing that all the judges applying them are prag-

the most serious and best known are to be found in the work of Herbert Wechsler and Alexander M. Bickel. Both sought to anchor their jurisprudence to constitutional principle, to a view of the Constitution that comprehends the fundamental law as the embodiment of the nation's political principles. As such, they provide a healthy antidote to much of the pragmatic thrust of twentieth-century constitutional jurisprudence. In the end, however, their solutions prove unsatisfactory. The purpose of the following brief review of their positions is to provide a setting for the approach to judicial application of constitutional principle that will be suggested in the remaining pages.

Herbert Wechsler's jurisprudence represents an effort to develop a reason-oriented approach toward constitutional interpretation. Accordingly, the test of virtue in interpretation, the criterion for evaluating the work of the Court, is reason. Decisions of the Court must be measured as "exercises of reason," not acts of will, as many of the realists and group-theorists have argued. The judicial process must be generally principled, and judgment must be reached on the basis of constitutional principles that transcend the immediate case at hand.[8] Judicial fiat must be replaced by reasoned impartiality. Questions of expediency must not be allowed to influence judicial considerations. Judges are to be entirely principled, applying the law with even-handed exactness, never allowing the particular circumstances involved in a case to distort or subvert the demands of generality and neutrality, which constitute the main qualities of the law. Although in Wechsler's work there is no explicit definition of

matists parading under different labels. Obviously, as we saw in the preceding chapter on Justice Frankfurter, this is not the case. Rather, the argument is that a crucial element of both of these approaches (when they are elevated to judicial philosophies) is also a distinguishing characteristic of pragmatic jurisprudence—an absolute faith in the future (leading to relativism), or to quote Justice Holmes, a faith that "truth will win out in the marketplace." Thus, in an important sense, the activist libertarian and the deferential self-denier can be understood as advocating a similar pragmatic doctrine, maintaining that because there is no objective truth in the world, the Court, or in the case of the activists, the legislature, cannot be permitted to impose its view of the truth (constitutional or any other) in the place of the free flow and exchange of ideas.

8. Herbert Wechsler, "Toward Neutral Principles of Constitutional Law," *Harvard Law Review,* 73 (1959).

justice, we can infer that it relates to the rule of similar cases being treated equally under the law. Thus, while there is an effort to dissociate the Court from a blatantly result-oriented approach to adjudication, there is a sense in which the doctrine of neutral principles is calculated to achieve certain desirable political ends (or results).

Wechsler did not argue that value preferences can be completely eliminated from human decision making or that personal judgments can be kept entirely from intruding upon the work of judges.[9] His concept of neutrality meant that a judge should strive not to adjudicate according to his own economic and social preferences, but rather according to established rules of law which must be generally applied. If a rule of law should impede the advancement of a particular policy considered desirable by the judge, the rule of law must prevail. To illustrate this point, Wechsler cited his own position with respect to decisions in the area of race relations, an area that, he claimed, provided him with the most difficult test of his belief in principled adjudication. The *Brown* decision, for example, is criticized because it was not decided according to neutral principles. Wechsler indicated that he would like to think that there was a principled way to reach the Court's result, but "I confess that I have not yet written the opinion." As a result, despite the fact that *Brown* was among the decisions that "have the best chance of making an enduring contribution to the quality of our society of any that I know in recent years," Wechsler was prepared, if necessary, to sacrifice this enduring contribution upon the altar of principled adjudication.[10]

9. See, in this regard, Arthur S. Miller and Ronald F. Howell, "The Myth of Neutrality in Constitutional Adjudication," *University of Chicago Law Review,* 27 (1960). This article is a splendid illustration of realist jurisprudence applied to constitutional adjudication. If Wechsler's reason-oriented approach is deficient because it neglects result, this result-oriented approach is inadequate because it disparages reason. A viable jurisprudence must *attempt* to be generally principled at the same time it is attempting to secure desirable political ends. Miller and Howell wish to create a "teleological jurisprudence;" however, this article reflects the general failure of realists to understand that if, indeed, neutrality is a myth of constitutional adjudication, it is a beneficent myth, one that is a necessary concomitant of a purposive legal system.

10. Wechsler, "Neutral Principles," pp. 34, 27.

The central problem in Wechsler's formulation is thus related to his insistence upon analysing the Court only as a court of law and not as a political institution (political in either the narrow or broad sense). The analysis is consequently deficient because it fails to recognize the demands of prudence; indeed, it takes the prudence out of jurisprudence. The judge who is truly reason oriented, who formulates neutral principles, who writes perfectly logical, consistent opinions, who, in short, measures up to Wechsler's norms, may actually be a very poor jurist. The Court, in the American context, is unavoidably a political institution, and it therefore behooves a judge to appreciate the primary political virtue, prudence. Because reason is posited as the end of law, there is no consideration of the possible conflict between reason (narrowly defined by Wechsler to mean logical, consistent thinking) and justice. If reasoned principles of constitutional law do not in fact lead to a just political order, then it is necessary to question the basic premises of such an approach to constitutional interpretation.

Pragmatic jurisprudence, it should be recalled, was a response to a mechanical, inflexible jurisprudence that ignored the social realities of its time and place. The latter was characterized by a refusal to civilize the absolute right to private property; hence, it subverted constitutional principle. Wechsler's solution shies away from natural rights; however, its antiempirical orientation may lead to similar undesirable consequences, as illustrated in the segregation cases. The principles of the Constitution are not neutral principles. They are positive principles that require careful study of the circumstances surrounding their application. This is the essence of constitutional judgment, and it is precisely this judgment that is lacking in Wechsler's scheme. The pragmatists and the realists do not possess a judicial monopoly over the facts involved in constitutional adjudication. The alternative we are seeking need not concede, as Wechsler does implicitly, the validity of the pragmatists' claim to be the only ones not oblivious to the world around them.

This is a point well understood by Alexander M. Bickel, whose constitutional philosophy carefully steered a middle course between the reason-oriented approach of Professor Wechsler and the result-oriented solutions idealized in the writings of the legal realists.

Bickel began from an understanding of the Supreme Court as a deviant institution in American politics. Unlike those who understand the Court's power to rest upon democratic foundations,[11] Bickel viewed the Court as an inherently undemocratic institution, whose power of judicial review has the dangerous potential to sap the vitality of the democratic process. Thus, it must exercise its power cautiously, recognizing that it "labors under the obligation to succeed."[12] As a result of its unique position, Bickel believed that a major function of the Court is to derive principles of enduring value (a function that he seemed to question in a more recent book),[13] principles without which no good society can exist.

At the same time, however, the Court must recognize the political context in which it adjudicates. It must, therefore, be cognizant of the importance of prudence and compromise. Bickel stated the problem of the Court in terms of a "Lincolnian tension;" that is, compromise is supportable only when principles are maintained and upheld. As a student of history, he observed that on every occasion when the Court had misjudged the limits of its own power, its power and prestige, and hence also the purpose for which it was intended, had been seriously undermined. Judges must always remember that law is not "self-executing through its own institutions," that the Court requires the cooperation of the other branches of government in order for it to prosper, and that, most important, a law is bad law if it manages to engender widespread opposition among the general population.[14] The Court is an institution of "neither Force nor Will," and consequently, according to Bickel, it should declare as law only such principles as will in time acquire general assent.

Bickel's solution to the problem confronting the Court emerges from his consideration of the options available to the Court in the exercise of its duty. The Court may overrule, legitimate, or do nothing. The first two options are constitutional adjudications and

11. See Note 3, *supra.*
12. Alexander M. Bickel, *The Least Dangerous Branch* (Indianapolis, 1962), p. 239.
13. Alexander M. Bickel, *The Supreme Court and the Idea of Progress,* p. 99.
14. Alexander M. Bickel, *Politics and the Warren Court* (New York, 1965), p. 111.

therefore must be principled; the last is a technique of avoidance that enables the Court to reconcile principle and expediency. Thus are developed the "passive virtues"—the key to Bickel's jurisprudence—enabling the judge to maneuver successfully within the context of the "Lincolnian tension."

Ultimately, however, Bickel's extreme circumspection forced him, as one critic pointed out, to walk a tightrope that was unable to support the weight of his noble endeavor.[15] Unable to support that weight, the pronouncement of these enduring principles that is so much a part of the Court's work must inevitably suffer. Indeed, it is quite easy to see how Bickel's approach might very well induce an erosion of principle, forcing the well-intentioned judge into a corner of hopeless moral relativism. It is a relativism more Burkean than Deweyan, and in his last work Bickel expressly acknowledged his huge debt to the eighteenth-century English political philosopher. Preferring the Whig model, which begins, he felt, with a real society rather than with theoretical rights (the premise of the "liberal contractorian model"), Bickel explicitly called for relativism in constitutional adjudication.[16] He found in Edmund Burke's powerful arguments in behalf of continuity, evolution, flexibility, and experience the theoretical support for his prescriptions regarding the exercise of judicial power by the Supreme Court. He went too far, however, in his efforts to dichotomize the two traditions. Burke himself did not categorically reject the natural rights philosophy of the contractorian model if, and this is crucial, that

15. Gunther, "The Subtle Vices." For Gunther, the "passive virtues" are "subtle vices" which lead to the abandonment of principle. His criticism results from a disagreement with Bickel's fundamental premises. First, he accused Bickel of being too preoccupied with the legitimation problem—guesses about the political impact of Court decisions are "treacherous sources of precepts for Court behavior." Second, he denied the existence of the Lincolnian tension, and in doing so maintained, á la Wechsler, that doctrinal integrity must be more than a sometime goal. Finally, he argued that jurisdictional issues (the basis of the passive virtues) are themselves imbued with principle, and thus this manipulation through prudential considerations ultimately becomes law-debasing. Much of Gunther's criticism is well-taken, although occasionally for the wrong reasons. His denial that the "Lincolnian tension" is relevant to the Court is an unproven assertion made by one who, writing from a Wechslerian perspective, underestimated the political demands upon the Court's activity.

16. Alexander M. Bickel, *The Morality of Consent* (New Haven, 1975), p. 4.

philosophy was firmly embedded in the traditions of a given society. Thus it was possible for the evolving principles of society to be rooted in "theoretical" rights. Had Bickel not perceived these traditions to be mutually exclusive, and had he viewed American constitutional development as a reflection of both Burke and Locke, he would undoubtedly have written the definitive statement on the subject of judicial statesmanship.

The fear of legitimation that leads to avoidance techniques and colloquies with other institutions may have the effect, as a result of Bickel's dichotomy, of subverting the function Bickel considered to be the rationale for judicial review. If the Court is to declare as enduring values only those principles likely to achieve general acceptance, then there will be some question as to the moral quality and integrity of the values that emerge. Why, for example, is the principle of integration any more sacred in 1954 than in 1896? If the answer is that a majority favored it in 1954 whereas a different majority opposed it in 1896, then why is the latter legitimation any less entitled to be classified as an enduring value than the former? If, having finally declared legal segregation to be repugnant to the Constitution and the ideals behind the Constitution, the Court then, as Bickel advocated, avoids the issue of miscegenation because it is too emotion-laden, what becomes of the principle? The Supreme Court cannot claim to be guardian of the society's enduring values through such excessive solicitude.

Bickel was certainly not mistaken in his view that a basic ingredient of good law is the capacity to secure popular assent. In order to complete Bickel's insight, however, it becomes necessary to add that the securing of popular assent is related to the effectiveness with which the Court argues the case for the regime's political principles. Of course, the Court cannot simply ignore public opinion—the art of statesmanship, as we know, involves great subtlety. The Court must understand the beliefs and fears of those whom it seeks to educate. But it cannot surrender to those beliefs and fears; it must overcome them. In the final analysis, good law embodies the principles of a just regime and attracts the support of those to whom it applies.[17]

17. Nothing herein is intended to detract from Bickel's significant con-

Certainly Bickel was on the right track. His "passive virtues," while born of practical considerations, do not represent a pragmatic calculus. His judge, though usually harbored in the waters of self-restraint, is not, at least according to Bickel's modus operandi, opposed to judicial activism. Activism and self-restraint are tactics. Once they are elevated into ends in themselves, they tend to obscure both the character and the purpose of the Supreme Court in American political life.[18]

When it elaborates upon the enduring principles of our society, the Court must engage in creative interpretation, it must adjust its tactics to the object at hand, as defined by the immediate situation. A situation may demand self-restraint or it may demand activism— the actual choice is to be determined by whatever appears necessary to affirm constitutional principle and purpose. With this understanding, the mental gymnastics, for example, of those who were advocates of judicial self-restraint prior to 1937 and then suddenly found themselves defending judicial activism (while concurrently groping for a principled way in which to explain the abrupt reversal of their judicial philosophy), might have been avoided. Much of the embarrassment and hypocrisy that developed reflected the inability or unwillingness of scholars and judges to confront the essential role of the Court. Constitutional principles (such as, for example, "preferred freedoms") were usually derived from the approach to judicial power that required a defense. The reverse process, however, should have occurred. Any particular approach to judicial power ought to be derived from a constitutional principle

---

tribution. His avoidance techniques are valuable judicial tools if exercised properly. However, the retreat to passivity, if used consistently as a means to accommodate the interests of principle and expediency, may ultimately operate to the detriment of both.

18. Relevant here are the comments of Professor Eidelberg. "Without material power, without popular and party mandates—nevertheless the Court is to adjust and modify the operation of the laws according to the rule of that higher law, the Constitution. Without material power, but through creative interpretation of the "great outlines" and "objects" of that Constitution, the Court is to influence, so far as prudence will allow, the very course and character of American life. It is to do this, however, not by judicial activism, but by judicial activism *under* judicial self-restraint." Paul Eidelberg, *The Philosophy of the American Constitution* (New York, 1968), pp. 245–246.

(which, more than the approach, requires defense), and the approach must therefore vary according to the circumstances surrounding the application of such principles. In short, one must be on guard against the old problem, characteristic of pragmatism (but not only of pragmatism), of confusing constitutional means and ends.

CHANGE AND THE CONSTITUTION

The linkage between pragmatism and democracy was seen in Chapter 3 to be grounded to a considerable extent in the emphasis that each attaches to the desirability of change. The Darwinian teaching that change carries with it implications of perfection was part of the democratic ethos described by Tocqueville, and it also constituted a significant element in pragmatic thought, particularly in the writings of John Dewey.[19] There is, of course, nothing unique to the pragmatic understanding of the inevitability of change. Writers as disparate in their thinking as Marx and Disraeli, Dewey and Burke, could not find fault with Heraclitus' position on the permanence of change. The pragmatists, lacking any fixed standards, were inclined not to distinguish very sharply between change and progress.[20] The major criticism leveled against the pragmatic view of change was precisely that it failed to provide an unchanging standard by which to evaluate the particular merits of change, that it reflected an inadequate appreciation of progress as a matter of controversy. The pragmatic view, like Tocqueville's democracy, made of change an object of reverence, but having done so, permitted this reverence to evolve into blind worship.

19. See Chapter 3, *supra.* Also see, Edward S. Corwin, "The Impact of the Idea of Evolution on the American Political and Constitutional Tradition," in *Evolutionary Thought in America.* Said Corwin: "Its [pragmatism's] extension of certain implications of evolutionary thought challenges some of the more fundamental elements of classical American political thought. The cornerstone of the latter at its inception was the notion of a natural law of final moral and political values which were the discovery of reason." Ibid., pp. 196–197.

20. Or as Bertrand Russell has written: "Change is one thing, progress is another. 'Change' is scientific, 'progress' is ethical; change is indubitable, whereas progress is a matter of controversy." Bertrand Russell, *Unpopular Essays* (New York, 1951), p. 8.

The fact remains, however, that unless law is rendered adaptable to change, it will fail in its effort to order wisely the lives of men, and through such failure, it will lose the allegiance of those to whom it is directed. Change is a function of two inter-related factors, societal transformation and evolution of public opinion. Those charged with the responsibility of interpreting the law cannot be oblivious to the demands that these forces make upon the polity. However, it is here that the advocate of fixed principles—whether of human nature or constitutional law—is most vulnerable. He must, if he is to be taken seriously, demonstrate that his absolutes do not make the judge an ostrich whose head is buried in the sands of inflexible principle while the world passes him by.

The American judge whose work most graphically effects such a demonstration is John Marshall. Faulkner's study of Marshall describes how the chief justice applied the Lockean natural rights philosophy to mold the early law of the Constitution to the changing contours of a developing society. In so doing, Marshall was not out of step with his times. Opportunity and ability enabled him to become the principal exponent of the jurisprudence of the founding fathers. This does not mean, of course, that Marshall and his contemporaries were all in agreement in this interpretation of the Constitution. However, the attachment to fixed principles of natural right was a jurisprudential commitment common to even the most bitter political enemies. Jefferson and Marshall, for example, could not have been further apart politically, within the limited American spectrum, yet even they reflected this common commitment. "Jefferson's sanguine expectations from progress and democracy qualify his nonetheless *genuine adherence* to fixed Lockean institutions; 'only the imperishable rights of man' supply a permanent touchstone."[21] Both he and Marshall, in other words, despite their disagreement over the relative merits of progress and democracy, were united in their allegiance to a common source of political principle.

Quite often, however, Jefferson is seen as an eighteenth-century precursor of the pragmatic movement in politics and philosophy. It is hardly surprising, in view of his reflections on progress and democracy, that he was John Dewey's favorite founding father; but

21. Faulkner, *John Marshall,* p. 187. Emphasis added.

it is simply inaccurate and misleading to ascribe to Jefferson the philosophical orientation of his latter-day admirer.[22] According to Daniel J. Boorstin, perhaps the leading exponent of this interpretation, "the naturalistic emphasis of the Jeffersonians . . . became transfigured into the systematic and explicit pragmatism of the nineteenth century. Many of the presuppositions, doctrines, and attitudes of that latter-day pragmatism were the extreme logical conclusion—in some cases perhaps the *reductio ad absurdum*—of the presuppositions, doctrines and attitudes of Jeffersonian thought."[23] To be sure, one can observe certain elements of Jeffersonian thought in pragmatic philosophy, but these elements, taken together, do not add up to pragmatism. Boorstin and others assume that anyone who exhibits a concern for empirical knowledge, who possesses a futuristic orientation, who sees that institutions must keep pace with social change, and who is generally sympathetic to the tenets of democracy, qualifies as a pragmatist.[24] This, however, is precisely the view that ought to be challenged. While these may be necessary conditions of pragmatism, they are not sufficient conditions. It is possible for a statesman to care deeply about socioeconomic realities and institutional change without expressing his concern through pragmatic channels.

Jefferson, though never a judge, had a good deal to say about the law and how it ought to be interpreted. Boorstin's view of the pragmatic Jefferson is reflected in the work of scholars who have studied Jefferson's observations on jurisprudence.[25] These writers

22. Dewey's admiration for Jefferson was expressed in a book he introduced and edited, entitled *The Living Thoughts of Thomas Jefferson* (London, 1946).

23. Daniel J. Boorstin, *The Lost World of Thomas Jefferson* (Boston, 1948), pp. 241–242.

24. Notice, for example, why, according to Boorstin, some of Jefferson's contemporaries are not really "pragmatic." "The thought of men like John Adams, John Marshall, Fisher Ames—and Hamilton itself—while in a sense pragmatic in temper, was supported by appeal to the past, to history and traditions. They were not stirred by the peculiar American hope that out of the naked processes of nature, and man's integration into those processes, a new and prosperous society would emerge." Ibid., p. 241. In other words, these men were conservatives; hence, they could not be pragmatic. Whereas Boorstin was wrong about Jefferson's pragmatism, he was right about the above men, but for all the wrong reasons.

25. Charles Wiltse, whose work contains many excellent insights into

base their judgments principally upon Jefferson's many comments urging that the law keep pace with the changing times. If it does not, it will no longer prove effective, it will fail the test of experience. But the person who evaluates the law according to the test of experience is not a legal pragmatist if his criteria for evaluation are grounded in permanent principles.[26] This point is worth remembering as we proceed to examine certain features of Jefferson's jurisprudence. John Courtney Murray's reflections, in this regard, warrant careful consideration.

The structure of the state [to the founding fathers] was not ultimately defined in terms of a pragmatic calculus. The rules of politics were not a set of operational tools wherewith to further at any given juncture the dialectic process of history. On the contrary, they thought, the life of man in society under government is founded on truths, on a certain body of objective truth, universal in its import, accessible to the reason of man, definable, defensible. If this assertion is denied, the American Proposition is . . . eviscerated at one stroke. *It is indeed in many respects a pragmatic proposition; but its philosophy is not pragmatism.* For the pragmatist there are, properly speaking, no truths; there are only results. But the American Proposition rests upon the more traditional conviction that there are truths, that they can be known; that they must be held; for if they are not held, assented to, consented to, worked into the texture of institutions, there can be no hope of founding a true City, in which men may dwell in dignity, peace, unity, justice, well-being, freedom.[27]

Jefferson's jurisprudence, observed that the "administration of the law is essentially a pragmatic process in Jefferson's view." Charles Wiltse, *The Jeffersonian Tradition in America* (Chapel Hill, 1935), p. 166. Other scholars agree. Caleb P. Patterson indicated that Jefferson's constitutionalism is predominantly pragmatic. Caleb Perry Patterson, *The Constitutional Principles of Thomas Jefferson* (Austin, 1953), p. 63. He did, however, indicate that Jefferson *was* "bound by universal and invariable laws of nature." Ibid., p. 63.

26. As John Courtney Murray has written, "when a law ceases to be supported by a continued experience of its goodness, it becomes a dead letter, an empty legal form." Murray went on to say that "although pure pragmatism cannot be made the philosophy of law, nonetheless the value of any given law is importantly pragmatic." Murray, *We Hold These Truths*, p. 80.

27. Ibid., pp. 8–9.

Jefferson, the author of the Declaration of Independence, believed in such truths and, however much he talked about change, they were to remain as immutable standards against which experience was to be measured.

Jefferson may very well have been one of the few founding fathers with a theory of change as one of his constitutional principles,[28] and he stated his theory in flamboyant, if not irresponsible, language. Thus, when the sage of Monticello suggested that we could all profit from a rebellion every twenty years or so, he simply may have been warning those in power to keep on their toes, but his rhetoric was not framed in that spirit of moderation which nurtures the liberties of a free people.[29] In more reflective moments he would observe that "as new discoveries are made, new truths disclosed, and manners and opinions change with the change of circumstances, institutions must advance also, and keep pace with the times." "Let us provide in our Constitution," he urged, "for its revision at stated periods. . . . Each generation is as independent of the one preceding, as that was of all which had gone before."[30] These words were similar to sentiments that appeared in a letter written twenty-seven years earlier to James Madison. The author of *Federalist* 49, that great defense of continuity and stability in the law, may have been a bit put off when he read: "No society can make a perpetual law. The earth belongs always to the living generation: they may manage it, then, and what proceeds from it, as they please, during their usufruct."[31]

It does not require unusual perception to understand how these sentiments might have lent themselves to a pragmatic interpretation. We have seen how similar arguments were employed by the legal

28. Patterson, *Constitutional Principles*, p. viii.

29. Adrienne Koch wrote of this suggestion: "His defense of revolutions, so frequently misinterpreted as literal advice to nourish the tree of liberty with bloodshed every twenty years, is really part of his desire to provide a framework of freedom and liberty for social changes." *The Philosophy of Thomas Jefferson* (Chicago, 1964), p. 187. Koch was correct in her interpretation of Jefferson's intent, although somewhat uncritical regarding whether his words are calculated to achieve the intended effect.

30. Letter to Samuel Kercheval, July 12, 1816, in Adrienne Koch and William Pedin, *The Life and Selected Writings of Thomas Jefferson* (New York, 1945), pp. 674, 675.

31. Letter to James Madison, September 6, 1789. Ibid., p. 491.

pragmatists who rejected the old Fieldian jurisprudence of the late nineteenth century. Like Jefferson, these challengers of the status quo argued that the present generation ought not to be burdened by the past, that contemporary problems demanded contemporary solutions, that the Constitution must be rendered adaptable to the flux of events, that the life of the law has been experience not logic.[32] But there is nothing necessarily pragmatic about this. "Jefferson's famous doctrine," according to Harry V. Jaffa, "that the earth belonged only to the living, and that no constitution or law should have a longer tenure than nineteen years (the approximate life of one generation), however impracticable, indicated an enduring bias in American thought, a bias as hostile to the past and to precedent as the First Commandment."[33] The intensity of the bias described by Jaffa varies widely across the spectrum of American political thought; men such as Adams and Hamilton were much less hostile to the past than Jefferson or Dewey. This hostility, however, may very comfortably coexist with a seventeenth-century natural rights philosophy. Such philosophy is not dependent upon history; rather on reason. This reason, we may recall, is precisely what is to be reconstructed by Dewey's reconstruction in philosophy. Thus, Jefferson's words, had they been written by John Dewey (and, in fact, they can be found in nearly the same form in Dewey's jurisprudential writings), would clearly constitute one building block in the structure of legal pragmatism. For Jefferson, however, who shared Dewey's disdain for the past, but who was bound by his commitment to Lockean natural rights philosophy, they served as a reminder that fixed principles retain their viability only if they are continually reapplied to new social conditions and problems in order to derive timely and appropriate political solutions.

Jefferson's concern for *principled* change was nicely reflected in his "Statute of Virginia for Religious Freedom" (1786).

32. Thus Wiltse, for example, comments: "The final test of any political philosophy is not the logical but the pragmatic test . . . . Jefferson realized the futility of trying to fix in one generation political forms that should be valid for all time . . . . His legacy is not his solution of the political problem, but his realization that the problem must be solved anew in each succeeding era." Wiltse, *The Jeffersonian Tradition*, p. 213.
33. Jaffa, *Equality and Liberty*, pp. 125–126.

And though we well know that this Assembly, elected by the people for the ordinary purposes of legislation only, have no power to restrain the acts of succeeding Assemblies constituted with powers equal to our own, and that therefore to declare this act irrevocable would be of no effect in law; yet we are free to declare . . . that the rights hereby asserted are of the natural rights of mankind, and that, if any act shall be hereafter passed to repeal the present resolution or to narrow its operation, such act will be an infringement of natural right.[34]

Succeeding generations and their majorities, Jefferson was saying, are not obliged to accept the laws of their predecessors, but they must accept certain principles as just, not because history has stamped them with legitimacy, but because they are of the natural rights of mankind. "A generation," Jefferson wrote in a letter to John Cartwright, "may bind itself as long as its majority continues in life; when that has disappeared, another majority is in place, holds all the rights and powers their predecessors once held, and may change their laws and institutions to suit themselves. *Nothing then is unchangeable but the inherent and unalienable rights of man.*"[35] Each generation has a green light to alter its laws and institutions as it pleases, but the clear implication of the second sentence is that all such changes must somehow incorporate what is unchangeable, what remains fixed in the midst of flux. The specific forms may change, but the essence is to remain inviolate. "It is still certain that though written constitutions may be violated in moments of passion or delusion, yet they furnish a text to which those who are watchful may again rally and recall the people; they fix, too, for the people the principles of their political creed."[36] The principles of the American political creed, were, of course, those penned by Jefferson in the Declaration of Independence. The natural rights referred to in that document were, through the Constitution, to be translated into the rights of citizenship guaranteed to all men living under its law. Here, once again, Jefferson and Mar-

34. "Statute of Virginia for Religious Freedom," in *The Political Writings of Thomas Jefferson,* ed. Edward Dumbauld (Indianapolis, 1955), p. 35.
35. Letter to John Cartwright, June 5, 1824, in ibid., p. 126. Emphasis added.
36. Letter to Joseph Priestly, June 19, 1802, in ibid., p. 128.

shall were in fundamental agreement. Together, they stand in disagreement with the legal pragmatists, in that the Declaration, as a natural rights document, cannot be reconciled with pragmatic principles. Some have tried, arguing that despite the apparent "deep gap between natural rights and pragmatism" there is nothing inharmonious about combining them, and in fact, it is claimed, both can be found in the Declaration of Independence.[37] The words of the Declaration do not admit of such interpretation. No individuals were more explicit in their disavowal and rejection of natural rights principles than the pragmatists themselves, who believed, as we saw in Chapter 2, that such principles were obstacles in the way of social progress. Jefferson and the framers of the Constitution, however, perceived these principles as obstacles only to undesirable change. They were to serve at once to circumscribe power and to ensure that, when exercised, power would be directed toward the common good.

By 1823 a generation had passed since the delegates met in Philadelphia to deliberate on a Constitution. Yet here was Jefferson, proponent of each new generation's right to chart independently its own path, giving advice on the subject of constitutional interpretation: "On every question of construction, carry ourselves back to the time when the Constitution was adopted, recollect the spirit manifested in the debates and, instead of trying what meaning may be squeezed out of the text or invented against it, conform to the probable one in which it was passed."[38] Such advice, though at first glance appearing at variance with Jefferson's antipathy toward the past, is actually quite consistent with his, and the founding statesmen's, general orientation in matters of constitutional construction. That is to say, rather than constituting an uncharacteristic concession to history's determined effort to retain control over the present, Jefferson is here expressing the view that the present ought to be informed by the same "spirit" that guided the work of the founders of the regime. That spirit, however, was itself trans-

37. See Henry Steele Commager, "The Pragmatic Necessity for Freedom," in his *Civil Liberties under Attack* (Philadelphia, 1951), pp. 4–6.

38. Letter to William Johnson, June 12, 1823, in Dumbauld, *Political Writings,* p. 148.

cendent of history, issuing forth, as it were, from a source over-arching the artificial barriers that separate the generations. Recall, in this context, what was said in Chapter 3 about Dewey and the pragmatists, for whom the work of the founding fathers was less the object of reverence than of denigration. Accepting the sociological basis of all philosophy, they (particularly Dewey) viewed the work of the constitutional period as one might an ancient artifact, more for antiquarian interest than for its contemporary utility. The "belief in political fixity" was "one of the stumbling blocks in the way of orderly and directed change." For Jefferson (this is a point missed in most of the work done on him), the timelessness of certain fixed ideas rendered them especially useful in the process of orderly and directed change. Hence, the political wisdom reflected in the constitutional debates might very well be of service to those in future generations seeking institutional reform.

It is impossible to say what kind of judge Jefferson would have been had he sat on the Court. The early political wars cast him in the role of a defender of judicial self-restraint, but we can only speculate about his understanding of the judicial role as it might have been formed by the perspective of the judiciary. Most likely he would have placed more emphasis on the amendment process than on judicial innovation. "But whatever be the constitution, great care must be taken to provide a mode of amendment when experience or change of circumstances shall have manifested that any part of it is unadapted to the good of the nation."[39] The judges might still, however, have an indirect role in the amendment process. Whenever Jefferson expressed his well-known faith in the people, he was careful always to emphasize the role of education. "I know no safe depository of the ultimate powers of the society but the people themselves, and if we think them unenlightened enough to exercise their control with a wholesome discretion, the remedy is not to take it from them but to inform their discretion by education. This is the true corrective of abuses of constitutional

39. Letter to Adamantios Corey, October 31, 1823, ibid., p. 119. And in a letter to Robert J. Garnett, February 14, 1824: "The real friends of the Constitution in its federal form, if they wish it to be immortal, should be attentive by amendments to make it keep pace with the advance of the age in science and experience." Ibid., p. 125.

power."[40] If, then, constitutional change is necessary to keep pace with developments in society, might it not be to the judges that we ought to turn for instruction in legal evolution? Though the Constitution be amended its spirit shall not be violated, and it could not but have occurred to Jefferson that there was one branch of the government best situated to illuminate the true nature of that spirit. This, of course, is highly speculative, but Jefferson did possess a theory of constitutional change that enabled him to distinguish change from progress when the two, as frequently is the case, did not coincide.[41]

CONSTITUTIONAL PRINCIPLE: MEANING AND APPLICATION

To understand the art of judicial statesmanship, the student of public law should analyze the opinions of our most skilled legal craftsmen. One of the best such examples is the majority opinion of Chief Justice Hughes in *Home Building and Loan Association v. Blaisdell.*[42] Hughes's opinion suggests norms for judicial decision making in the arena of public law that avoid the inflexibility of the mechanical jurisprudence of the late nineteenth century, while also avoiding the abandonment of fixed constitutional principles that is required by the pragmatic solution. The decision splendidly reveals how the prudent judge interprets the Constitution. As will be seen, Hughes was not interested simply in legal growth, but rather in principled, purposive legal growth. Unlike the old, property-minded Court of the turn of the century, he understood that judicial doctrine must reflect the temper and needs of the time; and unlike the pragmatic reaction to the jurisprudence of the old Court, he also understood that the lifeblood of a "living Constitution" consists of a permanent body of political principles.

During the period between tenures as justice and chief justice,

40. Letter to William G. Jarvis, September 28, 1820, ibid., p. 154.
41. Adrienne Koch's comments are quite appropriate here and worth considering as we proceed to the final section: "Jefferson sincerely believed that there is a 'best' form of government, a limiting ideal toward which legislators, statesmen, and educators may look for inspiration and guidance. But the wise man would understand that this political ideal, like any other, needs careful and loyal tending—needs the appropriate time, place, and guidance to make it mature." Koch, *Thomas Jefferson,* p. 132.
42. 290 U.S. 398 (1934).

Charles Evans Hughes delivered a series of lectures on the Supreme Court. In one of these lectures he had occasion to quote approvingly from an opinion written by Justice Sutherland in 1926. "While the meaning of constitutional guaranties never varies, the scope of their application must expand or contract to meet the new and different conditions which are constantly coming within the field of their operation. In a changing world, it is impossible that it should be otherwise. But although a degree of elasticity is thus imparted, not to the *meaning*, but to the *application* of constitutional principles, statutes and ordinances, which, after giving due weight to the new conditions, are found clearly not to conform to the Constitution, of course, must fall."[43]

Justice Sutherland was clearly expressing an unpragmatic view of constitutional interpretation. The pragmatists did not distinguish in the above manner between meaning and application. The application of a principle, constitutional or other, gave to that principle its meaning; or stated pragmatically, truth was to be made in the course of experience. Chief Justice Hughes is thus remembered, through the influence of pragmatism, not for his more serious reflections on the judicial process but rather for the aphorism that "the Constitution *is* what the Supreme Court says it is."[44]

In subscribing to Sutherland's view, however, Hughes was implicitly rejecting the standard interpretation of his aphorism (a pragmatic one), and was instead accepting an older understanding that the Constitution consists of a body of permanent political principles, the interpretation and application of which may or may not conform to the demands of those principles. Notice that Sutherland's unpragmatic stance is not necessarily an impractical one. He

43. *Euclid* v. *Ambler County*, 272 U.S. 365 (1926), as quoted in Charles Evans Hughes, *The Supreme Court of the United States* (New York, 1928), pp. 198–199.

44. Professor Eidelberg has suggested that this famous line may be reconciled with a radically unpragmatic jurisprudence. "The only way in which the judges can determine what the Founders would have willed here and now is to inquire into their *general* principles and purposes. But insofar as judges are guided by such an inquiry they cannot but preserve the general principles and purposes of the Constitution—in which case, however, it might be said that the Constitution *is* what the Supreme Court says it is!" Eidelberg, *Philosophy of the American Constitution*, p. 223.

was not ignoring the facts of social change; on the contrary, he called attention to the necessity for judicial recognition of the new and different conditions of social life. At the same time, though, he concluded that such recognition must not entail the abandonment of constitutional principle. In other words, the viable adaptation of constitutional law to changing factual circumstances requires the guiding force of political principle.

To expound these principles necessitates intensive examination into the intent of those who gave us the Constitution. Many scholars claim this to be an impossible task, arguing either that there were a multiplicity of intents (some contradictory), that there is no available statement of constitutional intent, or that even if constitutional intent could be ascertained, it would have no relevance to the modern problems that confront the Constitution and the nation.[45] Thus, even when there may be no express commitment to legal pragmatism, this historiographical problem may in fact lead the judge or constitutional scholar to the same ends as those that emerge from the application of pragmatic jurisprudential principles. From this perspective, the application of a particular clause of the Constitution will serve, just as for the pragmatist, to establish its meaning, the assumption being that prior to judicial interpretation the meaning of the clause was at best beclouded by mystery and uncertainty.

One cannot, of course, deny what many justices, through their own misadventures, have discovered—that the use of history too easily leads to its abuse. On the other hand, the pitfalls of the historical journey should not prevent the judge from embarking upon it. Doubtless, most judges will stumble and fall along the way, but then most judges are unequipped by training, intellect, and character to carry the enormous burden of judicial statesmanship. With this in mind, let us turn to the case of *Home Building and Loan Association* v. *Blaisdell*.

The pertinent facts of the case can be briefly stated. In 1933, at

45. See in this regard, William Anderson, "The Intention of the Framers: A Note on Constitutional Interpretation," *American Political Science Review*, 49 (1955); John G. Woffard, "The Blinding Light: The Uses of History in Constitutional History," *University of Chicago Law Review*, 31 (1964).

the height of the depression, Minnesota passed a mortgage moratorium law authorizing the extension of the period of redemption from foreclosure sales until May 1, 1935. It was, simply put, a debtors' relief statute, passed in order to prevent the loss of mortgaged property by individuals temporarily unable to meet their financial obligations. It was also, as Benjamin F. Wright has pointed out, "obviously a carefully drafted statute, one which attempt[ed] to protect the interests of the creditors as well as those of the debtor."[46] Despite the care that went into drafting the statute, it did alter the arrangements of existing contracts, and thus it raised the question of whether or not the act was an unconstitutional impairment of the obligations of contract.

Hughes, writing for the majority, upheld the constitutionality of the statute, and in so doing, provoked a vigorous dissent from Justice Sutherland. This clash of opinions is especially interesting in light of Hughes's extrajudicial agreement with Sutherland's views on constitutional interpretation, expressed eight years earlier in *Euclid* v. *Ambler Realty Co.* The *Blaisdell* case, involving as it does the meaning of the contract clause, and its application to an unusual set of facts (the Depression), may serve to indicate which of these two judges was more faithful to the jurisprudence to which they both avowed common allegiance.

Sutherland began his dissent by explaining that the decision in the immediate case involved a great deal more than the Minnesota statute. The majority opinion, he suggested, would almost certainly undermine the Constitution as a document limiting the arbitrary exercise of power. "A provision of the Constitution, it is hardly necessary to say [but made necessary by the majority opinion], does not admit of two distinctly opposite interpretations. It does not mean one thing at one time and an entirely different thing at another time."[47] Sutherland retained the distinction between meaning and application, but he insisted that what the Minnesota legislature had done was more than just a flexible application of a constitutional provision. Rather, it was a blatant violation of the Constitution. And as such, the action could not stand. "The pro-

46. Wright, *The Contract Clause,* p. 109.
47. *Blaisdell,* at 448.

visions of the Federal Constitution, undoubtedly, are pliable in the sense that in appropriate cases they have the capacity of bringing within their grasp every new condition which falls within their meaning. But their *meaning* is changeless; it is only their *application* which is extensible."[48] Once the meaning of a constitutional provision has been ascertained (through examination of the intent of the founders), the official oath taken by the judge precludes giving to any such provision a construction not warranted by the intentions of the founders. Thus far, Sutherland was entirely consistent with his statement in *Euclid* where he had indicated that after giving due consideration to new conditions, any statute that clearly does not conform to the Constitution must be overturned.

Sutherland then proceeded to undertake a rather extensive survey of some familiar history in order to prove that the statute contravened the clause. He described the economic conditions prevailing at the time the Constitution was written, pointing out that not only was the clause in question directed against debtors, but, more importantly, it was also specifically intended to prevent the states from mitigating the painful effects resulting to debtors in times of emergency. Thus, to argue in the manner of the majority, by asserting that the emergency conditions created by the Depression legitimated the action of the state, explicitly violates the intentions of the men who wrote the Constitution. "With due regard for the processes of logical thinking, it legitimately cannot be urged that conditions which produced the rule may now be invoked to destroy it."[49]

Sutherland's strategy was quite ingenious. By arguing that the founders had economic emergencies in mind when they wrote the contract clause, he was in effect saying that any application of the constitutional principle to support moratorium legislation in the face of new conditions was a negation of the meaning of the constitutional principle. He was thus able to preserve the theoretical distinction between meaning and application while rendering it useless in practice. In this manner he managed to write a much

48. *Blaisdell,* at 451. Justice Sutherland had in mind the commerce clause, the application of which must adapt to the new modes of transportation that have developed over the years.
49. Ibid., at 472.

more persuasive and powerful opinion than if he had simply relied, as had Field and others, upon the absolute character of the contractual obligation. The effect, of course, was the same—in both cases the law was ruled unconstitutional. Sutherland, at least, does not become subject to the charge that he was using the shield of natural rights to protect private property while concurrently blinding himself to the realities of the social order. Sutherland's inflexibility (and under the circumstances, extreme intransigeance) was given the appearance of responsible adjudication.

The majority opinion of Chief Justice Hughes anticipated and addressed itself to the objections raised in Justice Sutherland's dissent. Hughes was aware of the fundamental injustice of ruling against Minnesota amidst the terrible conditions of the Depression; but he also understood and respected the principle embodied in the contract clause. His opinion retains as much of the principle as anyone could retain and still uphold the legislation.

The chief justice began by rehearsing, in considerable detail, the economic conditions that had prompted the Minnesota legislature to provide relief under its police powers. Hughes, following Justice Louis Brandeis, meticulously examined the social and economic facts involved in constitutional litigation. He soon turned his attention to constitutional history, focusing upon the intent behind the contract clause and the context in which that clause was written. This inquiry led one well-known pragmatic realist, writing in the thirties, to comment as follows: "Hughes still feels he must [in *Blaisdell*] pay heavy attention to what was said by the Founding Fathers and in the early precedents a hundred years ago. He feels he must go through the arduous rigmarole of judicial ceremony which court tradition has hallowed, even where he is making a decision in the face of a national 'emergency.' "[50] The author, Beryl H. Levy, agreed with the outcome in the case, but he found it unnecessary to go beyond a pragmatic justification for the decision.

In this regard, it might be worth noting an earlier Supreme Court decision, the facts of which were quite similar to the *Blaisdell*

50. Beryl H. Levy, *Our Constitution: Tool or Testament?* (New York, 1941), p. 244. Levy then proceeded to express the hope that the new members of the Court will "lead us out of the conventional morasses of opinion-writing."

case, and which included a majority opinion by Justice Holmes that was unencumbered by the "rigmarole" of the Hughes opinion. The case is *Block* v. *Hirsh*,[51] involving an act of Congress designed to alleviate the rent burdens of tenants by establishing a commission with power to extend a tenant's right of occupancy beyond the expiration date written in his lease. Its provisions, the act declared, were necessitated by emergencies growing directly out of the war. Holmes's opinion, the brevity of which contrasts sharply with Hughes's lengthy exposition, upheld the legislation on the ground that Congress' decision deserved great respect, especially in times of emergency. Under the circumstances, the result achieved by Holmes was just and appropriate; but the reader is left unconvinced that the action taken was in fact consistent with the words and spirit of the Constitution. The pragmatic considerations that determined the outcome for Holmes are not the kind that illuminate the great clauses of the Constitution.[52] The legal pragmatist looks for the result, not necessarily illumination, in the opinions of the Court.

Hughes's reading of history did not differ much from that of Sutherland. However, he did not simply, as one commentator has written, "[admit] that history is not on his side and [then proceed] to decide the case on other principles."[53] Although he temporarily left history for the more solid ground of judicial precedent, he later returned to it with an introduction that consisted of a description of how social and economic conditions had changed since the time of the founding fathers. "Where, in earlier days, it was thought that only the concerns of individuals or of classes were involved, and that those of the state itself were touched only remotely, it has later been found that the fundamental interests of the state are directly affected; and that the question is no longer merely that of one party to a contract as against another, but of the use of reasonable means to safeguard the economic structure upon which the good of all

51. 256 U.S. 135 (1921).
52. Perhaps in fairness to Holmes it ought to be pointed out that Justice McKenna's dissenting opinion was much less persuasive than was Sutherland's dissent in *Blaisdell*.
53. Miller, *Uses of History*, p. 43.

depends."[54] Because the economy had become vastly more complex, Hughes argued, the interests of the state (which meant the interests of all of the people) were now affected by contracts entered into by private individuals.

Hughes went on to argue that the "founders of our government" would have interpreted the contract clause in the same manner as the Court was doing in this case, and that in doing so they would have been "preserv[ing] the essential content and the spirit of the Constitution." "With a growing recognition of public needs and the relation of individual right to public security, the Court has sought to prevent the perversion of the clause through its use as an instrument to throttle the capacity of the States to protect their fundamental interests. This development is a growth from the seeds which the fathers planted."[55] Here is the answer to Sutherland's historical argument. The dissenter was correct in asserting that the contract clause was intended to protect creditors from their debtors (even in emergencies). Beyond this, there was a deeper intent, which was to promote the conditions of economic stability. This, in view of the developments in the economy, was precisely what the moratorium law had been designed to accomplish.[56]

54. *Blaisdell*, at 442.
55. Ibid., at 443–444.
56. Professor Miller's criticism of Hughes is unclear on this aspect of the case: "Behind both the Constitution and the contract clause lay the conviction that economic prosperity and the form of government enjoyed by Americans were intertwined. By failing to substantiate any theoretical difference between the eighteenth and twentieth centuries on the role of government in the economy, Chief Justice Hughes' statement of the practical differences suffers, and along with it the justification of the *Blaisdell* decision on the basis of historical change." Miller, *Uses of History*, p. 49. Miller believed Hughes was "rationalizing a progressive result" (p. 50) by justifying the present in terms of the past, but the view here is that Hughes was *defending* a progressive result on the basis of old constitutional principles. In this context, Professor Corwin would seem to have overstated the difference between the approaches of Hughes and Sutherland. "In brief, the issue between the Chief Justice and Justice Sutherland is purely one of *approach* to the constitutional problem before the Court. The latter treats the Minnesota statute *as if* it had been enacted contemporaneously with the Constitution; while the former treats the Constitution as contemporary with the Minnesota statute, that is, with today." Edward S. Corwin, "Moratorium over Minnesota," *University of Pennsylvania Law Review*, 82 (1934), 316. Rather, it is the case, that Hughes rendered the Constitution applicable to today by preserving the wisdom of yesterday.

Thus, as Sutherland had said in *Euclid*, "while the meaning of constitutional guarantees never varies, the scope of their application must expand or contract to meet the new and different conditions which are constantly coming within the field of their operation." Hughes did not cavalierly ignore the fact, as Sutherland suggested, that the founders had intended the constitutional protection to operate in times of emergency; rather, he redefined the nature of an emergency to make it conform to contemporary reality. "The policy of protecting contracts against impairment presupposes the maintenance of a government by virtue of which contractual relations are worthwhile—a government which retains adequate authority to secure the peace and good order of society."[57]

It must be emphasized in all of this that Hughes, while permitting the impairment of a particular contract in the face of economic emergency, went out of his way to respect the importance of the contractual obligation. The residual police power of the state cannot be employed to trample upon constitutional principle. This was made clear in the following way: "Undoubtedly, whatever is reserved of state power must be consistent with the fair intent of the constitutional limitation of that power. The reserved power cannot be construed so as to destroy the limitation, nor is the limitation to be construed to destroy the reserved power in its essential aspects. They must be construed in harmony with each other. This principle precludes a construction which would permit the State to adopt as its policy the repudiation of debts or the destruction of contracts or the denial of means to enforce them. But it does not follow that conditions may not arise in which a temporary restraint of enforcement may be consistent with the spirit and purpose of the constitutional provision and thus be found to be within the range of the reserved power of the State to protect the vital interests of the community."[58] It would be difficult to find a more appropriate passage to illustrate the character of judicial statesmanship. Hughes established a constitutional basis for impairing the obligations of a specific contract as a means toward the preservation of the principle embodied in the clause itself.

Unlike so many others, both on and off the Court, who have

57. *Blaisdell,* at 435.
58. Ibid., at 439.

had a tendency to dichotomize liberty and authority and perceive them in opposition to each other, Hughes sought consistency and harmony, between the liberty to enter freely into a contractual relationship, and the power of the state to restrict such relationships for the good of society. Nowhere in Hughes's opinion is there to be found any repudiation, implicit or explicit, of the principle embodied in the contract clause. Indeed, the principle was affirmed in the opinion even if the decision might suggest (especially to those who care only about decisions) that it had been violated. Contrary to the predictions of some at the time that the *Blaisdell* decision would signal the demise of the sanctity of the contractual relationship,[59] the Court, as Benjamin F. Wright has shown, quickly upheld, with Chief Justice Hughes in agreement, a number of contracts against impairment by state laws that did not adequately safeguard the rights of creditors.[60] Justice Sutherland was, of course, in accord with these decisions, believing them to have been a healthy departure from the doctrine of *Blaisdell*. But they were not inconsistent with the *Blaisdell* opinion, which had carefully stipulated the conditions and procedures that would have to be met in order to legitimate legislation impairing the obligations of contracts.

Thus, the opinion by Chief Justice Hughes illustrates an approach to constitutional decision-making that can serve as a model of judicial statesmanship. The opinion is not burdened by inflexible judicial absolutes, yet it respects fixed political-constitutional principles; it adapts the Constitution to changing socio-economic conditions, yet it does not abandon the vision of the founding fathers; it

59. For example, a note in the *Harvard Law Review* claimed that *Blaisdell* "bids fair to revolutionize a tradition of constitutional interpretation." "Constitutionality of Mortgage Relief Legislation: *Home Building and Loan Association* v. *Blaisdell*," *Harvard Law Review*, 47 (1934), 661. And later: "For while the preservation of a venerable code as a living rule of conduct requires some growth and adaptation by judicial exposition, the evolution of a doctrine to the point where it deserts the very roots of its inception is a far more significant matter." Ibid., p. 668.

60. See Wright, *The Contract Clause*, pp. 11–19. The principal cases are *W. B. Worthen Company* v. *Thomas*, 292 U.S. 426 (1934); *W. B. Worthen Company* v. *Kavanaugh*, 295 U.S. 426 (1935); *Louisville Joint Stock Land Bank* v. *Radford*, 295 U.S. 555 (1935); *Treigle* v. *Acme Homestead Association*, 297 U.S. 189 (1936); and *Richmond Mortgage and Loan Corporation* v. *Wachovia Bank and Trust Company*, 300 U.S. 124 (1937).

responds to the call of public opinion, while seeking all the while to inform it.

In order to appreciate Hughes's technique, it might be helpful to summarize briefly the constitutional principles in the case, the set of facts to which the principles were applied, and the judicial doctrine that emerged from such application. The point, of course, is that Hughes did more than simply bring the Constitution up to date; rather, he enabled it to grow along the lines of development established and prescribed by the document itself.

Two basic constitutional principles were respected, preserved, and applied by Chief Justice Hughes. These had to do with the original intent of the contract clause and with the reserved police power of the state. The purpose of the contract clause was to safeguard credit, and this in turn, the authors of the clause believed, was necessary to insure economic stability without which it would be impossible to promote the conditions and establish the confidence essential to prosperous trade and commerce. Although the importance of the contract clause in constitutional litigation in the twentieth century was considerably less than it had been in the previous century, Hughes was nevertheless in implicit agreement with Chief Justice Marshall's sentiment to the effect that one could not look back to the Constitutional Convention "without being sensitive of the great importance which was at that time attached to the tenth section of the first article."[61] The protection given to private property against state interference was "the reflection of an ethical principle coterminous with civil society, the principle that men should honor their promises."[62] In such a society it was necessary, as Marshall put it, to create the means with which to preserve "confidence between man and man" and the "sanctity of private faith."[63]

The importance of establishing constitutional intent is implicit in Hughes's explication of the state's police power, which, he argued, must always be exercised in a manner consistent with the spirit and purpose of the Constitution. Thus, as there are certain inalienable

61. *Ogden v. Saunders*, 12 Wheat., 213, 354 (1827).
62. Eidelberg, *Philosophy of the American Constitution*, p. 219.
63. *Ogden v. Saunders*, at 355.

rights, there exists also the principle of inalienable powers, enabling the state to accomplish the ends of its creation, which is to say, the protection of inalienable rights. As we noted in Chapter 2, the police power may be construed as "society's natural right to self-defense," authorizing the exercise of governmental power to the extent necessary to support the conditions which nourish the liberties of a free people. The principles espoused by Hughes are fixed and determinate, yet they are enunciated in such a way as to facilitate their adaptation to the socio-economic conditions of modern America.

Hughes was quite explicit in his account of precisely what the facts were and what had changed in 150 years of national development. The emergency conditions created by the Depression had threatened the stability vital to the existence of sound financial arrangements in a commercial economy. An appropriate response to this problem required a recognition of the radical changes that had occurred in the nation's economy since the time of the founding fathers. Its new complexity, a consequence of modern industrialization, commerce, and technology, meant that the interests of the society were intimately intertwined with the interests of the parties joined in a private contract. The statesmanlike application of the above constitutional principles demanded that these facts be placed into the judicial equation.

What, then, was the judicial doctrine that emerged from this application of principles to facts? First, the reasonable exercise of the protective power of the state is included in all contractual relations between private individuals. Second, the constitutional protection against the impairment of contractual obligation does not necessarily prohibit the state from preventing the enforcement of contracts in times of great public chaos and calamity, provided that the action of the state is of a temporary and limited nature. Doctrine is thus made consistent with, and reflective of, both constitutional principle and social reality.

The reader of Hughes's opinion, like the reader of the great Marshall opinions, the best example of which is *McCulloch* v. *Maryland*,[64] cannot but be impressed with the structural and logical

64. 4 Wheat. 316 (1819).

brilliance of the opinion, and the impressive manner in which the author consciously weaves principles and facts into a judicial fabric strong and resilient enough to withstand the wear and tear of modern society, while remaining faithful to a design established long ago. In short, the reader is treated to a lesson in the fine art of judicial statesmanship.

CONCLUSION AS BEGINNING

One of the guiding assumptions of this study has been that the opinions of the Court are important, not simply as vehicles for the announcement of decisions, but also as instruments for the elucidation of the fundamental principles underlying the regime.[65] Now, let us assume for the moment that no one reads these opinions, that as a consequence, they have no educational or moral impact, and that further, the prestige of the Court is totally unrelated to the quality of its opinions. Are they still important? Yes. For even if we concede all of the above to be true, the writing of a judicial opinion that investigates and reflects upon the fundamental principle involved in a particular case is critically important to the judge who writes the opinion. That is to say, the agony of judicial judgment, of deciding issues that are difficult and important, may be alleviated through a process whereby the jurist forces himself to expound the enduring principles of the polity in order to shed light on his immediate predicament. The principles, then, function to inform his judgment while providing order to the facts confronting him.

A judge, for example, is asked to rule on the constitutionality of a state law granting limited aid to parochial schools. He is bewildered by the maze of facts and statistics before him, some pur-

---

65. The quality of judicial opinions has long received the attention of scholarly critics of the Court. Critics of the Warren Court have made their views known to the public at large. See, for example, Alexander M. Bickel, "Is the Warren Court Too 'Political'?" *New York Times Magazine,* September 25, 1966; and Philip B. Kurland, "The Court Should Decide Less and Explain More," *New York Times Magazine,* June 9, 1968. For an interesting exchange of views on the subject see Henry Hart, "Foreword: The Time Chart of the Justices," *Harvard Law Review,* 73 (1959), 84–125; and Thurman Arnold, "Professor Hart's Theology," *Harvard Law Review* 73 (1960), 1298–1317.

porting to show how such aid is necessary to sustain religious education, others claiming to demonstrate the destructive effect of such governmental assistance on public education. Arguments descend upon him from both sides—supporters imploring him to defer to the legislative judgment of the facts, opponents urging him to overturn the legislation based upon the scientific evidence they have submitted for his consideration. Both sides manage, of course, to say something about the establishment clause, but, in the pragmatic spirit, they are content to "let the facts speak for themselves," differing only as to whose version of the facts ought to be decisive. The judge is confused. He has his own views on the wisdom of this kind of public policy, but he feels that justice demands that he attempt to transcend his own particular bias. At this point he turns to the principle behind the Constitution's two religion clauses, hoping that the articulation of the principle will develop relevant implications for the case at hand. The principle that emerges turns out to be religious pluralism—government must be neutral insofar as the preference of any religion is concerned, but it may provide limited assistance in situations where this assistance is necessary to support the end of free exercise.[66] Applying this principle to the facts before him does not immediately resolve all of his problems, but it does enable the judge to consider his facts alongside fixed standards of evaluation. To the extent that the principle he has derived accords with history, logic, and the political philosophy of the founding fathers, and to the extent that his factual information is reasonably reliable, to that extent will he possess the assurance that the decision he renders is the best that he is capable of rendering.

Nothing, obviously, is as easy as it can be made to sound on paper, and while the example given above may, through its over-

66. The most obvious example of such compensatory assistance is government support of military chaplains, where in order to enable servicemen freely to exercise their religion the government has to become involved in the support of organized religion. This is, of course, an exceedingly complicated issue concerning which there is a large body of literature. Suffice it to say, in this context, that religious pluralism, whereby the establishment clause is interpreted so as to implement the free exercise clause, is the principle that both conforms to the intentions of the founding fathers and avoids a reading of the two clauses that results in their being interpreted at cross-purposes.

simplification, distort some of the realities of judicial decision-making, it does illustrate (as would the same scenario constructed for any number of other issues) the possibility of formulating rules of law that are responsive to the immediate demands of the society and that conform to the political principles supportive of that society.

Suppose these political principles, if indeed they can be ascertained and identified, fail to provide unambiguous guidance. If, perchance, they do offer clear prescriptions, does statesmanship require that they always be binding? These are important questions, particularly since "under the influence of pragmatism in philosophy . . . most people now understand that meaning and application are at least interdependent, or that they are identical, or even that meaning depends upon application rather than the other way around."[67] Thus, it can no longer be assumed, unlike at an earlier day, that it is a generally accepted article of faith that the Constitution embodies immutable standards of justice and right conduct.

It is not necessary to rely upon faith in this crucial matter. The theoretical, if not any more the practical, consequence of denying the intractable character of the Constitution's political principles is to render questionable the institution of judicial review. Alexander Hamilton, responding to the charge that judicial review supposes a superiority of the judicial to the legislative branch, had this to say: "It only supposes that the power of the people is superior to both, and that where the will of the legislature, declared in its statutes, stands in opposition to that of the people, declared in the Constitution, the judges ought to be governed by the latter rather than the former. They ought to regulate their decisions by the fundamental laws rather than by those which are not fundamental."[68] Hamilton went on to point out that if judges failed to interpret the essence of this fundamental law they would call into question the very reason for their existence as a distinct institution.[69] If the Constitution was not intended to embody immutable standards of

67. Miller, *Uses of History,* p. 151.
68. Clinton Rossiter, ed., *The Federalist Papers* (New York, 1961) No. 78, p. 468.
69. Ibid., p. 469.

justice, if the clauses of the fundamental charter were not designed to embrace fixed political principles establishing general guidelines for those involved in the conduct of public affairs, then by what right can the Supreme Court claim the authority to nullify decisions of the elected representatives of the people?

Hamilton, to be sure, assumed that the members of the Supreme Court would be wise men, whose tenure, independence, and lack of effective sanctions would enable and encourage them to make good and just decisions. But this alone cannot justify their exercise of the power of judicial review, for its logic would also justify the transformation of the American regime into an aristocracy. Hamilton added that the justices of the Supreme Court are wise men, not primarily as a function of superior intellect and broad experience, but because their wisdom is not their exclusive preserve, it is not simply their own. Their own particular abilities are directed by the wisdom derived from careful interpretation of the Constitution. In their role as judges they are making available to us the wisdom of the founders, which is to say, the original will of the people. This role of spokesmen for a body of permanent political principles legitimizes their power in a constitutional democracy.

Consider what occurs when the justices apply the prohibition against *ex post facto* laws and bills of attainder, and when they enlist into service the commands of the First, Fourth, Fifth, Thirteenth, Fourteenth, and Fifteenth Amendments. Are they not measuring and evaluating conduct against standards of right conduct, rooted in nature, that reflect an awareness of both the dignity and the fallibility of man? The fundamental legal status of the Constitution, to use Hamilton's words, is attributable to its supremacy over ordinary legislation *and* to the fact that it "constitutes" testimony to some fundamental truths about human nature. The Constitution, as its Preamble indicates, is intended to "establish Justice," not justice according to any principles, but according to the principles set out in the document. The justice who interprets the clauses of this document also has the opportunity to expound the principles upon which they rest. When the clauses are violated, their violation represents a repudiation of more than the words of a written document. They represent actions offensive to the ends and purposes that are reflected in the principles behind the words. When, for example, the government performs an arbitrary act in violation of the Fifth Amendment, the Supreme Court is authorized to invalidate that act because the justices are uniquely situated to discern the contemporary implications of the original will of the people. This role legitimates the great power that they wield and is the necessary condition for judicial statesmanship.

Of course, as we observed in the *Blaisdell* case, the exigencies of the moment may require that the enforcement of principles on occasion be limited, but only to insure their survival in the long run. Statesmanship requires a recognition of the binding character of these principles and the ability to know when the compromise of principle lapses into the abnegation of principle.

Finally, we should not despair when, as frequently occurs, these principles do not provide unambiguous guidance for those responsible for their interpretation. The more we neglect them (which, unfortunately, is one of the consequences of judicial pragmatism) the longer will they remain ambiguous.

Selected Bibliography

Abraham, Henry J. *Justices and Presidents: A Political History of Appointments to the Supreme Court.* New York: Penguin Books, 1975.

Allen, Carleton Kemp. "Justice and Expediency." In Paul Sayre, ed., *Interpretations of Modern Legal Philosophies.* New York: Oxford University Press, 1947, 15–28.

Anderson, William. "The Intention of the Framers: A Note on Constitutional Interpretation." *American Political Science Review,* 49 (1955), 340–352.

Aristotle. *Politics.* Translated by Ernest Barker. New York: Oxford University Press, 1962.

Arnold, Thurman. "Professor Hart's Theology." *Harvard Law Review,* 73 (1960), 1298–1317.

Aronson, Moses J. "Cardozo and Sociological Jurisprudence." *Journal of Social Philosophy,* 4 (1938), 5–44.

———. "The Juristic Thought of Mr. Justice Frankfurter." *Journal of Social Philosophy,* 5 (1940), 150–173.

———. "Roscoe Pound and the Resurgence of Juristic Idealism." *Journal of Social Philosophy,* 6 (1940), 47–83.

Austin, John. *The Province of Jurisprudence Determined.* London: Weidenfield and Nicolson, 1955.

Bailyn, Bernard. *The Ideological Origins of the American Revolution.* Cambridge, Mass.: Harvard University Press, 1967.

Beard, Charles A. *An Economic Interpretation of the Constitution.* New York: Free Press, 1941.

Bedau, Hugo Adam. "Egalitarianism and the Idea of Equality." In J. Roland Pennock and John W. Chapman, eds., *Nomos IX—Equality.* New York: Atherton Press, 1967, 3–27.

Benn, Stanley. "Egalitarianism and the Equal Consideration of Interests." In J. Roland Pennock and John W. Chapman, eds., *Nomos IX—Equality*. New York: Atherton Press, 1967, 61–78.

Bentley, Arthur F. *The Process of Government*. Chicago: University of Chicago Press, 1908.

Berns, Walter F. "Buck v. Bell: Due Process of Law?" *Western Political Quarterly*, 6 (1953), 762–775.

———. *Freedom, Virtue, and the First Amendment*. Chicago: Henry Regnery, 1965.

———. "Oliver Wendell Holmes, Jr." In Morton J. Frisch and Richard G. Stevens, eds., *American Political Thought: The Philosophic Dimensions of American Statesmanship*. New York: Charles Scribner's Sons, 1971, 167–190.

Bickel, Alexander M. "Applied Politics and the Science of Law: Writings of the Harvard Period." In Wallace Mendelson, ed., *Felix Frankfurter: A Tribute*. New York: Reynal and Co., 1964, 164–198.

———. "Is the Warren Court Too 'Political'?" *New York Times Magazine*, September 25, 1966, 30–31, 130–132.

———. *The Least Dangerous Branch*. Indianapolis: Bobbs-Merrill Co., 1962.

———. *The Morality of Consent*. New Haven: Yale University Press, 1975.

———. *Politics and the Warren Court*. New York: Harper and Row, 1965.

———. *The Supreme Court and the Idea of Progress*. New York: Harper and Row, 1970.

Black, Charles L., Jr. *The People and the Court*. Englewood Cliffs: Prentice-Hall, 1960.

Blackstone, William. *Commentaries on the Laws of England*. Volume I. New York: Harper and Brothers, 1859.

Bodenheimer, Edgar. *Jurisprudence*. New York: McGraw-Hill, 1940.

Boorstin, Daniel J. *The Genius of American Politics*. Chicago: University of Chicago Press, 1953.

———. *The Lost World of Thomas Jefferson*. Boston: Beacon Press, 1948.

Brecht, Arnold. *Political Theory: The Foundations of Twentieth Century Political Thought*. Princeton: Princeton University Press, 1959.

Brody, Burton F. "Pragmatic Naturalism of Mr. Justice Holmes." *Chicago-Kent Law Review*, 46 (1969), 9–36.

Brown, Robert E. *Charles Beard and the Constitution: A Critical*

Analysis of "An Economic Interpretation of the Constitution." New York: Norton, 1956.

Browne, Stuart M., Jr. "Black On Representation: A Question." In J. Roland Pennock and John W. Chapman, eds., *Nomos X— Representation.* New York: Atherton Press, 1968, 144–149.

Cahill, Fred V. *Judicial Legislation.* New York: The Ronald Press Co., 1952.

Cardozo, Benjamin N. *The Growth of the Law.* New Haven: Yale University Press, 1924.

———. *The Nature of the Judicial Process.* New Haven: Yale University Press, 1921.

———. *The Paradoxes of Legal Science.* New York: Columbia University Press, 1928.

Claude, Richard. *The Supreme Court and the Electoral Process.* Baltimore: Johns Hopkins Press, 1970.

Cohen, Morris R. *American Thought.* Glencoe, Ill.: Free Press, 1954.

Commager, Henry Steele. "The Pragmatic Necessity for Freedom." In Henry Steele Commager, ed., *Civil Liberties under Attack.* Philadelphia: University of Pennsylvania Press, 1951, 1–22.

Cortner, Richard C. *The Apportionment Cases.* Knoxville: University of Tennessee Press, 1970.

Corwin, Edward S. *Constitutional Revolution, Ltd.* Claremont: Claremont Colleges, Administration Offices, 1941.

———. *Court over Constitution.* Princeton: Peter Smith, 1938.

———. "The Impact of the Idea of Evolution On the American Political and Constitutional Tradition." In Stow Persons, ed., *Evolutionary Thought in America.* Hamden: Archon Books, 1968, 182–199.

———. *Liberty against Government.* Baton Rouge: Louisiana State University Press, 1948.

———. "Moratorium over Minnesota." *University of Pennsylvania Law Review,* 82 (1934), 311–316.

———. *The Twilight of the Supreme Court: A History of Our Constitutional Theory.* New Haven: Yale University Press, 1934.

Cox, Archibald. *The Warren Court: Constitutional Decision as an Instrument of Reform.* Cambridge, Mass.: Harvard University Press, 1968.

De Grazia, Alfred. *Apportionment and Representative Government.* New York: Praeger, 1963.

De Tocqueville, Alexis. *Democracy in America.* 2 volumes. Henry Reeve Text. New York: Vintage Books, 1945.

Dewey, John. *Characters and Events: Popular Essays in Social and*

Political Philosophy. 2 volumes. Edited by Joseph Ratner. New York: Henry Holt, 1929.

——. *The Living Thoughts of Thomas Jefferson.* London: Cassell, 1941.

——. *Logic: The Theory of Inquiry.* New York: Henry Holt, 1938.

——. "My Philosophy of Law." In *My Philosophy of Law, Credos of Sixteen American Scholars.* Boston: Boston Law Book Co., 1941, 71–88.

——. *Philosophy and Civilization.* New York: Capricorn Books, 1963.

——. *The Public and its Problems.* New York: Henry Holt, 1927.

——. *Reconstruction in Philosophy.* Boston: Beacon Press, 1920.

——. "Theory of Valuation." *International Encyclopedia of Unified Science.* Vol. II. Chicago: University of Chicago Press, 1939, entire volume.

Diamond, Martin. "Democracy and *The Federalist:* A Reconsideration of the Framers' Intent." *American Political Science Review,* 53 (1959), 52–68.

Dixon, Robert G., Jr. *Democratic Representation: Reapportionment In Law and Politics.* New York: Oxford University Press, 1968.

——. "The Warren Court Crusade for the Holy Grail of 'One Man–One Vote'." 1969 *Supreme Court Review,* 219–270.

Donoso, Anton. "John Dewey's Philosophy of Law." *University of Detroit Law Journal,* 36 (1959), 579.

Dumbauld, Edward, ed. *The Political Writings of Thomas Jefferson.* Indianapolis: Bobbs-Merrill Co., 1955.

Dye, Thomas. "Malapportionment and Public Policy in The States." *Journal of Politics,* 27 (1965), 586–601.

Eidelberg, Paul. *The Philosophy of the American Constitution.* New York: Free Press, 1968.

Elliott, Ward E. Y. *The Rise of Guardian Democracy: The Supreme Court's Role in Voting Rights Disputes, 1845–1969.* Cambridge, Mass.: Harvard University Press, 1974.

Elliott, William Yandell. *The Pragmatic Revolt in Politics.* New York: The MacMillan Co., 1928.

Faulkner, Robert K. *The Jurisprudence of John Marshall.* Princeton: Princeton University Press, 1968.

Federalist Papers. Edited by Clinton Rossiter. New York: New American Library, 1961.

Foley, John P. *Natural Law, Natural Right and the "Warren Court."* Rome, Italy, 1965.

Frank, Jerome. "Cardozo and the Upper-Court Myth." *Law and Contemporary Problems,* 13 (1948), 369–390.

——. "Modern and Ancient Legal Pragmatism—John Dewey and Co. vs. Aristotle." *Notre Dame Lawyer,* 25 (1950), 207–257.

Frankfurter, Felix. *The Commerce Clause.* Chicago: Quadrangle Books, 1964.

——. "John Marshall and the Judicial Function." *Harvard Law Review,* 69 (1955), 217–238.

——. *Law and Politics.* New York: Capricorn Books, 1962.

——. "Memorandum on 'Incorporation' of the Bill of Rights Into the Due Process Clause of the Fourteenth Amendment." *Harvard Law Review,* 78 (1965), 746–783.

——. "Mr. Justice Holmes and the Constitution." *Harvard Law Review,* 41 (1948), 121–164.

——. *Mr. Justice Holmes and the Supreme Court.* 2d ed. New York: Atheneum, 1965.

——. *Of Law and Life and Other Things That Matter.* New York: Atheneum, 1969.

——. *Of Law and Men.* New York: Harcourt, Brace and Co., 1956.

——. *The Public and Its Government.* Boston: Beacon Press, 1964.

——, and James M. Landis. *The Business of the Supreme Court.* New York: The MacMillan Co., 1927.

Goedecke, W. Robert. *Change and the Law.* Tallahassee: Florida State University Press, 1969.

Goldwin, Robert, ed. *Representation and Misrepresentation: Legislative Reapportionment in Theory and Practice.* Chicago: Rand McNally, 1968.

Gray, John Chapman. *The Nature and Sources of the Law.* Boston: Beacon Press, 1963.

Gregg, Paul L., S. J. "The Pragmatism of Mr. Justice Holmes." *Georgetown Law Journal,* 31 (1943), 262–295.

Grimes, Alan P. *Equality in America: Religion, Race, and the Urban Majority.* New York: Oxford University Press, 1964.

Gunther, Gerald. "The Subtle Vices of the 'Passive Virtues'—A Comment on Principle and Expediency in Judicial Review." *Columbia Law Review,* 64 (1964), 1–25.

Hacker, Andrew. *Congressional Districting: The Issue of Equal Representation.* Washington, D.C.: Brookings Institution, 1963.

Haines, Charles G. *The Revival of Natural Law Concepts.* Cambridge, Mass.: Harvard University Press, 1930.

Hall, Jerome. *Living Law of Democratic Society.* Indianapolis: Bobbs-Merrill, 1949.

Hall, Margaret E., ed. *The Selected Writings of Benjamin Nathan Cardozo.* New York: Fallon Law Book Co., 1947.

Hamilton, Walton H. "Cardozo: Craftsman of the Law." *University of Chicago Law Review,* 6 (1938), 1–22.

——. "The Path of Due Process of Law." *Ethics,* 48 (1938), 269–296.

Hand, Learned. *The Spirit of Liberty.* New York: Alfred A. Knopf, 1953.

Hart, Henry. "Foreword: The Time Chart of the Justices." *Harvard Law Review,* 73 (1959), 84–125.

——. "Holmes' Positivism—An Addendum." *Harvard Law Review,* 64 (1951), 929–937.

Hartshorne, Charles, and Paul Weiss, eds. *Collected Papers of Charles Sanders Peirce.* Cambridge, Mass.: Harvard University Press, 1960.

Hartz, Louis. *The Liberal Tradition in America.* New York: Harcourt, Brace and World, 1955.

Hill, A. Spencer. "The Reapportionment Decisions: A Return to Dogma." *Journal of Politics,* 31 (1969), 186–213.

Hofferbert, Richard. "The Relation Between Public Policy and Some Structural and Environmental Variables in the American States." *American Political Science Review,* 60 (1966), 73–82.

Hofstadter, Richard. *Social Darwinism in American Thought.* Boston: Beacon Press, 1944.

Holmes, Oliver Wendell, Jr. *The Common Law.* Boston: Little, Brown, 1963.

——. "Holmes on Marshall." In Mark deWolfe Howe, ed., *John Marshall.* Chicago: University of Chicago Press, 1967, 129–134.

——. "The Path of the Law." *Harvard Law Review,* 10 (1897), 457–478.

Horwitz, Robert. "John Dewey." In Leo Strauss and Joseph Cropsey, eds., *A History of Political Philosophy.* Chicago: Rand McNally, 1963, 746–764.

Howe, Mark deWolfe. "The Positivism of Mr. Justice Holmes." *Harvard Law Review,* 64 (1951), 529–546.

Hughes, Charles Evans. *The Supreme Court of the United States.* New York: Columbia University Press, 1928.

Irwin, William P. "Representation and Election: The Reapportionment Cases in Retrospect." *Michigan Law Review,* 67 (1969), 729–754.

Jacob, Herbert. "The Consequences of Malapportionment: A Note of Caution." *Social Forces*, 43 (1964), 256–261.

Jacobs, Clyde E. *Justice Frankfurter and Civil Liberties*. Berkeley: University of California Press, 1961.

Jaffa, Harry V. *Crisis of the House Divided*. Garden City, N.Y.: Doubleday, 1959.

———. *Equality and Liberty: Theory and Practice in American Politics*. New York: Oxford University Press, 1965.

Jaffe, Louis L. "The Judicial Universe of Mr. Justice Frankfurter." *Harvard Law Review*, 62 (1949), 357–412.

James, William. "The Moral Philosopher and the Moral Life." In William James, *The Will to Believe and Other Essays in Popular Philosophy*. New York: Longmans, Green, and Co., 1915, 184–215.

———. *Pragmatism*. New York: Longmans, Green, and Co., 1907.

———. "The Will to Believe." In William James, *Pragmatism and Other Essays*. New York: Washington Square Press, 1962, 193–213.

Kenyon, Cecilia. "Republicanism and Radicalism in the American Revolution: An Old-Fashioned Interpretation." *William and Mary Quarterly*. Third Series. 19 (1962), 153–182.

Koch, Adrienne. *The Philosophy of Thomas Jefferson*. Chicago: Quadrangle Books, 1964.

———, and William Pedin. *The Life and Selected Writings of Thomas Jefferson*. New York: Modern Library, 1944.

Konefsky, Samuel J. *The Legacy of Holmes and Brandeis*. New York: The MacMillan Co., 1956.

Konvitz, Milton R., and Gail Kennedy, eds. *The American Pragmatists*. New York: Meridian Books, 1960.

Kurland, Philip B. "The Court Should Decide Less and Explain More." *New York Times Magazine*, June 9, 1968, 34–35, 122–126.

———, ed. *Felix Frankfurter on the Supreme Court: Extrajudicial Essays on the Court and the Constitution*. Cambridge, Mass.: Harvard University Press, 1971.

———. *Politics, the Constitution, and the Warren Court*. Chicago: University of Chicago Press, 1970.

Lash, Joseph, ed. *From the Diaries of Felix Frankfurter*. New York: Norton, 1974.

Lerner, Max. "Holmes and Frankfurter." *The Nation*, November 19, 1938, 537–539.

Lerner, Ralph. "The Supreme Court as Republican Schoolmaster." *1967 Supreme Court Review*, 127–180.

Levi, Edward H. *An Introduction to Legal Reasoning.* Chicago: University of Chicago Press, 1948.

Levinson, Sanford V. "The Democratic Faith of Felix Frankfurter." *Stanford Law Review,* 25 (1973), 1185–1202.

Levy, Beryl H. *Cardozo and the Frontiers of Legal Thinking.* New York: Oxford University Press, 1938.

——. *Our Constitution: Tool or Testament?* New York: Alfred A. Knopf, 1942.

Lewis, Anthony. "Earl Warren." In Richard H. Sayler, Barry B. Boyer, and Robert E. Gooding, Jr., eds., *The Warren Court: A Critical Analysis.* New York: Chelsea House, 1969.

MacDonald, Forrest. *We the People.* Chicago: University of Chicago Press, 1958.

McCloskey, Robert G. *American Conservatism in the Age of Enterprise, 1865–1910.* New York: Harper and Row, 1951.

——. "Economic Due Process and the Supreme Court: An Exhumation and Reburial." In Leonard W. Levy, ed., *American Constitutional Law: Historical Essays.* New York: Harper and Row, 1966, 159–187.

McKay, Robert B. *Reapportionment: The Law and Politics of Equal Representation.* New York: Twentieth Century Fund, 1965.

McKeon, Richard, ed. *Introduction to Aristotle.* New York: Modern Library, 1947.

Marx, Karl. "Theses on Feuerbach." In Karl Marx and Friedrich Engels, *The German Ideology.* New York: International Publishers, 1947, 197–199.

Mason, Alpheus Thomas. *The Supreme Court from Taft to Warren.* New York: Norton, 1964.

Mendelson, Wallace. *Justices Black and Frankfurter: Conflict in the Court.* Chicago: University of Chicago Press, 1961.

——. "Mr. Justice Frankfurter and the Process of Judicial Review." *University of Pennsylvania Law Review,* 103 (1954), 295–320.

Miller, Arthur Selwyn. *The Supreme Court and American Capitalism.* New York: Free Press, 1968.

——, and Ronald F. Howell. "The Myth of Neutrality in Constitutional Adjudication." *University of Chicago Law Review,* 27 (1960), 661–695.

Miller, Charles A. *The Supreme Court and the Uses of History.* Cambridge, Mass.: Harvard University Press, 1969.

Mitchell, E. T. "Social Ideals and the Law." In Jerome Hall, ed.,

Readings in Jurisprudence. Indianapolis: Bobbs-Merrill Co., 1938, 250–252.

Moore, Edward C. *American Pragmatism: Peirce, James, and Dewey.* New York: Columbia University Press, 1961.

Murphy, Jay Wesley. "John Dewey—A Philosophy of Law for Democracy." *Vanderbilt Law Review,* 14 (1960–1961), 291–317.

Murray, John Courtney, S.J. *We Hold These Truths.* Garden City, N.Y.: Image Books, 1964.

Navasky, Victor. *Kennedy Justice.* New York: Athenaeum, 1971.

North, Alfred A. *The Supreme Court: Judicial Process and Judicial Politics.* New York: Appleton Century Crofts, 1966.

Northrop, F. S. C. "Ethical Relativism in the Light of Recent Legal Science." *The Journal of Philosophy,* 52 (1955), 649–662.

Note. "Constitutionality of Mortgage Relief Legislation: *Home Building and Loan Association* v. *Blaisdell.*" *Harvard Law Review,* 47 (1934), 660–668.

Note. "Holmes, Peirce, and Legal Pragmatism." *Yale Law Journal,* 84 (1975), 1123–1140.

Patterson, Caleb Perry. *The Constitutional Principles of Thomas Jefferson.* Austin: University of Texas Press, 1953.

Patterson, Edwin W. "John Dewey and the Law: Theories of Legal Reasoning and Valuation." *ABA Journal,* 36 (1950), 619–622, 699–701.

———. *Jurisprudence: Men and Ideas of the Law.* Brooklyn: Foundation Press, 1953.

———. "Pound's Theory of Social Interests." In Paul Sayre, ed., *Interpretations of Modern Legal Philosophies.* New York: Oxford University Press, 1947, 558–573.

———. "Pragmatism as a Philosophy of Law." In Edwin W. Patterson, ed., *The Philosopher of the Common Man.* New York: G. P. Putnam's Sons, 1940, 172–204.

Perry, Ralph Barton. *The Thought and Character of William James.* New York: George Braziller, 1954.

Persons, Stow. "Darwinism and American Culture." In Cushing Strout, ed., *Intellectual History in America,* II. New York: Harper and Row, 1968, 1–9.

Pitkin, Hannah. *The Concept of Representation.* Berkeley: University of California Press, 1967.

Plato. *The Laws.* Translated by Trevor J. Saunders. Middlesex, England: Penguin Books, 1970.

———. *The Republic.* Translated by Allan Bloom. New York: Basic Books, 1968.

———. *Statesman.* Translated by J. B. Kemp. Indianapolis: Bobbs-Merrill Co., 1957.

Polsby, Nelson, ed. *Reapportionment in the 1970s.* Berkeley: University of California Press, 1971.

Pound, Roscoe. *Interpretations of Legal History.* New York: The MacMillan Co., 1923.

———. *An Introduction to the Philosophy of Law.* New Haven: Yale University Press, 1922.

———. "Mechanical Jurisprudence." *Columbia Law Review,* 8 (1908), 605–623.

———. *Outlines of Lectures on Jurisprudence.* 4th ed. Cambridge: The University Press, 1928.

———. *Social Control through Law.* New Haven: Yale University Press, 1942.

———. "The Theory of Judicial Decision." *Harvard Law Review,* 36 (1923), 641–662.

———. "A Theory of Social Interests." In Jerome Hall, ed., *Readings in Jurisprudence.* Indianapolis: Bobbs-Merrill Co., 1938, 238–246.

Pritchett, C. Herman. "The Limits on Judicial Self-Restraint." In Walter F. Murphy and C. Herman Pritchett, eds., *Courts, Judges, and Politics: An Introduction to the Judicial Process.* New York: Random House, 1961, 691–694.

———. *The Roosevelt Court.* Chicago: Quadrangle Books, 1969.

Purcell, Edward A., Jr. *The Crisis of Democratic Theory: Scientific Naturalism and the Problem of Value.* Lexington, Ky.: University of Kentucky Press, 1973.

Rodell, Fred. "It is the Earl Warren Court." *The New York Times Magazine,* March 13, 1966, 30–31, 93–100.

———. "Judicial Activists, Judicial Self-Deniers, Judicial Review and the First Amendment—Or, How to Hide the Melody of what You Mean behind the Words of what You Say." *Georgetown Law Journal,* 47 (1959), 483–490.

———. *Nine Men.* New York: Random House, 1955.

Rostow, Eugene V. "The Democratic Character of Judicial Review." *Harvard Law Review,* 66 (1952), 193–224.

Rumble, Wilfred E., Jr. *American Legal Realism.* Ithaca: Cornell University Press, 1968.

Russell, Bertrand. *Unpopular Essays.* New York: Simon and Schuster, 1951.

Sabine, George H. "The Pragmatic Approach to Politics." *American Political Science Review*, 24 (1930), 865–885.

Schwartz, Bernard. *A Commentary on the Constitution of the United States—Part II: The Right of Property*. New York: Macmillan, 1965.

Shapiro, Martin. *Law and Politics in the Supreme Court*. New York: The Free Press, 1964.

Simon, Yves. *The Philosophy of Democratic Government*. Chicago: University of Chicago Press, 1951.

Smith, David G. "Pragmatism and the Group Theory of Politics." *American Political Science Review*, 58 (1964), 600–610.

Somjee, A. H. *The Political Theory of John Dewey*. New York: Teachers College Press, 1968.

Stevens, Richard G. "Felix Frankfurter." In Morton Frisch and Richard G. Stevens, eds., *American Political Thought: The Philosophical Dimensions of Statesmanship*. Chicago: Scribner and Sons, 1971, 237–260.

———. "Reason and History in Judicial Judgment: Mr. Justice Frankfurter's Treatment of Due Process." Ph.D. dissertation, University of Chicago, 1963.

Stone, Julius. *The Province and Function of Law*. Sydney: Associated General Publications, 1946.

Storing, Herbert J. "William Blackstone." In Leo Strauss and Joseph Cropsey, eds., *A History of Political Philosophy*. Chicago: Rand McNally, 1963, 536–548.

Strauss, Leo. *Natural Right and History*. Chicago: University of Chicago Press, 1953.

———. "Plato." In Leo Strauss and Joseph Cropsey, eds., *A History of Political Philosophy*. Chicago: Rand McNally, 1963, 7–63.

Strout, Cushing, ed. *Intellectual History in America*. 2 volumes. New York: Harper and Row, 1968.

———. *The Pragmatic Revolt in American History: Carl Becker and Charles Beard*. Ithaca: Cornell University Press, 1966.

Sumner, William Graham. *Folkways*. Boston: Ginn and Co., 1907.

Swisher, Carl Brent. *Stephen J. Field: Craftsman of the Law*. Hamden: Shoe String Press, 1963.

Taylor, A. E. *Plato: The Sophist and the Statesman*. London: Thomas Nelson and Sons, 1961.

Thayer, H. S. *Meaning and Action: A Critical History of Pragmatism*. Indianapolis: Bobbs-Merrill Co., 1968.

Thomas, Helen Shirley. *Felix Frankfurter: Scholar on the Bench*. Baltimore: Johns Hopkins Press, 1960.

Van Alstyne, William W. "The Fourteenth Amendment, the 'Right' to Vote, and the Understanding of the Thirty-Ninth Congress." 1965 *Supreme Court Review*, 33–86.

Ward, Paul W. *Intelligence in Politics*. Chapel Hill: University of North Carolina Press, 1931.

Wechsler, Herbert. "Toward Neutral Principles of Constitutional Law." *Harvard Law Review*, 73 (1959), 1–35.

White, Morton. *Social Thought in America: The Revolt against Formalism*. Boston: Beacon Press, 1947.

Wiener, Philip P. *Evolution and the Founders of Pragmatism*. Cambridge, Mass.: Harvard University Press, 1949.

Wiltse, Charles A. *The Jeffersonian Tradition in American Democracy*. Chapel Hill: University of North Carolina Press, 1952.

Woffard, John G. "The Blinding Light: The Uses of History in Constitutional History." *University of Chicago Law Review*, 31 (1964), 502–533.

Wood, Gordon. *The Creation of the American Republic, 1776–1787*. Chapel Hill: University of North Carolina Press, 1969.

Wright, Benjamin F., Jr. *The Contract Clause of the Constitution*. Cambridge, Mass.: Harvard University Press, 1938.

Wyzanski, Charles E. "Comment." In Arthur E. Sutherland, ed., *Government under Law*. New York: Da Capo Press, 1968, 490–494.

Zetterbaum, Marvin. *Tocqueville and the Problem of Democracy*. Stanford: Stanford University Press, 1967.

Index

Pragmatism, Statesmanship,
and the Supreme Court

Designed by R. E. Rosenbaum.
Composed by York Composition Company, Inc.,
in 10 point Linotype Times Roman, 2 points leaded,
with display lines in monotype Deepdene.
Printed letterpress from type by York Composition Company
on Warren's Number 66 text, 50 pound basis.
Bound by John H. Dekker & Sons, Inc.
in Joanna book cloth
and stamped in All Purpose foil.

Library of Congress Cataloging in Publication Data
(For library cataloging purposes only)

Jacobsohn, Gary J   1946-
   Pragmatism, statesmanship, and the Supreme Court

   Bibliography: p. 199
   Includes index.
   1. United States. Supreme Court.   I. Title.
KF8742.J33   347'.73'26   77-1921
ISBN 0-8014-1071-1